JOURNAL FOR THE STUDY OF THE NEW TESTAMENT
SUPPLEMENT SERIES
80

JSOT Press
Sheffield

Biblical Greek Language and Linguistics

Open Questions in Current Research

edited by

Stanley E. Porter

and

D.A. Carson

Journal for the Study of the New Testament
Supplement Series 80

Published by JSOT Press
JSOT Press is an imprint of
Sheffield Academic Press Ltd
343 Fulwood Road
Sheffield S10 3BP
England

Typeset by Sheffield Academic Press
and
Printed on acid-free paper in Great Britain
by Biddles Ltd
Guildford

British Library Cataloguing in Publication Data

Biblical Greek Language and Linguistics:
Open Questions in Current Research.—
(JSNT Supplement Series, ISSN 0143-5108;
No. 80)
I. Porter, Stanley E. II. Carson, D.A.
III. Series
487

ISBN 1-85075-390-3

CONTENTS

Preface   7
Abbreviations   12
List of Contributors   15

PART I
VERBAL ASPECT

D.A. CARSON
An Introduction to the Porter/Fanning Debate   18

STANLEY E. PORTER
In Defence of Verbal Aspect   26

BUIST M. FANNING
Approaches to Verbal Aspect in New Testament
Greek: Issues in Definition and Method   46

DARYL D. SCHMIDT
Verbal Aspect in Greek: Two Approaches   63

MOISÉS SILVA
A Response to Fanning and Porter on Verbal Aspect   74

PART II
OTHER TOPICS

STANLEY E. PORTER
An Introduction to Other Topics in Biblical Greek
Language and Linguistics   84

JEFFREY T. REED
To Timothy or Not? A Discourse Analysis of
1 Timothy   90

PAUL DANOVE
The Theory of Construction Grammar and its
Application to New Testament Greek   119

MICHEAL W. PALMER
How Do we Know a Phrase is a Phrase?
A Plea for Procedural Clarity in the Application of
Linguistics to Biblical Greek   152

MARK S. KRAUSE
The Finite Verb with Cognate Participle in the New
Testament   187

Index of References   207
Index of Authors   215

This collection, *Biblical Greek Language and Linguistics: Open Questions in Current Research*, brings together into one volume papers first delivered at the Society of Biblical Literature annual meetings in 1990 and 1991. These papers were all presented under the auspices of the then Consultation on Biblical Greek Language and Linguistics. This consultation was convened for the 1990 meeting, and, after two successful years, for the 1992 meeting has had its status elevated to that of a Section. It will continue in that capacity for at least the next five years.

When the original co-chairpersons of the Consultation, D.A. Carson and Stanley E. Porter, along with the two other original members of the steering committee, Daryl D. Schmidt and Moisés Silva, first discussed the possibility of instituting such a consultation, they did so because of a perceptible need within the discipline of New Testament studies and an apparent lack of opportunity at the Society of Biblical Literature's annual meetings. The annual meeting consisted of a variety of sessions focused upon various biblical topics, many of them hermeneutical and methodological in nature. There were sessions addressing questions of Hebrew language and linguistics, but none devoted in their focus to questions related to Greek language and linguistics. This struck us as significant, since the failure to provide a venue for concentrated examination of one of the two major biblical languages could only have serious repercussions for the discipline. It was not that issues of grammar did not arise in other sessions, to be sure, but that there was no place where one could choose to address solely grammatical issues, without necessarily feeling compelled to place them as subordinate to some other agenda, such as theology or history, as important as these may be in their own rights.

To go further, we considered the lack of opportunity to explore matters of language from self-consciously linguistic as well as more traditional grammatical perspectives to reflect sadly upon the general state of regard for such matters within the wider profession of New Testament studies. Over the last thirty years there has been the increasing recognition that the study of the biblical languages has fallen on difficult times. More and more institutions do not require that Greek be studied to any significant level of technical competence. Consequently, fewer scholars are devoting their careers to matters of Greek language, and publications in the area have become relatively scarce. One cannot help but wonder whether such a condition does not have implications regarding the level of linguistic competence displayed by the exegetes who are in fact attempting to comment upon the Greek text.

As a result of the above observations, and after determining that there was significant and widespread interest among a variety of other scholars, application was made for a Consultation on Biblical Greek Language and Linguistics. The application consisted of the following statement of purpose and orientation. This same statement was resubmitted as part of the application for elevation to the status of Section, and is reprinted here.

> The Section on Biblical Greek Language and Linguistics is designed to promote and publish the latest research into the Greek of both Testaments. The Section does not assume that biblical Greek is a distinct dialect within the larger world of *Koine*: on the contrary, the assumption is that biblical Greek is part and parcel of the hellenistic Greek that dominated the Mediterranean world from 300 BC to AD 300. If the Section focuses on the corpora of the Old and New Testaments, it is because these writings generate major interest around the world, not only for religious but also for historical and academic reasons.
>
> Research into the broader evidence of the period, including epigraphical and inscriptional materials as well as literary works, is more than welcome, provided the results are cast in terms of their bearing on biblical Greek. In the same way, the Section is devoted to fresh philological, syntactical, linguistic, and lexicographical study of the Greek of the biblical books with the subsidiary aim of displaying the contribution of such study to accurate exegesis.

The statement contains all of the essential requirements of the Section, including the material to be analysed, the methods to be used, and the purpose for which the research is done. The format for presentation of papers at the first two annual meetings has followed a consistent pattern that reflects the priorities of the statement of purpose. One session is devoted to a specified topic, with invited papers and responses, and the other session is open to papers proposed by individual scholars. The response to this idea was noteworthy from the start. The designated session of 1990 in New Orleans, Louisiana, USA featured a panel discussion of the lexicon of the Greek New Testament edited by J.P. Louw and E.A. Nida. David Aune is to be thanked for his organizing and chairing this highly successful first session of the new Consultation. The designated session of 1991 in Kansas City, Missouri, USA featured a panel discussion of two recent volumes on Greek verbal aspect. The audience for that occasion was impressive in its size, in the light of the perceived technicality of the subject matter. The subject is an important one, and one that promises not to go away in the next several years. If the proponents of the theory are correct, the semantic category of verbal aspect will prove vital to future analysis and exegesis of Greek, including that of the New Testament. The two major papers and two responses from that session are introduced and included in Part I, below.

The open sessions of 1990 and 1991 included a number of papers on a range of topics in current research, including various theoretical linguistic orientations and a range of applications and useful exegetical insights. There are several important questions to ask when deciding which essays to include in the collection of a group of disparate essays such as this. The question is not simply which papers are the best or worst, since virtually every one of the papers has at least something to commend it. The questions instead focus on which ones give an accurate sampling of the kinds of papers presented at the conference, and which ones possess the greatest significance in the light of issues of linguistic modelling, demonstrable discussion of grammatical categories, insights gained for exegesis of particular texts, and potential to stimulate further discussion, to name only a few. The fact that we have decided to include certain of the papers means that some of the papers have had to be excluded for one reason or another. We do not mean to imply that these papers were not good, but it was felt that they were not as significant in giving evidence of the current state of informed analysis of New Testament Greek as those included. New Testament studies is beginning to see results from its attempts to reassess the accepted methods of New Testament analysis. It would be rewarding for all of us, editors, contributors and participants, to discover that this collection in some way serves as a catalyst for others to begin or continue their own work in the area of Greek grammar and linguistics. They can be assured that there is a sympathetic venue for presentation of such results in the Section.

Because this volume divides itself so neatly into two sections, a separate introduction is provided to each part. Part I: Verbal Aspect includes the presentations and responses on the topic of Greek verbal aspect first read in Kansas City in 1991. It was rewarding to see that despite the specialized nature of the topic the papers prompted insightful responses and a number of penetrating questions in the time left after the formal presentations. The revisions to these papers consist only of incorporated responses to issues specifically raised during the session. Part II: Other Topics includes four papers selected from the eight presented in the two open sessions of 1990 and 1991. The constraints of time prevented the participants from being able to elucidate everything that they considered their subjects warranted, so the full papers are presented here, revised in the light of the informative question time following each.

The editors, who served as co-chairpersons of the original Consultation and who now serve as co-chairpersons of the Section, wish to recognize two groups of people who have enabled the Consultation on Biblical Greek Language and Linguistics to be as successful as it has been so far. The first vote of thanks must go to the various contributors. In the present climate of academic biblical studies, it is understandable that scholars would naturally gravitate towards exploration of the topics that appear to arouse the most interest and to constitute the heart of the discipline's current dominant concerns. One of the aims of this Consultation (and now Section) is to put issues of Greek grammar and linguistics back into the centre of the discussion. We are grateful to the contributors who have accepted this challenge. Many of them have had to work in relative isolation as they have developed interpretative grammatical strategies, and as they have dared to suggest that their grammatical matrixes have significant and even fundamental implications for how to interpret particular Greek texts. The second vote of thanks goes to those who have attended the various sessions. Even though attendance has varied depending upon the paper topics and format, it is fair to say that we have been pleasantly surprised to see the numbers in virtually every instance exceed our expectations. And the attenders have done more than simply occupy their seats. The discussion following papers has rarely suffered from a lack of participation. There are always more questions than there is time for their asking, resulting in many useful discussions after the formal sessions have ended.

Looking to the future, we anticipate more of the same. In particular, we would like to encourage grammarians to develop grammatical models to apply to ancient Greek, including that of the New Testament. We wish always to illustrate the connection between grammatical description and exegesis. We would also like to encourage studies of the Greek found outside of the New Testament, including the Greek of the Septuagint (LXX), of the papyri and inscriptions, and of non-biblical authors. There are also a number of fundamental topics where there is room for serious discussion and debate, including the nature of the Greek found in the New Testament in the light of possible Semitic influence, the contribution of discourse analysis and rhetorical models for analysis of the text of the New Testament, and the use of stylistics in evaluating questions of authorship and sources. Any or all of these topics may be addressed in designated sessions in the future. Individual papers on them are also welcome.

Stanley E. Porter
D.A. Carson

ABBREVIATIONS

AB	Anchor Bible
AnBib	Analecta biblica
ANRW	*Aufstieg und Niedergang der römischen Welt*
ASV	American Standard Version
AV	Authorized Version
BAGD	W. Bauer, W.F. Arndt, F.W. Gingrich and F.W. Danker, *Greek–English Lexicon of the New Testament*
BDF	F. Blass, A. Debrunner and R.W. Funk, *A Greek Grammar of the New Testament*
Bib	*Biblica*
BLG	Biblical Languages: Greek
BSac	*Bibliotheca Sacra*
BT	*The Bible Translator*
BTB	*Biblical Theology Bulletin*
CBQ	*Catholic Biblical Quarterly*
CR	*Critical Review of Books in Religion*
EBib	Etudes bibliques
ExpTim	*Expository Times*
FN	*Filología Neotestamentaria*
FRLANT	Forschungen zur Religion und Literatur des Alten und Neuen Testaments
GTJ	*Grace Theological Journal*
ICC	International Critical Commentary
JB	*Jerusalem Bible*
JBL	*Journal of Biblical Literature*
JSNT	*Journal for the Study of the New Testament*
JSNTSup	*Journal for the Study of the New Testament*, Supplement Series
JTS	*Journal of Theological Studies*
LCL	Loeb Classical Library
LSJ	Liddell–Scott–Jones, *Greek–English Lexicon*
NAB	*New American Bible*
NASB	*New American Standard Bible*
NCB	New Century Bible
NEB	*New English Bible*
Neot	*Neotestamentica*

NIV	New International Version
NKJV	New King James Version
NovT	*Novum Testamentum*
NRSV	New Revised Standard Version
NTS	*New Testament Studies*
PE	Pastoral Epistles
RNT	Regensburger Neues Testament
RSV	Revised Standard Version
SBLDS	Society of Biblical Literature Dissertation Series
SBLSBS	Society of Biblical Literature Sources for Biblical Study
SBLSP	Society of Biblical Literature Seminar Papers
THKNT	Theologischer Handkommentar zum Neuen Testament
TNTC	Tyndale New Testament Commentaries
TynBul	*Tyndale Bulletin*
UBS	United Bible Societies
UBSGNT	United Bible Societies' *Greek New Testament*
WBC	Word Biblical Commentary
WTJ	*Westminster Theological Journal*
ZNW	*Zeitschrift für die neutestamentliche Wissenschaft*

LIST OF CONTRIBUTORS

D.A. Carson is Research Professor of New Testament at Trinity Evangelical Divinity School, Deerfield, Illinois.

Paul Danove is Assistant Professor for New Testament Studies at Gonzaga University, Spokane, Washington.

Buist M. Fanning is Professor of New Testament at Dallas Theological Seminary, Dallas, Texas.

Mark S. Krause is Associate Professor of Biblical Studies at Puget Sound Christian College, Edmonds, Washington.

Micheal W. Palmer is Assistant Professor of New Testament, Greek and Philosophy at Bluefield College, Bluefield, Virginia.

Stanley E. Porter is Associate Professor of Religious Studies at Trinity Western University, Langley, British Columbia, Canada.

Jeffrey T. Reed teaches Greek and New Testament at Talbot School of Theology, Biola University, La Mirada, California.

Daryl D. Schmidt teaches at Pacific School of Religion, Berkeley, California.

Moisés Silva is Professor of New Testament at Westminster Theological Seminary, Philadelphia, Pennsylvania.

Part I
VERBAL ASPECT

AN INTRODUCTION TO THE PORTER/FANNING DEBATE

D.A. Carson

Students of elementary Greek tend to learn a large number of rules to which subsequent courses add the exceptions. The more reflective students ultimately ask themselves if the sheer number and variety of exceptions in some instances call in question the validity of the rule first articulated.

Few areas of Greek grammar have produced more puzzlement of this kind than the verbal system. The history of the study of the language betrays the difficulty of accurately describing the semantics of verbal morphology. There is not space here to trace these developments from the time of the early Greek grammarians (second century BCE) to the present. In the modern period, however, it would be fair to say that the prevailing influence of rationalism resulted in the view, throughout most of the nineteenth century, that time and tense-forms are isomorphic.[1] The number of exceptions was so daunting that some other key was sought. Various developments in comparative philology led many in the second half of the nineteenth century to link tense-forms not to time but to the kind of action that actually occurred—in short, to *Aktionsart*.[2] Some combination of these two models still controls most of the major Greek grammars. The first model, it is usually argued, operates in the indicative, and the second everywhere else in the Greek verbal system.[3] One of the most remarkable features

---

1. One thinks, for instance, of G.B. Winer, *A Treatise on the Grammar of New Testament Greek Regarded as a Sure Basis for New Testament Exegesis* (trans. W. F. Moulton; Edinburgh: T. & T. Clark, 3rd edn, 1882).

2. So K. Brugmann, *Griechische Grammatik* (ed. A. Thumb; Munich: Beck, 4th edn, 1913 [1885]).

3. So, more or less, J.H. Moulton, *A Grammar of New Testament Greek*. I. *Prolegomena* (Edinburgh: T. & T. Clark, 3rd edn, 1908); A.T. Robertson, *A Grammar of the Greek New Testament in the Light of Historical Research* (Nashville: Broadman, 4th edn, 1934); F. Blass and A. Debrunner, *A Greek*

of these grammars, however, is how the authors oscillate between an implicit definition of *Aktionsart* that grounds tense-form differences in the kinds of action to which reference is made, and an implicit definition that grounds tense-form differences in the decision of the author to describe or think of an action in a certain way. One model tries to tie tense-forms to what actually takes place; the other ties tense-forms to the author's depiction of what takes place. The two are constantly confused. Even where there is formal recognition that the two models are different (thus BDF §318 labels *Aktionsarten* as 'kinds of action' and aspects as 'points of view'), these grammars feel no embarrassment in assigning a tense-form to one or the other depending entirely on the apparent exigencies of the context.

In fact, aspect theory had been growing alongside the publication of these grammars, yet was largely unrecognized by them. Sometimes developments occurred that did not explicitly use the expression 'aspect theory' but nevertheless contributed to the field. For instance, at the end of the last century Donovan, in a series of articles, persuasively demonstrated that the common assertion that the present imperative exhorts to continuing action while the aorist imperative exhorts to beginning action simply will not stand up.[1] Although a number of subsequent studies have strongly buttressed his evidence,[2]

Grammar of the New Testament and Other Early Christian Literature (trans. and rev. by R.W. Funk; Chicago: University of Chicago Press, 1961); N. Turner, *A Grammar of New Testament Greek*. III. *Syntax* (Edinburgh: T. & T. Clark, 1963); F. Blass, A. Debrunner and F. Rehkopf, *Grammatik des neutestamentlichen Griechisch* (Göttingen: Vandenhoeck & Ruprecht, 14th edn, 1976)—to cite but a few.

1. J. Donovan, 'Greek Jussives', *Classical Review* 9 (1895), pp. 145-49; and, 'German Opinion on Greek Jussives', *Classical Review* 9 (1895), pp. 289-93, 342-46, 444-47.

2. See H.D. Naylor, 'More Prohibitions in Greek', *Classical Review* 20 (1906), p. 348; A. Poutsma, 'Over de tempora van de imperativus en de conjunctivus hortativus-prohibitivus in het Grieks', *Verhandelingen der Koninklijke Akademie van Wetenschappen te Amsterdam* 27/2 (1928), pp. 1-84; J.P. Louw, 'On Greek Prohibitions', *Acta Classica* 2 (1959), pp. 43-57; W.F. Bakker, *The Greek Imperative: An Investigation into the Aspectual Differences between the Present and Aorist Imperatives in Greek Prayer from Homer up to the Present Day* (Amsterdam: Hakkert, 1966).

the major grammars have not mentioned it.[1] More broadly, verbal aspect theory, largely a development generated by the study of Slavonic languages, became the focus of much work. Some of this filtered into the study of Greek. So far as I am aware, the first full-length treatment of verbal aspect in Greek was that of Holt (1943),[2] but his focus was not on the Greek New Testament. Mandilaras treated the Hellenistic papyri;[3] Comrie, followed by Dahl and Bache, produced full-length studies of verbal aspect as a semantic category.[4]

But it was left to Mateos,[5] and especially to McKay,[6] to attempt systematically to introduce verbal-aspect theory to Greek generally, and especially to the Greek of the New Testament. While preserving the traditional categories of *Aktionsart*, Mateos attempted to make space in the study of New Testament Greek for verbal aspect by tying

1. For example, Turner (*Syntax*, pp. 74-75) published his work after all but Bakker, yet does not mention any of the relevant studies by Donovan, Naylor, Poutsma or Louw.

2. J. Holt, *Etudes d'aspect* (Acta Jutlandica Aarskrift for Aarhus Universitet, 15.2; Copenhagen: Universitetsforlaget I Aarhus, 1943).

3. B.G. Mandilaras, *The Verb in the Greek Non-Literary Papyri* (Athens: Hellenic Ministry of Culture and Sciences, 1973).

4. B. Comrie, *Aspect: An Introduction to the Study of Verbal Aspect and Related Problems* (Cambridge: Cambridge University Press, 1976); Ö. Dahl, *Tense and Aspect Systems* (Oxford: Basil Blackwell, 1985); C. Bache, *Verbal Aspect: A General Theory and its Application to Present-Day English* (Odense: Odense University Press, 1985).

5. J. Mateos, *El aspecto verbal en el nuevo testamento* (Madrid: Ediciones Cristiandad, 1977).

6. Beginning in 1965, K.L. McKay has left a trail of important articles: 'The Use of the Ancient Greek Perfect down to the End of the Second Century AD', *Bulletin of the Institute of Classical Studies* 12 (1965), pp. 1-21; 'Syntax in Exegesis', *TynBul* 123 (1972), pp. 39-57; 'Some Linguistic Points in Marxsen's Resurrection Theory', *ExpTim* 84 (1972–73), pp. 330-32; 'Further Remarks on the "Historical" Present and Other Phenomena', *Foundations of Language* 11 (1974), pp. 247-51; 'On the Perfect and Other Aspects in the Greek Non-Literary Papyri', *Bulletin of the Institute of Classical Studies* 27 (1980), pp. 23-49; 'On the Perfect and Other Aspects in New Testament Greek', *NovT* 23 (1981), pp. 289-329; 'Repeated Action, the Potential and Reality in Ancient Greek', *Antichthon* 15 (1981), pp. 36-46; 'Aspects of the Imperative in Ancient Greek', *Antichthon* 20 (1986), pp. 41-58. See also his *Greek Grammar for Students: A Concise Grammar of Classical Attic with Special Reference to Aspect in the Verb* (Canberra: Australian National University, 1974).

the aspect of verbs to the kind of action reflected in their lexical meaning. McKay goes much further. The traditional labels attached to verbal morphology are inadequate, he insists, since they are connected in our minds with the time of event. Although he continues to use the labels 'perfect' and 'aorist', he introduces a new label, 'imperfective', to refer to the semantic weight of the present and imperfect verbal forms. Verbal aspect, he writes, is 'the way in which the writer or speaker regards the action in its context—as a whole act [aorist], as a process [imperfective], or as a state [perfect]'.[1] McKay insists that outside the indicative verbal aspect determines verbal meaning. Even in the indicative mood, he tends to minimize the extent to which the time of event is connected with verbal form.

Obviously I have mentioned only a few of the major players. Nevertheless this potted history sets the stage for Porter[2] and Fanning.[3] Their respective works are described and assessed (by each other and by others) in the following pages, and it is no part of my task to duplicate those efforts here. Still, it may be of use to students and to grammarians who have not wrestled with verbal-aspect theory if I briefly indicate where Porter and Fanning agree (and what an achievement this agreement signals), and where they disagree. The latter, though initially difficult to delineate precisely, is especially important: each ends up insisting the other has not really been consistent or even properly informed in his use of verbal aspect. An orientation to this polarization may make the debate somewhat easier to follow.

Both Porter and Fanning argue that verbal aspect is concerned with the 'viewpoint' of the author toward the event represented by the verb. Porter defines verbal aspect as

> a synthetic semantic category (realized in the forms of verbs) used of meaningful oppositions in a network of tense systems to grammaticalize the author's reasoned subjective choice of conception of a process.[4]

---

1. McKay, *Greek Grammar*, p. 44.
2. S.E. Porter, *Verbal Aspect in the Greek of the New Testament, with Reference to Tense and Mood* (Studies in Biblical Greek, 1; New York: Peter Lang, 1989).
3. B.M. Fanning, *Verbal Aspect in New Testament Greek* (Oxford Theological Monographs; Oxford: Clarendon Press, 1990).
4. Porter, *Verbal Aspect*, p. 88.

Somewhat similarly, Fanning writes,

> Verbal aspect in NT Greek is that category in the grammar of the verb
> which reflects the focus or viewpoint of the speaker in regard to the action
> or condition which the verb describes. . . To be more specific, aspect is
> concerned with the speaker's viewpoint concerning the action in the sense
> that it implicitly sets up a relationship between the action described and a
> reference-point from which the action is viewed. . . It is . . . a rather
> subjective category, since a speaker may choose to portray certain
> occurrences by one aspect or another without regard to the nature of the
> occurrence itself.[1]

To traditionalist grammarians, this level of agreement, in work
undertaken quite independently but building on a heritage of research
that has been overlooked far too long, is nothing short of stunning. It
means, for instance, that insofar as verbal aspect has been grammaticalized in the morphology of the Greek verb, one cannot immediately
leap to the kind of event to which reference is being made
(*Aktionsart*), or to the time of event to which reference is being made
(as in a time-based analysis of the verbal system), but to the writer's
or speaker's decision to depict the event in a particular way. The
bearing of this result on exegesis cannot easily be overestimated.

On the other hand, Porter and Fanning find themselves at odds over
several principles and countless details. If I understand them correctly, the heart of the issue between them is extremely important at
the level of fundamental theory—although, interestingly enough, in
many instances they would arrive at rather similar exegetical
conclusions even if their respective ways of arriving there are disparate. The issue between them can be simply put. Porter argues that
aspect and only aspect is grammaticalized in the tense-forms of Greek,
in all moods (which in his analysis are now renamed 'attitudes').
There are quasi-exceptions, such as the future, which has a place
apart, morphologically speaking, in the Greek verbal structure; or a
verb such as εἶναι, which does not offer a full range of tense-form
choices and is therefore 'aspectually vague', but in no case does the
tense-form carry an unambiguous semantic feature other than what is
aspectual (such as indication of time or *Aktionsart*). Fanning sharply
distinguishes aspect from *Aktionsart* at the theoretical level, but holds
that the actual semantic freight carried by any particular verbal form

---

1. Fanning, *Verbal Aspect*, pp. 84-85.

depends on complex interaction with lexis (the basic semantic range of the verb in question), context, temporal structures and much more. He is not saying merely that the sentence or the discourse carries this additional meaning, but that the verbal form itself takes it on board.

All the points of dispute between Porter and Fanning turn on these fundamentally different perceptions as to what meaning is conveyed by the verbal forms themselves. Fanning is greatly interested in the work of Vendler and Kenny[1] and their successors. Operating with philosophical rather than linguistic concerns, Vendler and Kenny, working independently, proposed rather similar taxonomies of verbs[2] and related these classifications to the kinds of action verbs might depict—that is to something akin to what Greek grammarians would call *Aktionsart*. One of Fanning's distinctive contributions is his attempt to relate the Vendler–Kenny taxonomy to aspect. In numerous instances this generates exegeses that have the feel of being fresh and nuanced. From Fanning's perspective, Porter's approach is reductionistic, failing to take into account the complexities that interrelate to convey meaning through the Greek tense-forms. Moreover, dependent as he is on Comrie's theoretical construction of aspect, Fanning objects to Porter's use of 'stative' as an aspect, judging that 'stative' is inseparably tied to *Aktionsart*. Porter, then, in Fanning's view, has not only failed to learn from the Vendler–Kenny taxonomy, but is reductionistic and even inconsistent.

Porter's approach to the subject is that of a working linguist. He adopts systemic linguistics as his model, a flexible and powerful (and astonishingly non-dogmatic) analytical tool developed by J.R. Firth and especially M.A.K. Halliday[3] (though as far as I can see his analysis

1.   Z. Vendler, 'Verbs and Times', *Philosophical Review* 66 (1975), pp. 43-60—reprinted and slightly revised in his *Linguistics in Philosophy* (Ithaca, NY: Cornell University Press, 1967), pp. 97-121; A. Kenny, *Action, Emotion and Will* (London: Routledge & Kegan Paul, 1963), pp. 151-86.

2.   Vendler's classification (to choose one of the two) is fourfold, in two groupings: A. Continuous verbs: (1) activities that 'go on in time in a homogeneous way'; (2) accomplishments that 'also go on in time' but 'proceed toward a terminus which is logically necessary to their being what they are', including a 'climax'; B. Non-continuous verbs: (1) achievements, which 'can be predicated only for single moments of time' or 'occur at a single moment'; (2) states, which 'can be predicated for shorter or longer periods of time' or may 'last for a period of time'.

3.   Probably their most important works are, respectively, J.R. Firth, *Papers in*

is not dependent on this model). Partly to avoid the confusion of using current labels in fresh ways, Porter adopts terminology common in Slavonic linguistics, and finds three fundamental aspects: perfective, grammaticalized in the aorist; imperfective, grammaticalized in the present and the imperfect, and the stative, grammaticalized in the perfect and pluperfect. Subtle adjustments are introduced into almost every dimension of Greek verbal morphology, but the result is that Porter argues that the *tense-forms* of Greek grammaticalize verbal aspect, and that alone. Of course, Porter is not unaware of the contributions to the meaning of verbs used in particular contexts made by lexis, context, and a complex web of markers that linguists sum up as *deixis*, but the entire focus of his work is on the semantics of the morphology of the Greek verb, not on pragmatics. From this perspective, a critic might disagree with many of Porter's brief exegeses without denting his theory in the slightest (in exactly the same way that traditionalist adherence to *Aktionsart* in moods outside the indicative could generate many different exegeses). From the vantage point of Porter, then, Fanning so seriously confuses semantics and pragmatics that his work is fatally flawed. Without any consistent, undergirding theory of the semantic contributions made by the morphology of the Greek verbal system Fanning's approach, in Porter's view, is methodologically arbitrary and linguistically without rigor.

At the consultation where these papers were first read, I found myself in the chair and therefore committed to neutrality. In introducing these essays, or at least the fundamental issue that has called them forth, I must maintain the same stance. But perhaps I might be permitted to venture one or two suggestions to the principal protagonists.

Porter has focused most of his considerable energies on developing a consistent semantic theory of Greek verbal morphology. Although he has not entirely ignored pragmatics, I suspect that his aspect theory will find wider and more rapid acceptance if he now devotes more attention to a systematic articulation of the ways in which a wide range of factors impinge on the meaning of a verb in a particular

Linguistics, 1934–51 (Oxford: Oxford University Press, 1951); and M.A.K. Halliday, *Halliday: System and Function in Language* (ed. G.R. Kress; Oxford: Oxford University Press, 1976).

context. The Vendler–Kenny taxonomy, for instance, could easily be adapted to dealing with the challenge of exegesis where the interpreter has adopted Porter's aspect theory. When Porter is charged with too forcefully stressing the subjective nature of the choice in tense-form made by the speaker or writer, he could develop at greater length than he has the kinds of factors (lexical, temporal, social and others) that might prompt the speaker to opt for one particular form. For instance, the fact that perhaps 85 per cent of finite aorists in the indicative are past-referring might owe a fair bit to the intrinsic likelihood that an action in the past will be presented as a 'complete' action: the speaker's or writer's choice of tense-forms (grammaticalizing aspects), theoretically as open-ended as the forms available, may be sharply constrained, or at least reduced within definable probabilities, by the pragmatics. Systematizing such reflections would go a long way toward deflating the protests of those grammarians who at this point are still unwilling to abandon all connections between verbal form and time in the indicative. It is not that Porter has done none of this work; rather one suspects that he will win more adherents by extending his theory along such lines in the future—or, more accurately put, by applying his theory to these kinds of problems.

Fanning has frequently demonstrated a fine sensitivity to the complexities of exegesis, and an admirably wide reading of many elements of aspect theory. On the long haul, however, if his theory is to prevail he must make explicit how morphology is tied to aspect (and other semantic elements?). More broadly, his future work on this topic will have to demonstrate a greater grasp of the fundamental distinction between semantics and pragmatics.

To both of these scholars all of us owe an immense debt of gratitude. Their work will be sifted and evaluated with profit for decades. For that reason the evaluations of Daryl Schmidt and Moisés Silva, published here, are not only invaluable in their own right, but harbingers of discussions to come. From now on, treatments of the verbal system of New Testament Greek that do not probingly interact with Porter and Fanning will rule themselves outmoded. Few works can claim so much; for their achievement we are grateful.

IN DEFENCE OF VERBAL ASPECT

Stanley E. Porter

Verbal Aspect as a Category in Greek Grammar and Linguistics

The growth and development of an academic discipline is never completely straightforward. There are at least as many false starts as successful hypotheses, but the false starts are often forgotten. Like the stories of wars, the history of scientific discovery is written by the victors. To use the useful terminology of T. Kuhn, the history of discovery for virtually every discipline that considers itself to be scientifically rigorous is one of periods of normal science disrupted by often tumultuous paradigm shifts.[1] These shifts are rarely graceful, since there is not only the issue of accuracy (or truth) at play, but there are numerous personal, political and social issues at stake as well.

In this progression, digression, retrogression and further progression, there are several possible reactions that bear directly upon discussion of verbal aspect. One is to ignore work which stretches the traditional categories and to pretend that all is normal and that normal is in fact the way things are. It is disheartening to find that few recent biblical commentators include insightful comments upon Greek grammar, and especially verbal structure. Perhaps it is out of ignorance, or perhaps it is out of fear that many 'assured' conclusions may not be so well grounded. Another reaction is to jump on any new hypothesis as the answer to all questions, thus circumventing further fruitful enquiry. One is reminded of rhetoric regarding redaction criticism as the panacea for understanding all Synoptic difficulties. A

---

1. T. Kuhn, *The Structure of Scientific Revolutions* (Chicago: University of Chicago Press, 2nd edn, 1970); cf. most recently V. Poythress, *Science and Hermeneutics* (Foundations of Contemporary Interpretation, 6; Grand Rapids: Zondervan, 1988), esp. pp. 39-49.

third reaction is to recognize the validity of a new construct but—in
resisting its full force—to make multifarious attempts to reconcile and
harmonize the old perspective with the new. This pattern has been
repeated numerous times in the history of scientific enquiry, and biblical studies is particularly susceptible to it, since it tends to be a
reactionary discipline. Without analysing the basis of many of its
current beliefs, it often attempts to incorporate new ideas into its
existing structures, frequently failing to ask whether such a synthesis
is methodologically possible (or even desirable). Elsewhere I have
argued that work on reader-response criticism is of such a kind.[1]

The study of ancient languages, in particular of biblical languages,
is experiencing a commendable—and I would say necessary—re-
orientation in the light of developments in modern linguistics. As biblical scholars, we are at last responding to L. Rydbeck's call.[2] Modern
linguistics is, as the name implies, a fairly recent discipline, delimited
and developed within the twentieth century. Contrary to some, it
cannot be equated simply with the ability to speak many languages
(i.e. being a polyglot) or with the traditional concerns of classical
philologists regarding the history of the language, the primacy of its
literary remnants, and reconstructions of rather arcane etymologies.
Instead, modern linguistics has its own assumptions (even if not all
linguists agree what they are) and its own way of treating this phenomenon called language.[3] This is not the place to define these
assumptions, except to say that most linguists are what might (for
simplicity's sake) be called synthetic, viewing language as an
autonomous system of interdependent structures, each warranting its
own analysis but not fully comprehensible apart from those linguistic
elements to which it is connected. This is a significant insight from
modern linguistics, one which needs to be appreciated in examination

1. See S.E. Porter, 'Why Hasn't Reader-Response Criticism Caught on in New
Testament Studies?', *Journal of Literature and Theology* 4 (1990), pp. 283-84.
2. L. Rydbeck, 'What Happened to Greek Grammar after Albert Debrunner?',
NTS 21 (1974–75), pp. 424-27. I hope that the response is not in the direct shadow
of Blass–Debrunner, however. See S.E. Porter, 'What Should a Modern Grammar
of an Ancient Language Look Like?: A Critique of the Schmidt Proposal for a New
Blass/Debrunner/Funk', *Forum* (in press).
3. See R. Hudson, 'Some Issues on which Linguists Can Agree', *Journal of
Linguistics* 17 (1981), pp. 333-43.

of any language, including the Greek of the New Testament.[1]

For whatever reason—and speculation could be quite profitable— the discipline of biblical studies hesitates to appropriate fully developments in other related and potentially productive areas of knowledge. These include, for example, sociology, literary interpretation of various kinds, psychology and modern linguistics. But recent developments in modern linguistics have been momentous and the pace and nature of its development continue. Recent research has moved beyond traditional linguistic concerns (e.g. phonology and morphology) into syntax, semantics, pragmatics and discourse analysis, among other areas. As far as biblical studies is concerned, this research includes what may be called primary research, such as that by K.L. McKay and J.P. Louw into verbal aspect;[2] M. Silva, Louw and Porter into semantics;[3] D.D. Schmidt and J.T. Reed into syntax;[4] and Louw and

---

1. See S.E. Porter, 'Studying Ancient Languages from a Modern Linguistic Perspective: Essential Terms and Terminology', *FN* 2 (1989), pp. 147-72.

2. K.L. McKay, 'Syntax in Exegesis', *TynBul* 23 (1972), pp. 39-57; *idem*, 'On the Perfect and Other Aspects in New Testament Greek', *NovT* 23 (1981), pp. 289-329; *idem*, 'Aspect in Imperatival Constructions in New Testament Greek', *NovT* 27 (1985), pp. 201-26; *idem*, 'Style and Significance in the Language of John 21.15-17', *NovT* 27 (1985), pp. 319-33; and *idem*, *Greek Grammar for Students: A Concise Grammar of Classical Attic with Special Reference to Aspect in the Verb* (Canberra: Australian National University, 1974); J.P. Louw, 'On Greek Prohibitions', *Acta Classica* 2 (1959), pp. 43-57; *idem*, 'Die Semantiese Waarde van die Perfektum in Hellenistiese Grieks', *Acta Classica* 10 (1967), pp. 23-32; *idem*, 'Verbal Aspek in Grieks', *Taalfasette* 15 (1971), pp. 13-26; *idem*, 'Verbal Aspect in the First Letter of John', *Neot* 9 (1975), pp. 98-104.

3. M. Silva, 'The Pauline Style as Lexical Choice: γινώσκειν and Related Verbs', in D.A. Hagner and M.J. Harris (eds.), *Pauline Studies* (Festschrift F.F. Bruce; Exeter: Paternoster Press, 1980), pp. 184-207; *idem, Biblical Words and their Meaning: An Introduction to Lexical Semantics* (Grand Rapids: Zondervan, 1983); J.P. Louw, *Semantics of New Testament Greek* (Philadelphia: Fortress Press, 1982); S.E. Porter, 'Is *dipsuchos* (James 1.8; 4.8) a "Christian" Word?', *Bib* 71 (1990), pp. 469-98; *idem*, καταλλάσσω in Ancient Greek Literature, with Reference to the Pauline Writings (Estudios de Filología Neotestamentaria, 5; Córdoba: Ediciones El Almendro, 1992 [in press]).

4. D.D. Schmidt, *Hellenistic Greek Grammar and Noam Chomsky: Nominalizing Transformations* (SBLDS, 62; Chico, CA: Scholars Press, 1981); J.T. Reed, 'The Infinitive with Two Substantival Accusatives: An Ambiguous Construction?', *NovT* 33 (1991), pp. 1-27.

E.A. Nida into discourse analysis;[1] among others. There have also been a significant number of works of secondary research, 'translating' modern linguistics for those who do not have the time, energy, inclination or requisite background for studying or developing primary works in linguistics.[2]

Verbal aspect is a notion of fairly recent provenance. For most linguists it falls under the category of semantics, in other words it is a category—no matter what its other linguistic properties—related to meaning. In this area, work in biblical Greek has not lagged far behind discussion of the topic in other linguistic circles.[3] B. Comrie did a tremendous service in his book, *Aspect*, first published in 1976. This was the first full-length monograph in English on the topic of

1. J.P. Louw, 'Discourse Analysis and the Greek New Testament', *BT* 24 (1973), pp. 101-18; *idem*, *A Semantic Discourse Analysis of Romans* (2 vols.; Pretoria: Department of Greek, University of Pretoria, 1987); E.A. Nida *et al.*, *Style and Discourse, with Special Reference to the Text of the Greek New Testament* (Roggebai, South Africa: Bible Society, 1983).

2. These include the following works: M. Silva, *God, Language and Scripture: Reading the Bible in the Light of General Linguistics* (Foundations of Contemporary Interpretation, 4; Grand Rapids: Zondervan, 1990), on general linguistics (see the short review by S.E. Porter in *JSNT* Booklist 45 [1992], p. 127); D.A. Black, *Linguistics for Students of New Testament Greek: A Survey of Basic Concepts and Applications* (Grand Rapids: Baker, 1988), on grammatical topics (he has written a number of articles using the methodology of Louw and Nida) (see the review by S.E. Porter in *CR* [1991], pp. 172-73); A.C. Thiselton, 'Semantics and New Testament Interpretation', in I.H. Marshall (ed.), *New Testament Interpretation: Essays on Principles and Methods* (Exeter: Paternoster Press, 2nd edn, 1979), pp. 75-104, on semantics; P. Cotterell and M. Turner, *Linguistics and Biblical Interpretation* (London: SPCK, 1989), on semantics and pragmatics (see the review by S.E. Porter in *CR* [1991], pp. 77-79); D.A. Carson, *Exegetical Fallacies* (Grand Rapids: Baker, 1984), on some of the linguistic errors of exegetes; and S.E. Porter, *Idioms of the Greek New Testament* (BLG, 2; Sheffield: JSOT Press, 1992), in an intermediate level grammar.

3. Two noteworthy articles deal with these topics in meaningful ways even though they were not perhaps fully aware of the larger linguistic issues: F. Stagg, 'The Abused Aorist', *JBL* 91 (1972), pp. 222-31; C.R. Smith, 'Errant Aorist Interpreters', *GTJ* 2 (1981), pp. 205-26. There are exceptions of course, in particular J. Thorley, 'Subjunctive Aktionsart in New Testament Greek: A Reassessment', *NovT* 30 (1988), pp. 193-211; *idem*, 'Aktionsart in New Testament Greek: Infinitive and Imperative', *NovT* 31 (1989), pp. 290-313.

verbal aspect,[1] followed by the useful monographs by Ö. Dahl and C. Bache.[2] McKay, whose publications on this topic began in 1965, has done the most significant work over the longest period of time on Greek, especially of the New Testament.[3] There are now two full-length monographs by Porter and B.M. Fanning (582 and 471 pages respectively) devoted to verbal aspect in the Greek of the New Testament or New Testament Greek, depending upon whose title one adopts.[4] (The difference in the titles is significant, because the first discusses the New Testament as one among many corpora of Hellenistic Greek texts, while the second treats the New Testament with few significant references to extra-biblical Greek and as a bit of

---

1.   B. Comrie, *Aspect: An Introduction to the Study of Verbal Aspect and Related Problems* (Cambridge Textbooks in Linguistics; Cambridge: Cambridge University Press, 1976). Also of relevance is his *Tense* (Cambridge Textbooks in Linguistics; Cambridge: Cambridge University Press, 1985). My evaluation of his work is found in S.E. Porter, *Verbal Aspect in the Greek of the New Testament, with Reference to Tense and Mood* (Studies in Biblical Greek, 1; New York: Peter Lang, 1989), pp. 45-47, although his perspective was widely used in formulation of my linguistic model of verbal usage in ch. 2.

2.   Ö. Dahl, *Tense and Aspect Systems* (Oxford: Basil Blackwell, 1985), and C. Bache, *Verbal Aspect: A General Theory and its Application to Present-Day English* (Odense University Studies in English, 8; Odense: Odense University Press, 1985). These two works proved highly instructive in the formulation of my linguistic model of verbal usage, and the interplay between the use of individual tense-forms and their recurrence in various discourse types (see Porter, *Verbal Aspect*, pp. 75-108). See also J. Forsyth, *A Grammar of Aspect: Usage and Meaning in the Russian Verb* (Cambridge: Cambridge University Press, 1970).

3.   Besides the works noted above, see K.L. McKay, 'The Use of the Ancient Greek Perfect down to the End of the Second Century AD', *Bulletin of the Institute of Classical Studies* 12 (1965), pp. 1-21; 'On the Perfect and Other Aspects in the Greek Non-Literary Papyri', *Bulletin of the Institute of Classical Studies* 27 (1980), pp. 23-49; 'Aspects of the Imperative in Ancient Greek', *Antichthon* 20 (1986), pp. 41-58. Louw's work precedes McKay's, but it was not published in places as accessible or languages as widely known.

4.   Porter, *Verbal Aspect* and B.M. Fanning, *Verbal Aspect in New Testament Greek* (Oxford Theological Monographs; Oxford: Clarendon Press, 1990). One needs only to look at the publication dates of the two works, and the substantial list of publications that anticipate them, to see that Fanning's statement that 'NT verbal aspect has received no recent comprehensive treatment' (p. 6) is somewhat hasty. See my short review in *JSNT* Booklist 43 (1991), pp. 127-28.

an oddity in the linguistic panoply of the ancient world.)[1] Although the works were done in Great Britain (as was Comrie's), they were done independently, with neither seeing the other's work until published. As one might expect, since the two authors were analysing essentially the same primary material, and drawing upon the same traditions of research, the two works have similarities. But they have a significant number of differences as well.

Areas of Agreement between Porter and Fanning

As I see them, the works by Porter and Fanning have in common the following basic features. Since these features are treated similarly or at least are compatible with each other in a number of ways, I will not fully explicate them. They are, nevertheless, worth recounting. Both works realize the importance of the semantic category of verbal aspect for understanding the structure of the Greek verbal system, as well as its potential implications for exegesis. The Greek verb is seen as part of a coordinated system of verbal structure, so that talking about the aorist tense (for example) has implications for talking about the present tense and the perfect tense. Both works place their discussions within the context of the historical discussion of Greek grammar, in particular of verbs, and attempt to chronicle the progress of the discussion. Both works have a number of functional categories into which to place particular instances of a given verbal usage. The results of analysis of a number of passages are often consonant. For example, both Fanning and I have a place for gnomic (or as I prefer, omnitemporal) use of the tenses, where we list Jas 1.11 and 1 Pet. 1.24 as gnomic aorists; for past use of the aorist tense and of the present tense (so-called historic present), where we list numerous examples found in strategic places in narrative; for the future-referring use of the tenses, where we list Mt. 26.45 and Mk 10.33 as examples of the future use of the present tense and Jn 13.31 and Jude 14 as examples of the aorist tense; for the present use of the aorist and present tenses;

---

1. The debate over the nature of the Greek of the New Testament is surveyed in S.E. Porter (ed.), *The Language of the New Testament: Classic Essays* (JSNTSup, 60; Sheffield: JSOT Press, 1991), which collects statements by A. Deissmann, J.H. Moulton, C.C. Torrey, M. Black, J.A. Fitzmyer, H.S. Gehman, N. Turner, L. Rydbeck and M. Silva.

and the like. These functional categorizations are similar, even though our theoretical underpinnings may be distinctly different (more on this below). And these are not seen by us as surprising exceptions— and *usually* not (although more often for Fanning than for me) as Semitically motivated. Both recognize the importance of acknowledging the difference in the mood forms. Both treat the indicative uses of the various verb tenses, and devote rather lengthy sections to examining instances of usage of the verbs in non-indicative contexts. Both have discussions of the use of the imperative, where we are agreed that the oft-repeated distinction between aorist and present for inceptive and continuing action cannot be sustained (although we arrive at very different analyses of what the difference between the two is).

In fact, Fanning and I have very similar definitions of what verbal aspect is. I define verbal aspect as 'a synthetic semantic category (realized in the forms of verbs) used of meaningful oppositions in a network of tense systems to grammaticalize the author's reasoned subjective choice of conception of a process'.[1] In a linguistic situation, among the many choices that a language user must make is the conception of a process. A Greek speaker had a choice of three verbal forms to grammaticalize three verbal aspects (note the relation of form and function): the aorist tense grammaticalized the semantic feature labelled 'perfective', the present tense 'imperfective', and the perfect tense 'stative'.[2] This language is not meant to imply that the choice by a language user was always (or ever!) conscious, but that the 'choice' was presented or required by the structure of the verbal system of the language. In defining the semantic features of this system, my formulation utilizes contrastive substitution to illustrate that absolute temporal categories (such as past, present and future) are not grammaticalized by the verb forms even in the indicative mood and that a particular verbal aspectual semantic feature is grammaticalized by a given verb form. In this analysis, such significant instances

1. Porter, *Verbal Aspect*, p. 88.
2. It must always be remembered that these labels are given to the verbal aspect grammaticalized by a tense-form, and in no way are fully descriptive of their meanings or functions. It must further be remembered that the given terminology is to be interpreted within its respective context. I use the term 'stative' within the context of the terminology of verbal aspect, and as elucidated in Louw, 'Die Semantiese Waarde van die Perfektum in Hellenistiese Grieks'; cf. Porter, *Verbal Aspect*, pp. 251-59.

mentioned above as the gnomic tenses, the historic present, and the like constitute important data that cannot be neglected. It is not only that such usage often goes beyond the parameters implied by the label given to a tense-form, since the names of the tense-forms are only markers, often formulated for various idiosyncratic reasons; it is also that such instances constitute legitimate and widely found verbal usage that must be semantically defined by the system. That semantic feature may indeed be shaped by use in a given context, but part of what using the form means is for it to have this particular meaning. The subjective factor involved means that the choice of verbal aspect rests upon the user, although patterns of usage, for example in various discourse types, mean that choice of verbal aspect is *not* random. The interpreter's latitude is circumscribed by the semantic features of the given form, and in this sense analysis of verbal aspect is objective.

Fanning's definition of verbal aspect is similar:

> Verbal aspect in NT Greek is that category in the grammar of the verb which reflects the focus or viewpoint of the speaker in regard to the action or condition which the verb describes. . . To be more specific, aspect is concerned with the speaker's viewpoint concerning the action in the sense that it implicitly sets up a relationship between the action described and a reference-point from which the action is viewed... Thus, aspect has nothing inherently to do with temporal sequence, with procedural characteristics of actual situations or of verbs and verb-phrases, or with prominence in discourse. It is instead a rather subjective category, since a speaker may choose to view or portray certain occurrences by one aspect or another without regard to the nature of the occurrence itself.[1]

I have selected these areas of agreement in large part because they are areas that distinguish these 'new' approaches to verb structure, and illustrate rightly the place that categories from modern linguistics can play in describing grammatical phenomena of ancient languages such as Greek. Traditional treatments typically (to make a gross generalization) looked at a particular tense-form in isolation, imposed absolute temporal reference upon it, were baffled by fairly commonplace 'exceptions', and even fossilized study of Greek grammar with the rather absurd assertion that nineteenth-century comparative philology,

---

1. Fanning, *Verbal Aspect*, pp. 84-85. He continues by referring to such things as procedural character and the nature of the action, both of which I dispute as relevant to a strict discussion of verbal aspect.

or even the ancient Greeks themselves, had answered all of the 'problems' of Greek grammar and linguistics. A slightly well-known (at least in some circles, none of them linguistic) professor once said this very thing to me.[1]

Areas of Disagreement between Porter and Fanning

Fanning and I are not far apart in our analyses of Greek verbal structure in so far as we recognize the importance of verbal aspect and have a fairly similar idea of what it is. But I do not want to minimize the significant differences in our treatments of verbal aspect and the Greek in which it appears, either. Many grammatical models can adequately treat a reasonably large number of common instances in a given language, but the difficult instances prove which is the most effective model and go the furthest to making the best grammatical rules. To the differences in our discussions of verbal aspect I now turn.

To refer back to the characteristic reactions I cited at the beginning of this paper, my treatment perhaps comes across as one that appears to circumvent further discussion. I posit rather boldly a scheme for analysis of the Greek verbal system that does not suffer exceptions gladly, since I believe that—especially for ancient languages—one must begin from the dictum that where there is a difference of form there is a difference in meaning or function. In the period since my initial work on verbal aspect, and after having pursued much further research in this area, I believe now more than ever that I was essentially correct in my analysis of the Greek verbal structure as a coordinated system of three verbal aspects grammaticalized by three major tense-forms, in which temporal reference is not grammaticalized in either the indicative or the non-indicative mood-forms. The *three* verbal aspects (of which the future form is *not* one, as will be discussed below) are conveniently and explicitly analysed in a set of semantic oppositions, which I illustrate by way of a system network.[2] The semantic relation of the verbal aspects can also be discussed in terms of other useful metaphorical expressions, such as the visual

1.   See also Rydbeck, 'What Happened to Greek Grammar', p. 427.
2.   See Porter, *Verbal Aspect*, p. 109. The necessary theory behind systemic linguistics is discussed in the introduction, pp. 1-16.

analogy of a parade and the description of discourse prominence.[1] My subsequent research has taken forward several of my initial comments regarding discourse analysis.[2] The concept of verbal aspect—at least as I define it—has proved useful. Some of the results of this work appear in several journal articles, a forthcoming commentary on Romans, and my *Idioms of the Greek New Testament*, an intermediate level grammar.[3] I believe that there is much to be said for the aorist serving as the background tense, the present as the foreground tense, and the perfect as the frontground tense in understanding many of the basic contours of units of discourse. Much more waits to be done regarding verbal aspect in various discourse types. Some of the potential for future research is well illustrated in the differences between the basic structures of narrative and exposition. In narrative the aorist tense or perfective aspect lays down a basic framework upon which more prominent items in the narrative—whether they be events or descriptions—are placed. In exposition, items are selected for description, analysis and the like, in which the present tense or imperfective aspect may be supported by the aorist tense or further heightened by the use of the perfect tense or stative aspect.

---

1. See Porter, *Verbal Aspect*, pp. 91-92, 92-93. Fanning (*Verbal Aspect*, p. 72) has stated that he believes that discourse functions are not the primary meanings of the verbal aspects, an idea in some ways mirrored in Silva's general comments on minimizing the exegetical significance of changes in tense form (*God, Language and Scripture*, pp. 117-18). Furthermore, even in English, the aspectual choice between the progressive and simple forms of the verb in 'When Sally got home, her husband was cooking dinner' and 'When Sally got home, her husband cooked dinner' has meaningful semantic implications regarding the conception and sequence of events.

2. Ch. 6 in Porter, *Verbal Aspect* (pp. 291-320), regarding conditional structures, was an attempt in this area, since it illustrated how verbal aspect could be applied to units larger than the clause. But the premise was functioning throughout the entire work, as illustrated in ch. 2 in discussion of forms of discourse (pp. 102-107), among other places.

3. E.g. S.E. Porter and J.T. Reed, 'Greek Grammar since BDF: A Retrospective and Prospective Analysis', *FN* 4 (1991), pp. 143-64; S.E. Porter, 'Greek Language and Linguistics (Keeping up with Recent Studies 17)', *ExpTim* 103 (1991–92), pp. 202-208; *idem*, *Idioms of the Greek New Testament*, esp. chs. 1 and 21; S.E. Porter *et al.*, *The Book of Romans: A Grammatical–Rhetorical Commentary* (Leiden: Brill, forthcoming).

Fanning's treatment, it seems to me, falls victim to the last reaction noted above, that is, of feeling compelled to harmonize the new paradigm with the old. The result is a less than satisfactory synthesis. Fanning presents a revisionist view of the history of verbal aspect, going to great lengths to preserve the traditional categories and terminology. He stresses his belief that the comparative philologists of the nineteenth century were in actual fact discussing verbal aspect, even if they did not call it this or recognize it as such.[1] I find this highly problematic. Research in linguistics regarding the category of verbal aspect, as the technical term has come to be understood, while needing to acknowledge earlier work which may have foreshadowed or paved the way for verbal aspect, has changed the terms of discussion.[2] This is well illustrated by the important discussion between H. Jacobsohn and E. Hermann in 1926–33, in which Jacobsohn usefully distinguished between subjective aspect, which is very similar to what is now defined as verbal aspect in the linguistic literature, and objective *Aktionsart*, the notion central to much earlier discussion.[3] Furthermore, the technical definition of verbal aspect is not readily compatible with the definition of the function and use of the verb tenses as typically conceived of in the pre-verbal aspect literature, as Fanning tacitly acknowledges in his critique of *Aktionsart*.[4] Fanning does not realize the full force of his criticism, for example, regarding the fact that the discussion of *Aktionsart* failed to consider its subjective nature (that is it regarded the way the action transpired as objective) and made semantic judgments on the basis of the meanings of individual lexical items. Fanning has a vested interest in maintaining

1. E.g. Fanning, *Verbal Aspect*, p. 12.
2. Two names are important here, the first being G. Curtius (*Elucidations of the Student's Greek Grammar* [trans. E. Abbott; London: Murray, 2nd edn, 1875], pp. 207-18) and the second being J.M. Stahl (*Kritisch-historischer Syntax des griechischen Verbums der klassischen Zeit* (Indogermanische Bibliothek, 4; Heidelberg: Winter, 1907]). But their work was to a large extent ignored and did not have the redefining forcefulness it perhaps should have. It is clear that they are outside the mainstream of the discussion of their times.
3. H. Jacobsohn, Review of *Vorlesungen*, by J. Wackernagel, *Gnomon* 2 (1926), pp. 369-95, esp. 378-86; E. Hermann, 'Objective und subjektive Aktionsart', *Indogermanische Forschungen* 45 (1927), pp. 207-28; H. Jacobsohn, 'Aspektfragen', *Indogermanische Forschungen* 51 (1933), pp. 292-318.
4. Fanning, *Verbal Aspect*, pp. 30-34.

this line of continuity, since he devotes a large section of chapter 1 and all of chapter 3 to defining the effect of inherent lexical meaning upon the meaning of the verbal aspects.[1] The result is a conflation of grammatical and lexical semantic categories in which lexis takes predominance over grammar (Fanning does not really ask the question of what constitutes inherent lexical meaning). As Fanning recognizes, this methodology is surprisingly similar to the method found, for example, in the work of K. Brugmann,[2] in which he posited categories of meaning and then gave examples, some of them in Greek and some in German, without establishing firm Greek-based criteria for how one is to estimate whether use of a verb is iterative or punctiliar (to use categories from Brugmann) or unbounded or durative (to use categories from Fanning).[3] At this point it seems that any principled formal basis for discussing verbal aspect as a grammatical category which describes verbal structure as a coordinated system of tense-forms has collapsed.

Like McKay, Fanning assumes, but does not argue in any rigorous way, the traditional view that the tense-forms in the indicative mood and when used as participles are time-based.[4] This poses problems. One is the methodological inconsistency it creates with his own definition of verbal aspect, which posits that it has nothing to do with temporal sequence. Another is the internal inconsistency with explaining—if his definition is correct—how the indicative functions as it does and how such examples as the future-referring use of the aorist

1.   Fanning, *Verbal Aspect*, pp. 42-50 and 126-96 respectively.

2.   K. Brugmann, *Griechische Grammatik* (ed. A. Thumb; Munich: Beck, 4th edn, 1913 [1885]), esp. pp. 538-41.

3.   This is not the place to discuss the apparent theological criteria which go into Fanning's categorization of verbs, so that he places verbs such as ἁγιάζω and ἁγνίζω, as well as verbs of 'dying', into the category of climaxes, that is verbs denoting instantaneous transitions. In the light of his treatment of usage in ch. 4, I believe that his statement on p. 127 n. 2 of *Verbal Aspect* is disingenuous.

4.   E.g. Fanning, *Verbal Aspect*, pp. 29 and n. 71, 185, 198, 407; cf. McKay, *Greek Grammar*, pp. 136-41; cf. pp. 214-24. Several grammarians before the advent of verbal aspect argued that participles were non-temporal, including E.D.W. Burton (*Syntax of the Moods and Tenses in New Testament Greek* [Chicago: University of Chicago Press, 3rd edn, 1898; repr. Grand Rapids: Kregel, 1976], p. 54 and *passim*) and A.T. Robertson (*A Grammar of the Greek New Testament in the Light of Historical Research* [Nashville: Broadman, 4th edn, 1934], p. 1111); cf. McKay, *Greek Grammar*, pp. 219-20.

participle are to be explained.[1] Fanning, it seems to me, is incapable of shedding a time-based perspective on verbs. This comes through transparently in his treatment of the perfect and the future tenses. Regarding the perfect tense Fanning strongly resists overthrowing the traditional conception of the tense as speaking of 'a state or condition resulting from a completed action'.[2] He goes so far as to say that the perfect is not an aspect like the aorist and present in his essentially two-aspect system, but combines three elements of meaning: tense, *Aktionsart* and aspect. According to Fanning's own terminology—in particular, his conflation of *Aktionsart* and aspect—this definition presents serious problems. The most significant is that it is flatly contradictory given his own definitions of *Aktionsart* (which I have argued is itself inherently contradictory)[3] and verbal aspect.[4] Regarding the future form, after citing several major positions, Fanning simply posits (he does not argue) that the future form is a 'non-aspectual *tense* category'.[5] He apparently means that rather than a category of *Aktionsart* or intention, it simply refers to future time. He does not consider paradigmatic peculiarities of the form, or views which discuss its relation to mood. I argue that the future form is not fully aspectual and neither an indicative nor a non-indicative mood form. It occupies a unique place in the Greek verbal structure.[6] In fact, Fanning provides enough evidence to have concluded similarly, if he had been able to free himself from the traditional categories.[7]

1. See Porter, *Verbal Aspect*, pp. 385-87.
2. Fanning, *Verbal Aspect*, p. 103.
3. Porter, *Verbal Aspect*, pp. 32-35.
4. It is interesting that the very useful article by Louw which disputes the traditional conception of the perfect ('Die Semantiese Waarde van die Perfektum'), and which I have used in my own redefinition of the meaning of the tense-form, is listed in Fanning's bibliography but not cited in his discussion of the meaning of the perfect.
5. Fanning, *Verbal Aspect*, p. 123.
6. Porter, *Verbal Aspect*, ch. 9 (pp. 403-49).
7. Fanning's traditionalist perspective is perhaps best summarized in a quotation from his *Verbal Aspect*, p. 196:

> What is recommended for the interpreter of the NT is an understanding of the aspects as differences in the speaker's viewpoint concerning the occurrence, a general awareness of this range of other features which can affect aspect-function, and a sensitivity in looking for such features in texts where the use of one of the aspects may be important to interpretation. In many ways this is no different from the procedure to be followed in

A second major difference between Fanning's work and mine is the role that modern linguistics plays. Fanning admits that he is not a linguist.[1] More importantly, I get an impression—it is only an impression, but it is a strong one—that linguistics is seen by Fanning as a tool. It is something that aids him in his task, but it remains a device that is selectively applied to the jobs to be done, and once the tool is worn out or is not useful or he does not know how to exploit it further he casts it aside. Now that the concept of verbal aspect has practical utility or the terminology is being widely employed, it is readily accepted by him and incorporated into his work. Just as *Aktionsart* as a name was thrown over when it was no longer au fait to use it, the same I suspect will happen to the term 'aspect', as far as Fanning is concerned. But for Fanning the categories he uses for his actual discussion—that is the practical framework regarding how the Greek verb functions—are unaffected by the conceptual categories of modern linguistics.

This can be seen in two important areas. First, when he actually discusses tense usage, Fanning's categories are the time-honoured ones employed by such grammars as Blass–Debrunner–Funk and Dana and Mantey, among others.[2] Why? Is it because these categories are

any area of exegesis: applying linguistic and historical sensitivity, along with a generous dose of common sense, to a broad array of contextual factors in order to construe the sense. What is to be avoided in any interpretive task is an atomistic approach to the text and its linguistic elements, and this is certainly true in regard to verbal aspect in NT Greek.

1. Fanning, *Verbal Aspect*, p. vi. However, he wishes for his book to be viewed as linguistic. By this he probably means that it is about language, as opposed to theology or history.

2. F. Blass and A. Debrunner, *A Greek Grammar of the New Testament and Other Early Christian Literature* (trans. R.W. Funk; Chicago: University of Chicago Press, 1961); H.E. Dana and J.R. Mantey, *A Manual Grammar of the Greek New Testament* (Toronto: Macmillan, 1955). Fanning's categories for the present indicative (*Verbal Aspect*, pp. 198-240) are: progressive present, instantaneous present, iterative present, gnomic present, present of past action still in progress, conative present, futuristic present, historic present, perfective present; for the imperfect (pp. 240-53) are: progressive imperfect, customary or iterative imperfect, conative imperfect, inceptive imperfect; for the aorist indicative (pp. 255-82) are: constative aorist, ingressive aorist, consummative aorist, gnomic aorist, proleptic aorist, dramatic aorist, epistolary aorist; for the perfect indicative (pp. 290-305) are: perfect of resulting state, perfect of completed action, perfect with aoristic sense, gnomic

sacrosanct, or fundamental in some intrinsic sense? No, they are not, even by Fanning's own terms; in other words, in the light of his own definition of verbal aspect, these categories must themselves be justified before they can be reintroduced into the discussion. They are merely enshrined by time and convention. Secondly, one notices that the explanations given for the various categories are for the most part in terms virtually identical to those of pre-verbal-aspect grammarians. A representative example is Fanning's treatment of the historic present.[1] He assumes that the vivid use, in other words, the transferring of past events into the present, is the function of the historic present (an explanation directly from *Aktionsart* grammarians),[2] and that it is simply a temporal transfer, not some sort of aspectual effect. His survey of significant discussions of the historic present is enviable, but there is no sustained attempt to discuss this usage in terms of the category of verbal aspect, which has been ruled out of play from the start. But how can this be? By Fanning's definition verbal aspect has to do with subjective choice of viewpoint and it seems that the historic present, if it is in fact used vividly, or if it is used as a narrative tense, or if it is simply a legitimate use of the Greek verb, requires some sort of explanation in (grammatical) aspectual or subjective terms.[3] Furthermore, linguists such as S.C. Levinson dealing with the area of pragmatics will be dismayed to know that they have taxed themselves over something as mundane as the epistolary aorist, which Fanning characterizes as 'quite straightforward',[4] something in fact which it is not.[5]

One's interpretative perspective does make a difference. The two earliest grammatical treatments of verbs, by the Greeks themselves (whom Fanning does not treat), had two different perspectives on how to classify and categorize the Greek verb. Dionysius Thrax was concerned with the issue of time: his classificatory scheme lists the tenses

perfect, proleptic perfect; for the pluperfect (pp. 305-309) are: pluperfect of resulting state, pluperfect of completed action, pluperfect with past stative meaning.

   1.   Fanning, *Verbal Aspect*, pp. 226-39.
   2.   E.g. Brugmann, *Griechische Grammatik*, pp. 555, 556.
   3.   Cf. Porter, *Verbal Aspect*, pp. 189-98.
   4.   Fanning, *Verbal Aspect*, p. 281.
   5.   See S.C. Levinson, *Pragmatics* (Cambridge Textbooks in Linguistics; Cambridge: Cambridge University Press, 1983), pp. 73-74; Porter, *Verbal Aspect*, pp. 228-30.

we would call the imperfect, aorist, perfect and pluperfect as past tenses. But the Stoics recognized kind of action as important, classifying verb forms by meaningful pairs (or oppositions), such as present-imperfect, perfect-pluperfect. The aorist and future remained an enigma, but were placed in opposition, perhaps illustrating a common semantic misunderstanding.[1] The same categories of time and kind of action have more recent practitioners in the rationalists of the eighteenth and nineteenth centuries, who described the verbs using highly time-bound categories,[2] and the comparative philologists (especially the New Grammarians) of the nineteenth century, who described verbs in terms of objective action.[3]

More recent examples are found in discussion of Rom. 2.12 and 3.23. If one is using a time-based scheme, one may well look, for example, to J.D.G. Dunn, who in commenting upon the use of the aorist in 2.12 says, 'Here the aorist (ἥμαρτον) is used, since at the final judgment the whole of life can be summed up as a single past event (though cf. 3.23 and 5.12)'. At 3.23 Dunn says that the 'aorist is used either because the perspective is that of the final judgment (as in 2.12, q.v.) or because the perspective is that of the decisive and universal character of man's fall (see further on 5.12)'.[4] This reflects the perspective of many commentaries, in which a mixed number of time-based and occasionally *Aktionsart*-based comments is made (although the tension in Dunn's analysis between past and future, many events and singularity is palpable). Fanning lists Rom. 3.23 as an example of

1. See Porter, *Verbal Aspect*, pp. 18-20 and 20-22, respectively.
2. See, e.g., W.E. Jelf, *A Grammar of the Greek Language Chiefly from the German of R. Kühner* (2 vols.; Oxford: James Henry Parker, 2nd edn, 1851), II, pp. 51-73; G.B. Winer, *A Treatise on the Grammar of New Testament Greek Regarded as a Sure Basis for New Testament Exegesis* (trans. W.F. Moulton; Edinburgh: T. & T. Clark, 3rd edn, 1882), esp. pp. 330-31.
3. See, e.g., Brugmann, *Griechische Grammatik*, esp. pp. 538-41; J.H. Moulton, *A Grammar of New Testament Greek*. I. *Prolegomena* (Edinburgh: T. & T. Clark, 3rd edn, 1908), pp. 108-51.
4. J.D.G. Dunn, *Romans 1–8* (WBC, 38A; Waco, TX: Word Books, 1988), pp. 96, 167. Dunn's commentary is selected not because it is necessarily the worst offender, but because of its temporal proximity to Fanning's work and mine on verbal aspect and its claim to being a major commentary on the Greek text. I know of two recent commentaries that take seriously discussion of verbal aspect: M. Silva, *Philippians* (Chicago: Moody, 1988), and esp. D.A. Carson, *The Gospel according to John* (Leicester: Inter-Varsity Press, 1991).

the constative or complexive aorist used to 'relate a *series* of repeated actions or states', in which the 'multiple situations may be either iterative… or distributive… The aorist in either case indicates a summary or composite of the repeated situations.'[1] I categorize Rom. 2.12 as an instance of the timeless use of the perfective aspect (on the basis of the context and in the light of the indefinite relative pronoun). I categorize Rom. 3.23 (and 5.12) as instances of the omnitemporal use of the perfective aspect (on the basis of the context and the use of πάντες).[2] To extend the implications of this analysis, it means that had the writer, Paul, chosen another tense-form (whether consciously or unconsciously is beside the point), for example the imperfect or present, the event he refers to would not have changed in and of itself but the aspectual semantics grammaticalized by the choice of another tense-form would have indicated a change in the writer's perspective. This would be true regardless of whether the change of tense-form resulted in a different translation in English.[3]

In keeping with my definition of aspect, I am less concerned with specifying precise temporal reference of a given tense-form (primarily because I do not believe that the verb forms in Greek grammaticalize absolute tense) than I am with explicating the semantic features that allow a given form to be used in a variety of contexts. It is clear in Dunn's case that he does not recognize the work of F. Stagg and others, much less of discussion of verbal aspect. He reflects the kind of understanding of Greek verbs found in elementary textbooks and the rationalist discussion of the eighteenth and early nineteenth centuries. His own comments illustrate that time-based categories are insufficient, however. Dunn never asks the important question of how these categories work together, quite possibly because the reference tools that he probably uses—such as Blass–Debrunner–Funk—do not ask

1. Fanning, *Verbal Aspect*, p. 258.
2. Porter, *Verbal Aspect*, pp. 237, 222. Cf. F.B. Denio, 'Translation of the Aorist Tense in the Indicative Mood', *BSac* 41 (1884), p. 388.
3. The difference between analysis of an ancient or epigraphic language and a modern language is often overlooked. The fact that speakers of, for example, modern English may know nothing about the workings of their language but can communicate in it has virtually no bearing upon the study of a language of which there are no native speakers and consequently there is no one with an innate knowledge of its system. All users of an epigraphic language must work from system to interpretation, whether or not they explicitly realize this.

these questions. What is perhaps more disappointing to see, but not entirely surprising in the light of my comments above, is that Fanning's treatment reads much like the discussion of *Aktionsart* found in nineteenth-century research. In other words, he shows more concern for the objective nature of the action than for the author's perspective on it. We cannot be dogmatic about the aorist as a past tense or as indicating one-time or punctiliar action, no matter how true we may believe the concepts to be (as Dunn illustrates), but neither can we see the aorist as reflecting objective action. The aorist, the present and the perfect tenses grammaticalize verbal aspects used by speakers to characterize processes, to make them, if you will, not simply to reflect them.

Many are willing to grant that modern linguistics has led to new ways of viewing language. One only needs to think of the fundamental re-orientation from diachronic to synchronic categories. It seems self-evident now—but this is because the categories of modern linguistics have had time to permeate our thoughts about language—that in analysing the Greek of the New Testament it is more important how the cases function in relation to each other or how the tenses form a system than whether the dative case is an amalgamation of three cases or the exact relation of the aorist to its Proto-Indo-European progenitor. The same re-orientation will become second nature in dealing with verbs as soon as the category of verbal aspect has had requisite time to permeate the linguistic vocabulary. By that I mean an accurate definition of the category. There will always be those who insist that the category is not viable; their insistence is the residual hesitance connected with any paradigm shift, according to Kuhn.

Not only is verbal aspect not simply *Aktionsart* in new clothing, or not simply another way of formulating the same temporal perspective on verbs, verbal aspect as a category of modern linguistics provides a new orientation to viewing the language itself. I would have preferred in my work merely to have defined the semantic force of, for example, the aorist or present or perfect tense and left it at that, a simple and elegant description of the semantics of the Greek tense-forms (I reject the notion that a grammatical analysis must have 'practical' or exegetical value to be valid or worth discussing). But semantics implies pragmatics,[1] and since temporal and other categories were

---

1. The distinction between semantics (the meaning of a form) and pragmatics

long-enshrined I was compelled to deal with such basic temporal notions as past, present and future. Along the way, I found it useful to include such terminology as omnitemporal and timeless, which place on the same plane categories that appear to be temporal but that expand the category to the point of breaking. One implies that a process cannot be pinned down to a specific time because it tends to happen all the time or at least regularly, and the other implies that a process cannot be pinned down to a specific time because there is no place on a timeline for such an event. The 'truths' of theology and mathematics are of this sort.[1] Once this is understood, one becomes acutely aware that it is difficult to pin down in any exact way the relation between a language event and any absolute conception of past, present and future *time* as well. This is true of Greek, Hebrew, English and any number of other languages—some more extremely so than Greek. So time, at least as a linguistic category, is no more absolute than any other, and I would contend that it is not grammaticalized, that is it is not enshrined by selection of a single tense-form in Greek, either in the non-indicative moods or in the indicative mood. The former has long been recognized by many serious students of Greek grammar, but the second moves beyond Fanning and even McKay. I am concerned to explicate what any of the verb tenses can be made by a speaker to do. The semantic category of verbal aspect can be imposed upon a process by a speaker, no matter when it may have occurred or how it may have actually occurred. This brings chills to some exegetes, because in their disjunctive (or tradition-bound) thinking they believe that this is another way of saying that the Greeks had no concern for time. I am in no way saying that time is unimportant. I am saying two things. The first is that when Greek speakers used a verb they had something other than temporal categories in mind with regard to what the verb form itself meant. They used the aorist form to mean one complex of things, and the present

(what the form means in context) is a useful one to differentiate between the level of definition and application. In fact, I would go further and contend that application cannot occur until the semantic framework is firmly in place.

1.   See J. Lyons, *Semantics* (Cambridge: Cambridge University Press, 1977), p. 680. Fanning obviously does not believe that these distinctions are worth making, since he conflates (or confuses?) the two. He defines the gnomic present in terms both of expressing 'timeless, universal occurrences' and of representing 'what occurs at *all* times' (*Verbal Aspect*, p. 208).

form to mean something else, and the perfect form for something else again. The second is that users could speak of when processes occurred, but they did not use verb forms alone to do so. They instead used various other tools in their language. For example, they would use deictic indicators such as temporal words or they would use discourse features, such as the type or kind of discourse.[1]

Conclusion

In conclusion, let me take this discussion beyond our two books. First, this is an important time in language study, since there is potential for rethinking many traditional categories in the light of work in theoretical and general linguistics. Secondly, the study of Greek, including that of the New Testament, is at a very promising point, when a new linguistic category—verbal aspect—is being analysed, assessed and even adopted. These new insights might well provide some of the needed impetus for renewing interest in the study of Greek at the undergraduate, theological college and seminary levels. Thirdly, this is an opportunity to go beyond the traditional strictures and confinements of discussion of the Greek New Testament to bring to bear a view of the language as a grammatical system, with all of the working parts functioning together. And verbal aspect, Fanning and I are agreed, should play a significant role in this linguistic revolution.

---

1. See Porter, *Verbal Aspect*, pp. 98-102; and *Idioms of the Greek New Testament*, chs. 1 and 21.

APPROACHES TO VERBAL ASPECT IN NEW TESTAMENT GREEK: ISSUES IN DEFINITION AND METHOD

Buist M. Fanning

It is remarkable that two major books on the topic covered here should have appeared within a year of each other. During the past seventy-five years, numerous monographs and major articles have been produced on verbal aspect in general linguistics and the study of other specific languages. But research on aspect in Hellenistic and New Testament Greek has been rare, usually limited in scope, and not widely known. Unfortunately, such study is still plagued by attitudes which regard grammatical issues as either already solved or rather unimportant.

So I welcome the opportunity to discuss these two books, as a way of clarifying what progress has been made and informing a wider readership of the issues involved. In the first section of my essay I intend to summarize the approach to verbal aspect which is given in my book, *Verbal Aspect in New Testament Greek*.[1] In the later section I will offer some evaluation of the approach to aspect taken by Stanley E. Porter in his *Verbal Aspect in the Greek of the New Testament, with Reference to Tense and Mood*.[2]

Summary of the Approach Taken in Fanning, Verbal Aspect in New Testament Greek

I think it will be clear to anyone who reads my book that it was written by a New Testament interpreter to help New Testament interpreters. I became interested in the topic initially in the midst of my own exegetical study of the New Testament and while trying to teach New Testament language and exegesis to seminarians. It became clear

1. Oxford: Clarendon Press, 1990.
2. New York: Peter Lang, 1989.

to me in the process that verbal aspect is a significant element in understanding many New Testament texts and that the traditional explanations of aspect are inadequate to give the kind of insight that an interpreter needs for his or her work. I embarked upon doctoral research in this area under the supervision first of George Caird and later of John Ashton, two New Testament exegetes and theologians who possessed a fine instinct for language and how it works, but who were not linguists in any technical sense. Caird especially tied me to the New Testament text from the very beginning, forcing me time after time to justify my insights by discussing actual examples of usage for which my ideas offered real help. He had very little patience for grand solutions worded in complicated linguistic jargon which claim to solve all problems, yet in fact offer little understandable help to the exegete. The goal of providing insight for the New Testament interpreter has molded my work in many ways (others will have to judge whether for good or for ill).

I want to summarize my approach to aspect by surveying a series of major conclusions for which I argue in the book. Many details will remain unmentioned and there is little space to give supporting discussion, so I will leave those things for someone to pursue on his or her own from the book itself.

a. *The Need to Distinguish Aspect itself from Related Features of Meaning*
Verbal aspect is difficult to define and work with because it always operates in a complex web of combinations with other features of meaning. The history of aspect studies has shown, I think, that the first step in understanding verbal aspect is to distinguish aspect itself from other features of meaning with which it is commonly confused. These other features include: the temporal meanings of the tenses; the lexical character of verbs themselves; meanings carried by verbal adjuncts such as objects, subjects, adverbs, prepositional phrases, and so forth; and certain features shown by the larger context. The development of aspect studies over the past 150 years has been consistently in the direction of more clearly distinguishing aspect itself from these other elements.

b. *The Importance of Maintaining a Strict Semantic Distinction between Aspect and Aktionsart*

These key terms are often used interchangeably by New Testament grammars, but in wider studies of aspect a distinction between the two concepts has been accepted, which makes a significant difference for understanding aspect. This distinction has been made on two levels, the second more rigorous than the first.

At a basic level the distinction involves defining aspect as the way in which a speaker views or portrays a situation, and defining *Aktionsart* as the procedural character or nature of the occurrence itself. It is often said at this level that aspect is more *subjective*, involving a free choice by the speaker to view the occurrence however he or she chooses, while *Aktionsart* is more *objective*, since it is dictated by the actual character of the action or state described. In this sense we would label as *Aktionsarten* a number of the contrasts traditionally associated with the difference between present and aorist in Greek: for example, durative/momentary, repeated/single, incomplete/accomplished, and so on. Aspect, on the other hand, is said to be concerned not with the actual occurrence but with how the speaker chooses to view the occurrence and is not dictated by the characteristics of the action itself. Along this line it is sometimes stated that *Aktionsart* is a matter of lexical meaning, while aspect is a matter of morphology or grammar since it is expressed by the grammatical category of present or aorist. In broad terms these statements are true, but the distinction must be taken further and qualifications need to be introduced.

A more rigorous distinction and qualifications of this contrast were made clear in a series of articles in the 1920s and 1930s by Porzig and Hermann,[1] and these have been picked up and refined more recently by Carl Bache (1982, 1985) and Carlota Smith (1983).[2] These writers argue, and I think I have shown it to be valid for New Testament

---

1. W. Porzig, 'Zur Aktionsart indogermanischer Präsensbildungen', *Indogermanische Forschungen* 45 (1927), pp. 152-67; and E. Hermann, 'Objektive und subjektive Aktionsart', *Indogermanische Forschungen* 45 (1927), pp. 207-28; *idem*, 'Aspekt und Aktionsart', *Nachrichten der Gesellschaft der Wissenschaften zu Göttingen* 5 (1933), pp. 470-80.

2. C. Bache, 'Aspect and Aktionsart: Towards a Semantic Distinction', *Journal of Linguistics* 18 (1982), pp. 57-72; *idem, Verbal Aspect: A General Theory and its Application to Present-Day English* (Odense: Odense University Press, 1985); and C.S. Smith, 'A Theory of Aspectual Choice', *Language* 59 (1983), pp. 479-501.

Greek, that a strict semantic distinction must be maintained between aspect and *Aktionsart*. What should be recognized is that features of verbal meaning commonly labelled *Aktionsarten* are of an entirely different order semantically than other features labelled 'aspects'. *Aktionsart* deals with matters of procedural character, including temporal properties (duration versus momentariness), kinetic properties (action versus state, process versus event, etc.), count features (single versus multiple), and matters of scope (general versus specific). Aspect, on the other hand, does not move on the same semantic plane. That is, it is not simply the same procedural features viewed subjectively, as though the present, for example, views an occurrence as durative or views it as a process. Instead, aspect reflects the focus or viewpoint of the speaker in reference to the occurrence, the perspective from which the occurrence is regarded, or the portrayal of the occurrence, totally apart from any features of procedural character.

To be more specific, aspect is concerned with the speaker's viewpoint concerning the action, in the sense that it implicitly sets up a relationship between the occurrence described and a reference point from which it is viewed. The crucial aspectual distinction is whether this reference point is internal or external to the occurrence. It may be viewed from a reference point *within* the occurrence, without reference to the beginning or end-point, but with focus instead on its internal structure or make-up. Or the occurrence may be viewed from a vantage point *outside*, with focus on the whole occurrence from beginning to end, without reference to its internal structure. A simpler way to articulate this is to say that one may take a *near* view, emphasizing the details of whatever may constitute the occurrence; or one may take a *distant* view, picturing the whole occurrence in summary without attention to the details. This difference of viewpoint or focus is the essential nature of verbal aspect, and it is semantically distinct from procedural character. I think this is what Porter means when he speaks of aspect as 'grammacaliz[ing] the author's reasoned subjective choice of conception of a process',[1] and so there is agreement between the two books on this point. I wonder, however, how his analysis of the perfect can be incorporated into the category of 'aspect as conception of a process', since *stative* (his label for the

1. Cf. Porter, *Verbal Aspect*, p. 88. His comments about visualization (p. 91) clearly fit the scheme of internal versus external viewpoint for present and aorist.

perfect) is an *Aktionsart*, not an aspect.[1] I think Porter has not been rigorous enough in grasping the difference between aspect and *Aktionsart* and in pursuing that all the way through his analysis.[2]

c. *The Recognition that neither Aspect nor Aktionsart is Totally Objective or Subjective*

Writers who recognize some sort of difference between aspect and *Aktionsart* as discussed above often emphasize the subjectivity of aspect and the objectivity of *Aktionsart*. Bache (1982) has argued convincingly, I think, that this distinction must be modified on both sides, although it does reflect an important general difference between the two.

He argues first that *Aktionsart* is not always objective in the sense of 'applying to the real world', since it frequently involves not actual differences in external facts but rather differing perceptions by the speaker (or by his speech-community) in which the action is *conceived* as durative or momentary and so on. Thus, he concludes that matters of *Aktionsart* '...are not to be regarded as physically measurable,

---

1.   My own approach to the perfect is an attempt to see aspect consistently as 'viewpoint' rather than procedural character and to apply that distinction to the perfect. Thus, there are significant oppositions between the perfect and the pure aspects (present and aorist), but they are not at the definition level. This treatment of the perfect as something different from the present and aorist is not idiosyncratic; it is the standard approach in recent aspect studies. See P. Friedrich, *On Aspect Theory and Homeric Aspect* (International Journal of American Linguistics, Memoir 28; Chicago: University of Chicago Press, 1974), pp. 16-19, 36; B. Comrie, *Aspect: An Introduction to the Study of Verbal Aspect and Related Problems* (Cambridge: Cambridge University Press, 1976), pp. 52-53; A.L. Lloyd, *Anatomy of the Verb: The Gothic Verb as a Model for a Unified Theory of Aspect, Actional Types, and Verbal Velocity* (Amsterdam: John Benjamins, 1979), pp. 117-18; and J. Bybee, *Morphology: A Study of the Relation between Meaning and Form* (Amsterdam: John Benjamins, 1985), pp. 141, 159-61. The three-part opposition as in Porter is found primarily in older Greek grammars and earlier linguistic studies.

2.   Thus, the description of my book in Porter's review in *JSNT* 43 (1991), p. 127, as 'an exposition of *Aktionsart*, not verbal aspect' is a distortion of my approach. I clearly articulate a view of aspect itself as viewpoint not *Aktionsart* (a point on which Porter's book is not clear), but go on to discuss secondary distinctions arising in combination with procedural character. This comment by Porter is akin to someone charging that his book is really an exposition of tense, since he gives attention to secondary functions which focus on temporal distinctions.

"objective" characteristics of situations but rather as psychological classifications of (objective and other) situations based on intuitive belief or conception'.[1]

He argues, on the other side, that aspect is not always subjective in the sense of 'offering an optional choice'. It is true that numerous examples can be found where in the description of a given action there is an open choice between one aspect or the other, depending on what a speaker wishes to emphasize. But in many instances the degree of optional choice is reduced and the speaker is limited to one aspect rather than another because of the combination of aspect with other features. In fact Bache argues that the only instance offering a truly free choice of aspects is one in which the situation is perceived as being durative, unbounded and non-stative.[2] But this can better be explained by going on to a fourth basic conclusion.

1. Bache, 'Aspect and Aktionsart', pp. 65-66, 70.
2. Bache, 'Aspect and Aktionsart', pp. 66-69; those not familiar with such discussions should read especially pp. 68-69. Bache details each restriction. Verbs or phrases denoting what is perceived to be a specific instantaneous act do not offer a free choice of portraying the act as perfective (aorist) *or* imperfective (present): the perfective would portray the single, momentary act, but the imperfective would denote either rapid iteration of the act or some prefaced action leading up to the act itself. Contrast the aorist in Acts 5.5 (ἐξέψυξεν) with the imperfect in Lk. 8.42 (ἀπέθνῃσκεν). Verbs or phrases denoting what is perceived to be a specific bounded process (an activity leading to a natural end-point or goal) likewise do not offer a free choice: the perfective denotes the accomplishment of the goal, while the imperfective refers to the process leading toward the goal but not reaching it. See Acts 5.39 (ἐπείσθησαν) versus Acts 7.26 (συνήλλασσεν). Verbs or phrases denoting a specific situation perceived to be stative also do not offer an optional choice: the perfective will shift the reference almost always to a focus on the act of entering the state, while the imperfective refers to the on-going condition in existence at that time. See Lk. 15.32 (ἔζησεν) versus Rom. 7.9 (ἔζων). In each of these cases, the speaker has a choice to be sure, but his choice is not fully subjective and does not operate purely at the level of viewpoint. Instead it is overlaid with various secondary contrasts which limit the speaker's free choice. Analysis of these uses which stops at the level of 'subjective conception' are simply incomplete.

Bache's discussion is crystal-clear, but it is not novel. Analyses like his of interactions between viewpoint and actional character are common fare and widely accepted in recent studies of aspect. He and others have demonstrated that fully subjective or optional choices between aspects are relatively rare and that analysis of oppositions between aspects is not complete without attention to such secondary contrasts.

d. *The Importance of Analyzing the Interaction between Aspect and other Linguistic Features*

I have argued throughout my book that aspect operates so closely with other linguistic features and is so significantly affected by them that no treatment of aspect can be complete without attention to these interactions. I think one of the weaknesses of Porter's treatment is that he does not pursue the meaning of aspect much beyond the most general or primary level. When he analyzes New Testament examples, he is usually content to state only that the difference is one of conception of the action.[1] But differences between the aspects in actual usage are always overlaid with various secondary distinctions produced by combination with other features. This should not lead us to confuse the viewpoint meanings of the aspects themselves with these other features, but it does require attention to the patterns of interaction which can be observed.

As Bache puts it (and others express a similar distinction), aspect should be analyzed both at a definitional level and at a functional level.[2] The *definitional* level focuses on the sense carried by the aspects themselves: that is, the meaning that the aorist or present has on its own apart from any other influence. The distinctions of internal versus external viewpoint come into play at the definitional level. On the other hand, the *functional* level moves to examine secondary or combinatory meanings produced in context when the sense of the aorist or present interacts with other features of meaning (such as the temporal meanings of the indicative forms, the lexical character of the verb itself, the nature of the subject or object phrase, use of various adverbs or prepositional modifiers, features of the broader context, and so forth). Porter refers to this sort of distinction (that is, of definition versus function), when he speaks of code versus text, semantics versus pragmatics, or primary versus secondary meanings for the aspects.[3] But he does not pursue the discussion. The point to be stressed is that a competent grasp of verbal aspect requires an

1. Cf. Porter, *Verbal Aspect*, pp. 324-34, 352-60.
2. Bache, *Verbal Aspect: A General Theory*, pp. 145-52; and 'The Semantics of Grammatical Categories: A Dialectical Approach', *Journal of Linguistics* 21 (1985), pp. 51-77. See also Smith, 'Aspectual Choice', pp. 482, 491-95. As Smith shows, the interpretation of aspect must be done both by maintaining a distinction between the two categories and by examining the interaction between the two.
3. Porter, *Verbal Aspect*, pp. 82-83, 97, 107.

interpreter or linguist to work on both levels of meaning but at the same time to be aware of the distinction between the two. I regard this to be very significant for the analysis of aspect in New Testament texts, and I tried to give as much attention to this as possible. Some of my suggestions along this line may need refinement, but I believe better understanding of aspectual usage will be gained by moving down this path of analysis.

In the wider literature on aspect, much has been done to lay the groundwork for analyzing the patterns of interaction displayed when aspect combines with other features of meaning. A well-known and widely accepted approach for working with part of these interactions is the Vendler–Kenny classification of actional types. This moves us to a fifth point.

e. *The Value of the Vendler–Kenny Taxonomy for Clarifying the Interaction between Aspect and Procedural Character*
In two essays prepared apparently without reference to each other (1957, 1963), Vendler and Kenny suggest a series of three or four verb classes or proposition classes based on distinctions of actional character.[1] This scheme was adopted and applied with some profit to New Testament verbal aspect by Mateos (1977).[2] Based on the work of these three writers, refinements suggested by others, and my own analysis, I posit in chapter 3 a five-part hierarchy of distinctions based on actional features of verbs in propositions. The fine points of such a scheme are extremely difficult to work out, and I am sure that details of my approach can be improved upon. I contend, however, that the broad outlines are correct and they provide significant help for analyzing the interaction of aspect with such procedural features. Porter at several points suggests that this avenue of research could be pursued with profit, but he does not follow it up in his book.[3]

In basic terms, these verb classes look for differences in procedural character as expressed in context by the lexical meaning of the verb

1. Z. Vendler, 'Verbs and Times', *The Philosophical Review* 66 (1957), pp. 43-60; reprinted in Z. Vendler, *Linguistics in Philosophy* (Ithaca, NY: Cornell University Press, 1967), pp. 97-121; and A. Kenny, *Action, Emotion and Will* (London: Routledge & Kegan Paul, 1963), pp. 151-86.
2. J. Mateos, *El aspecto verbal en el Nuevo Testamento* (Estudios de Nuevo Testamento, 1; Madrid: Ediciones Cristiandad, 1977).
3. Porter, *Verbal Aspect*, pp. 35 n. 15, 87, 96-97.

itself or by the combination of the lexical sense with other adjuncts (subject or object phrases, adverbs, etc.). So we would ask, for example, whether the verb is stative or active, a process or an instantaneous act, an activity which goes on without an inherent terminus or a process leading to a natural end point. The nature of noun phrases and other adjuncts is important because they help to show whether the action is done on a single, specific occasion or repeated at various times more generally. I think most would regard these to be obvious distinctions to look for in weighing the sense of a present or aorist within a context. Working with these kinds of observations has always been a part of competent, contextually sensitive interpretation of the aspects. What I have tried to do is to specify more carefully what other factors one should look for along these lines and to describe the predictable patterns of secondary meanings which are produced by these combinations.

These considerations are a natural concomitant of seeing aspect as a matter of viewpoint or focus. When a speaker chooses the internal viewpoint of the present, he signals a focus on the details of the occurrence. Thus we should examine the nature of that occurrence: is the emphasis on an unbounded process as it takes place, on an iterative series of acts, on a bounded process which at this point has not reached its terminus, or on a multiplicity of occurrences taking place on various occasions perhaps as a customary thing? The use of present aspect invites us to look further at the procedural character of the occurrence in this way. The aorist, on the other hand, looks at the occurrence in summary without attention to the details. But often it is valuable to inquire from context whether the occurrence itself is a single, specific act or a series of actions done at various times but narrated without emphasis on the repetition. Attention to this sort of thing is essential for giving an adequate account of aspectual function. While we end up examining matters of *Aktionsart* and wider features of meaning in the process, this is not a case of conflating aspect and *Aktionsart*. We must maintain a clear distinction between the two, but at the same time analyze the combinations with other features.[1]

---

1. This is seen most plainly in the articles and book by Bache cited above. He gives one of the clearest semantic distinctions between aspect and *Aktionsart*, yet insists on seeing how both areas of meaning work together pragmatically.

f. *Importance of the Secondary Distinction between General versus Specific Occurrence*

In the process of studying the use of the aspects in New Testament Greek, I have found one secondary distinction to be more significant than the literature on aspect would lead one to anticipate.[1] This is the difference of scope or frame of reference: that is, general versus specific occurrence. I find this to be a crucial feature of meaning to look for in the interpretation of aspect. The difference between so-called progressive use and customary use of the present or imperfect centers on the feature of scope: is the occurrence viewed in a narrow frame as taking place on a specific occasion or is it seen more generally as occurring at various times in a broader frame? Similarly the use of present and aorist in New Testament commands and prohibitions commonly exhibits a difference of this sort. The traditional distinction[2] of general precept versus specific command goes a long way towards explaining aspectual usage in New Testament commands and prohibitions. Thus, present imperatives are the most common usage in New Testament epistles and discourses, where 'rules for life' or 'whenever'-type commands are given (e.g., Gal. 6.1, καταρτίζετε— not 'keep on restoring' in some specific case or narrow frame, but 'restore' whenever the need arises in the community; 1 Cor. 11.28, dokimazétv—not 'be examining' but 'examine whenever. . . '). In narrative it is more common to find aorists, since the sense is often 'do this act on this occasion', but without intention to govern behavior more broadly. A number of exceptions to this do occur but the exceptions fall into predictable patterns.[3]

---

1. This difference is mentioned occasionally in standard grammars and in studies of aspect but not developed far enough, I think. One recent exception is P. Stork, *The Aspectual Usage of the Dynamic Infinitive in Herodotus* (Groningen: Bouma, 1982), pp. 51-88, 368-71, 392-95.

2. Cited, e.g., by F. Blass and A. Debrunner, *A Greek Grammar of the New Testament and Other Early Christian Literature* (trans. and rev. R.W. Funk; Chicago: University of Chicago Press, 1961), §335.

3. See ch. 5 of my book. It is disconcerting to see how cavalierly Porter (*Verbal Aspect*, pp. 340 n. 14, 351) dismisses this distinction. Perhaps he does not grasp the point at issue, since he claims to have difficulty with seeing the imperatives of 1 Cor. 16.13-14 as general rather than specific!

g. *Structural Relations between the Aspects to be Analyzed at the Functional Level, not at the Definitional Level*

I began my research on New Testament verbal aspect with a hypothesis that the aspects could be best explained by a system of two privative or binary oppositions, with the present as the marked member opposed to the aorist in one area of contrast and as the unmarked member opposed to the perfect in another contrast. As I pursued this scheme, I became dissatisfied with it and with other such systems which seek to explain aspect usage as oppositions at the macro level. While I can see that these have some value, I am convinced that the more important contrasts to study are the functional level oppositions. These oppositions take into account the other linguistic features which affect the meaning of aspect in specific contexts. In this way we can examine the speaker's choice of aspects more precisely by paying attention to its specific constraints. For example, given the use of a stative verb to describe a specific situation, what meaning would the present or imperfect carry in contrast to the aorist? (The aorist will almost always be ingressive, denoting the entrance into the condition, while the present aspect will focus on the existence of the state at that particular point.[1]) While these combinations are immensely complex and cannot be diagrammed in one grand chart, I think these are the kinds of structural oppositions which help to make sense of the aspects for the interpreter.

In conclusion, I have argued in my book that understanding verbal aspect requires us to grasp both the basic meanings of the aspects themselves and their function in combination with other linguistic features. The ways in which aspect interacts with these other features are complex, but they fall into predictable patterns. This welter of combinations, however, engenders problems, because it is easy to attach one of the combinatory senses (e.g., duration, repetition, specific act) to the aspect itself and expect to find that sense in all its occurrences. The semantic complexity of aspectual usage suggests that one must unpack several levels of meaning in order to give an adequate account of it.

The *definition* of the aspects should be stated in terms of the viewpoint which the speaker takes on an occurrence, whether internal or external, as explained above. Somewhat separate from this are

---

1. See pp. 136-40 of my book.

meanings like duration, completion, repetition, and so forth, which are *functions* of the aspects in combination with lexical and contextual features. It is true that some of the clearest contrasts of the aspects in actual usage are these combinatory variants. Such meanings are often stated as the basic definitions of the aspects by traditional grammars of New Testament Greek. The argument of my book is that such meanings must not be given as *definitions* of the aspects themselves but together with other kinds of distinctions should be clearly articulated as their secondary *functions* in combination with other elements. One must work on both levels to give an adequate account of aspect and provide help for the interpreter.

Evaluation of Porter, Verbal Aspect in the Greek of the New Testament

I have mentioned several points of evaluation concerning Porter's book in the first section of this essay. Now I wish to give my reactions to his book in a more organized way.

It is important to state at the outset my sincere appreciation and admiration for the work Porter has done. He has invested a prodigious amount of work in this book, and his expertise in linguistics and biblical studies contributes significantly to our discipline. His treatment touches on a wider range of issues than verbal aspect alone. He has already demonstrated by his publishing record that he has much to offer to the field. I applaud him in this and look forward to his continued contributions. It is also important for readers to note how many areas of agreement there are between our two books. Our results are complementary in many ways, and I hope we have given others a foundation on which to build or a greater understanding from which to offer better solutions.

However, since no treatment of these matters can be regarded as entirely correct or complete, I offer some suggestions for correction or further study. We must all be ready to learn from colleagues in our field, especially those who have worked carefully in the same area of study. While I have some stiff criticism to mention, I am trying to offer it in a collegial spirit and I hope it is received in that vein. It is no favor to step politely around areas of disagreement or suggested improvement as though they did not exist.

In broad summary, I see that Porter argues for three main

conclusions about Greek verbal aspect: (1) temporal meanings are not important, (2) we must distinguish *Aktionsart* from aspect by recognizing that aspectual choice is subjective, and (3) choices between the aspects are structured in a network of systemic oppositions.[1] I want to evaluate these conclusions in sequence.

First, I disagree with Porter's strict insistence that the Greek verbal forms carry no temporal value at all, and I do not think that his view of this offers the kind of ground-breaking contribution to the field that he has claimed for it. I believe Porter has made the best case for this view that anyone can make, but it is not persuasive. It is true that time is not as important for Greek tenses as for English ones and that the aspect values of viewpoint or conception of the process are of central importance in all the forms of the Greek verb (except the future). But the linguistic evidence is overwhelming that in the indicative forms the tenses carry a double sense of time and aspect together.

Porter's basic argument against this is as follows: examples of the present or aorist or perfect can be found which refer to past, present, or future or to omnitemporal events; therefore these forms cannot be said to grammaticalize any time value at all.[2] This sort of analysis is too simplistic, and the examples cited as contrasting pairs cry out for more careful examination. Are these instances normative or exceptional? Is there anything going on in these examples which causes departures from otherwise consistent patterns of temporal meaning? While they cannot be discussed in detail here, I argue that his examples are exceptional and that hard cases make bad law. A theory of Greek present and aorist which centers its evidence on things like historical presents, gnomic aorists and dramatic aorists has the wrong end of the stick. Porter has shown me that I have more to learn about these exceptional uses, but I am not convinced that our whole approach to the tense–aspect system should be molded to these.

Porter is ready to acknowledge that many or most aorist indicatives can be found in contexts narrating past events and many or most present indicatives are used in instances describing events going on in the present.[3] But such temporal indications come, he argues, from

1. Cf. Porter, *Verbal Aspect*, p. 107.
2. Porter, *Verbal Aspect*, pp. 75-79.
3. So the practical impact of his view is minimal, despite his broader claims.

deictic markers used along with the verbs or by standard association with certain contexts.[1] But the same argument can be made more easily for the opposite point: the broadly evidenced time values do attach directly to the indicative tenses, and occasional exceptions can be explained by other influences. I think he has missed the pattern evidenced by the vast body of usage in New Testament Greek in favor of a few anomalous instances. I understand Porter's argument that the typical or most frequent occurrence may not go to the heart of what the form expresses, but I believe he has been misled by trying to formulate a theory which brooks absolutely no exceptions.

Also, it seems to me that Porter spends so much time insisting on the absence of temporal meaning and assuming that this makes a vast difference, that he has neglected large areas of aspectual function which he should have pursued instead.

To follow this last point further, I want to move to comments on Porter's second major conclusion. He argues that *Aktionsart* must be distinguished from aspect by a recognition that aspectual choice is subjective. I strongly affirm the basic sense of this, but is it enough to stop at that conclusion and are the implications of it worked out as fully as they ought to be? As mentioned earlier, I think that in several important areas he has stopped short of a truly helpful or complete analysis of aspectual usage along this line.

First, he seems not to have grasped clearly the kind of strict semantic distinction between aspect and *Aktionsart* which I tried to trace earlier. This distinction is proposed (but not widely) in the literature on aspect, but Porter seems not to have grasped the point or its implications, even though he cites some of the works which clearly argue for it. It is not that he mentions this strict distinction and rejects it, or that it is incompatible with his larger theory; he just seems to have missed the point of the discussion in Porzig, Hermann, Bache and Smith.[2] In fact, he refers to Bache's critique of Comrie (1976) but he loses the main point of Bache's work by fixing his attention too much on temporal features.[3] The distinction is not merely whether there is

1. Porter, *Verbal Aspect*, pp. 81-83, 102-107.
2. Porter, *Verbal Aspect*, pp. 35-37, 46; Smith, 'Aspectual Choice', is listed in his bibliography but I find no reference to it in the book. See the references to these works cited earlier.
3. Porter, *Verbal Aspect*, pp. 46, 105.

a temporal element involved, but whether aspect itself has anything inherently to do with procedural character: that is, with semantic features such as process, event, state, activity and so on. I believe this clearer conception of the semantic nature of aspect as 'viewpoint' would strengthen Porter's work on aspect, and I hope that he will pursue it more clearly than he has in his book.

Secondly, Porter has insisted too much on the subjective conception of the occurrence, without realizing the limits on the optional choice available to the speaker under many circumstances.[1] My main discussion of this was given earlier, so I will not develop it again here.

Thirdly, Porter has not pursued the implications of the relationship between aspect and other features of meaning. This is ironic on two counts. First, he has laid the foundation for this work by his insightful comments on implicature: that is, on semantic categories and their pragmatic inferences in context, the difference between code and text, and the difference between primary meanings and secondary meanings of grammatical categories.[2] And at several places he hints that analysis of lexical and contextual influences on aspectual usage is important and 'should receive greater attention in future research'.[3]

At one point, Porter gives several valuable comments about such an endeavor: that is, in evaluating Smith's article on the aorist and Carson's response to it.[4] Here he agrees that 'the meaning of the Aorist in a given passage may be "shaped by the context"' and that it is '...misleading to deny that the Aorist has some essential semantic quality, and to forbid any further descriptive categories which may be used to describe the function of the Aorist in various pragmatic contexts'. But he rightly warns that: (1) we must make explicit the distinction between semantics and pragmatics, (2) the pragmatic meanings need not be limited to a set number or to the traditional

---

1. Cf. Porter, *Verbal Aspect*, pp. 88, 107, 225, 239, 335.

2. Porter, *Verbal Aspect*, pp. 82-83, 97, 107. Unfortunately he invokes implicature only in regard to temporal meanings and never procedural character and other implications. One wonders what Porter would have been able to see about wider functions of aspect if he had not been so intent on defending his non-temporal theory at every turn.

3. Porter, *Verbal Aspect*, pp. 35 n. 15, 87, 96-97, 184; quotation from p. 87.

4. Porter, *Verbal Aspect*, p. 184. The works discussed are C.R. Smith, 'Errant Aorist Interpreters', *GTJ* 2 (1981), pp. 205-26 and D.A. Carson, *Exegetical Fallacies* (Grand Rapids: Baker, 1984), pp. 72-74.

categories,[1] and (3) 'a distinction between the meaning of an entire
proposition in context and the individual semantic value of its component parts must be made'.[2] On these points he is exactly correct, but I
wish he had developed them in detail.

The other irony in this regard is that many other writers on aspect
in general linguistics and semantics have given attention to such matters and have included them as a central part of their discussion of
aspect.[3] A full treatment of aspect in New Testament Greek which
professes to be rooted in linguistic theory should hardly ignore or by-
pass such discussions. I am thinking here of Porter's almost complete
neglect of the Vendler–Kenny taxonomy of procedural character and
the refinements to it offered by many writers after their work. Porter
has no mention of Kenny's essay in his bibliography; he lists Vendler's
article, but never as far as I can tell does he mention it in his book; he
cites Mateos's work on New Testament aspect (which uses Vendler's
scheme) but cavalierly dismisses it;[4] he cites Comrie and Lyons[5] on
other points but never refers to the long sections in their treatments of
aspect where such matters are presented and regarded as significant
for aspect usage. In fact, in one place where a category such as this is
mentioned, he appears not to understand the basic difference between
bounded and unbounded verbs or propositions.[6] He evidences no
awareness of other careful discussions of the effect on aspect of other
linguistic features which occur with the verb.[7] Has he considered these

1. I see that my treatment may be criticized as too traditional on this point.
2. Porter, *Verbal Aspect*, p. 184.
3. See the range of works cited in section 3.1 of my book.
4. Mateos, *El aspecto verbal*. Cf. Porter, *Verbal Aspect*, p. 61.
5. Comrie, *Aspect*; and J. Lyons, *Semantics* (Cambridge: Cambridge University Press, 1977). On p. 97, Porter quotes with approval Lyons's aphorism that the structuralist's slogan is '*Tout se tient*—everything hangs together'. Actually the context in which Lyons cites this (p. 714) is in conclusion of his treatment of the interaction between aspect and the Vendler–Kenny classes of verbs. But Porter does not seem to appreciate the significance of Lyons's words.
6. Porter, *Verbal Aspect*, pp. 41-43, criticizing M.S. Ruipérez, *Estructura del sistema de aspectos y tiempos del verbo griego antiguo: Análisis funcional sincrónico* (Salamanca: Consejo Superior de Investigaciones Científicas, 1954). Ruipérez's distinction between 'transformational' and 'non-transformational' verbs reflects a basic difference of procedural character often discussed in studies of aspect. Porter's critique of Ruipérez on this point is obtuse.
7. Cf. D. Dowty, *Studies in the Logic of Verb Aspect and Time Reference in*

suggestions which are so common in the literature on aspect and found them invalid or incomplete? If so, this should be recorded in the book. If he did not consider them, it is a notable oversight and should be remedied in future treatment of the topic. Finally, I want to add a comment about Porter's third major conclusion. My comment here is closely related to the preceding point. Porter makes much of structuring the aspects in a network of systemic oppositions. I see some value in this for clarifying the sense of the aspect meanings in broad terms. But overall it strikes me as the sort of grand scheme that purports to explain everything but in fact provides little insight at the level of handling actual examples. Unfortunately, the history of aspect studies is filled with such theoretical constructs accompanied by grand claims and laced with disparaging comments about everything which came before. Skepticism in the face of such schemes and impatience with them is, I think, justified.

It is true that understanding the meaning and function of the aspects must always be done within a system of oppositions, since the choice of one aspect over another is not made in a vacuum but within a network of contrasts between them. I have no quarrel with this point. Why I am impatient with Porter's treatment is that the contrasts are seen only at the macro level. What is needed is discussion of more specific contrasts between the aspects within limited situations: for example, of certain verbs used with certain adjuncts and so on. Then the interpretative significance of aspectual choice can be seen more clearly and contribute in meaningful ways to exegesis.

I believe that Porter has a great deal of insight into linguistics and biblical studies, and I can only hope that he will continue to develop his ideas and be open to learning from others in the process. I look forward to seeing more of his work in the future.

English (Studies in Linguistics, 1; Austin: Department of Linguistics, University of Texas, 1972); H.J. Verkuyl, *On the Compositional Nature of the Aspects* (Foundations of Language Supplementary Series, 15; Dordrecht: D. Reidel, 1972); and Ö. Dahl, *Tense and Aspect Systems* (Oxford: Basil Blackwell, 1985).

VERBAL ASPECT IN GREEK: TWO APPROACHES

Daryl D. Schmidt

The appearance, almost simultaneously, of two thorough studies of verbal aspect in Greek is an important indication that the study of Greek grammar is reclaiming its rightful place as an essential discipline in the guild of biblical scholars. The more comprehensive study is Stanley E. Porter, *Verbal Aspect in the Greek of the New Testament, with Reference to Tense and Mood*.[1] More singularly focused on aspect is Buist M. Fanning, *Verbal Aspect in New Testament Greek*.[2] There is much to digest in these two volumes. This is not easy reading, especially Porter's book, which has very compact pages.

The details of each volume will surely be scrutinized for some time. However, an initial assessment of their individual and collective contributions would better focus on the overall approach taken in each of these works, and then a sample of some particulars.

Fanning divides his work into two parts: general matters (definition and meaning) and specific areas (related to mood). In arriving at the definition and meaning of aspect, Fanning traces how aspect became distinguished from four related areas.

1. Aspect is distinct from tense, which marks temporal sequence. Aspect is related internally, not externally, to temporal meaning (p. 29).

2. Aspect is distinguished from features related to procedural characteristics. This first appeared when aspect was defined as distinct from *Aktionsart*, though no consensus emerged on how to define the difference. In contrast to Comrie and Lyons, who treat aspect and

1.   (Studies in Biblical Greek, 1; New York: Peter Lang, 1989), a doctoral dissertation completed at the University of Sheffield.

2.   (Oxford Theological Monographs; Oxford: Clarendon Press, 1990), a doctoral dissertation completed at the University of Oxford in 1987.

Aktionsart as semantically equivalent, Fanning follows the more precise definition of Carl Bache.[1] Aspect is the more subjective category
for viewing a situation as either perfective, as a whole, or imperfective, an interior perspective, whereas *Aktionsart* is the more objective
category for the procedural oppositions that relate to a situation, such
as dynamic versus stative (pp. 38-40). Procedural features are characteristic of actual situations and are inherent in lexical verb classes (and
accompanying adverbial phrases). Other procedural oppositions
include: durative versus momentary, repetitive versus singular, complete versus incomplete, inceptive versus terminative (p. 50). While
aspect is related in various ways to these procedural features, it per-
tains only to the grammatical way the speaker portrays the situation.

3. Aspects are best described by 'structural oppositions'. Fanning
develops the meaning of aspects on this basis in chapter 2.

4. Aspect has a secondary discourse function to show the relative
prominence of events. Perfective verbs are used for foreground
events and imperfective verbs for background events (p. 75).

These 'four features of meaning...are closely related to aspect'
(p. 77), though in a complex relationship. The only invariant meaning
Fanning can find for aspect is 'the focus or viewpoint of the speaker in
regard to the action or condition which the verb describes' (p. 84).

Fanning's analysis in chapter 2 of 'the verbal forms in NT Greek
which are labelled "aspects"' yields only one invariant aspectual
contrast, that between aorist, which views the situation 'in summary',
'as a whole from the outside, without regard for the internal make-up
of the occurrence' (p. 97), and present, which views the situation in
its 'development or progress...in regard to its internal make-up,
without beginning or end in view' (p. 103). In the perfect verb,
Fanning finds a combination of features: aspect ('summary
viewpoint'), tense ('anteriority') and procedural characteristic or
Aktionsart ('stative', pp. 119-20), but in the future forms of the verb
he sees primarily tense. Fanning does not make explicit how

1. B. Comrie, *Aspect: An Introduction to the Study of Verbal Aspect and Related Problems* (Cambridge: Cambridge University Press, 1976), pp. 4-13; J. Lyons, *Semantics* (Cambridge: Cambridge University Press, 1977), pp. 705-13; C. Bache, 'Aspect and Aktionsart: Towards a Semantic Distinction', *Journal of Linguistics* 18 (1982), pp. 57-72.

morphology in general should be understood to function in relation to aspect.

Chapter 3 takes up in many ways some of the most interesting matters Fanning considers: how other features closely related to aspect affect aspectual function. The discussion often reflects Fanning's sensitivity to compositional features. He also provides helpful verb lists and correlates various categories of inherent meaning with aspect. For example, a stative verb such as φοβέομαι denotes a continuing state in the present ('be afraid'), but a change of state in the aorist ('become afraid').

The most important category related to aspect is the inherent lexical meaning of a verb stem. Fanning adopts the categories of Vendler and Kenny:[1] states and actions, activities and performances, accomplishments and achievements, to which Fanning adds climaxes and punctuals (p. 129). These correspond mostly to the 'procedural characteristics' identified earlier; for example, accomplishments are 'durative', achievements are not. Although this is an excellent start, much more will need to be done in terms of complementary verbs in the same semantic field. For example, both ἔρχομαι and πορεύομαι are used readily in both basic aspects, present and aorist, but their compound forms show peculiar patterns: ἀπέρχομαι, διέρχομαι, εἰσέρχομαι, ἐξέρχομαι, παρέρχομαι are predominantly used in the aorist, while διαπορεύομαι, εἰσπορεύομαι, ἐκπορεύομαι, παραπορεύομαι are never used in the aorist. A next step in the discussion should begin to account for such patterns, and the limitations implied for the speaker's 'choice' of aspect.

The recent work of Laurel J. Brinton treats these features as *Aktionsarten*.[2] Brinton argues that, unlike aspect, *Aktionsart* cannot be adequately represented by oppositions. In fact, Fanning seems to acknowledge as much in his grid on p. 163, where 'incidental features' are also listed under the 'distinctive feature' of each of the traditional categories.

One 'compositional feature' that warrants only brief attention in

1. Z. Vendler, 'Verbs and Times', in *Linguistics in Philosophy* (Ithaca, NY: Cornell University Press, 1967), pp. 97-121; A. Kenny, *Action, Emotion and Will* (London: Routledge & Kegan Paul, 1963), pp. 151-86.
2. *The Development of English Aspectual Systems* (Cambridge: Cambridge University Press, 1988).

Fanning (pp. 178-79) is 'aspectual verbs', such as ἄρχομαι and παύομαι. Fanning suggests that they are actually 'aktionsartlich', since they are more procedural than viewpoint. Brinton, in fact, argues that ingressive and egressive are two subcategories of a separate category of aspect, 'phase'. The relationship between the two categories of aspect and lexical *Aktionsart* will need much more study.

The lexical realization of aspect is demonstrated in Louw and Nida.[1] They include 'aspect' as domain 68 in their schema of 93 domains. Its subcategories are: begin, start; continue; complete, finish, succeed; cease, stop; try, attempt; do intensely or extensively; rapidity, suddenness. These do indeed correspond to the categories of meaning associated with features of verbal aspect inherent in verb forms.

The relationship between lexical realization and morphological realization can be illustrated in the Gospel of Mark. The use of ἄρχομαι at times directly parallels the imperfect:

Mk 4.1:   πάλιν ἤρξατο διδάσκειν παρὰ τὴν θάλασσαν.
Mk 2.13:   πάλιν παρὰ τὴν θάλασσαν...ἐδίδασκεν αὐτούς.

These can be seen as two different ways to grammaticalize the same aspectual feature, 'inception'. This relationship is conveyed in the new Scholars Version translation:

Mk 4.1:   Once again he started to teach by the sea.
Mk 2.13:   Again...by the sea...he started teaching.[2]

Fanning suggests that such an 'inceptive' sense of the imperfect 'is an effect of the context', derived from the sequence of two verbs (p. 252).

A valuable feature of Fanning is his consideration of discourse features (pp. 190-94), which he draws into his discussion in some key areas of his later analysis, such as historic present (pp. 232-33). However, the longer narrative sections that would better demonstrate this are only mentioned, not actually discussed; for example, the imperfects in Mk 5.1-20 are mentioned twice (pp. 191, 248), but never explored. Thus when the relatively high frequency of

1. J.P. Louw and E.A. Nida, *Greek–English Lexicon of the New Testament Based on Semantic Domains* (New York: United Bible Societies, 1988).
2. See D.D. Schmidt, *The Gospel of Mark, with Introduction, Notes, and Original Text, featuring the New Scholars Version Translation* (Scholars Bible, 1; Sonoma, CA: Polebridge Press, 1991).

imperfects in Mark is noted, Fanning merely passes along the traditional observation regarding Mark's 'desire to portray events in vivid fashion' (p. 255). Fanning had himself earlier noted the use of the imperfect in summary sections (p. 248).

In the new Scholars Version translation of the Gospels many of Mark's imperfects are understood to be 'pseudo-iteratives', that is, the narrative wants to convey that the activity being described was typical.[1] This corresponds to Fanning's '*generalized* narrative' with 'customary imperfects', which does not actually 'relate generalized, usually multiple, occurrences' (p. 247), but uses that style to convey such an impression. The appropriate English equivalent is 'would': 'they would bring all the sick and demon possessed to him. And the whole city would crowd around the door' (Mk 1.32-33).

Later in his discussion of the aorist, Fanning notes that 'the aorist may relate an *extended* action or state' when used with 'verbs with durative lexical character'. In noting the overlap here with the imperfect, he comments: 'In instances such as these the imperfect is a viable option for the speaker, since it would merely change the focus and emphasis, but not the basic sense: this is a place where the speaker's subjective choice and narrative style are free to operate' (p. 257). The footnote here makes an attempt to give each choice its own nuance, but the reader needs an analysis of a more extended text, or comparative examples that exemplify the nuance suggested in the footnote. Likewise, the list of examples may well illustrate the point, but the reader is not given direct help here in discerning how the examples relate to the general statement.

The difficulty may derive from the way Fanning approaches the second part of the book, aspect usage. The largest chapter is concerned with aspect in the indicative mood. Fanning accepts without critique the traditional categories that have long been used to describe the various usages of the tenses. Thus the discussion of the present indicative, for example, demonstrates how the position outlined in part 1 can account for the traditional subcategories of meaning: progressive or descriptive or specific, instantaneous, customary or iterative, gnomic, 'past action still in progress', conative, futuristic, historical, and perfective. For the aorist the categories are: constative or complexive, ingressive, consummative or effective, gnomic,

---

1. See Schmidt, *Gospel of Mark*, pp. 32-33.

proleptic or futuristic, dramatic or present state, epistolary. While it is helpful to see that there is an underlying conception that ties these together, the reader misses any discussion on the appropriateness of these categories.

Fanning more briefly applies aspect as viewpoint to non-indicative uses. In commands and prohibitions the distinction is between general and specific. The present aspect in commands has a 'customary' sense, 'make it your habit to do', not 'keep on doing' (p. 333). The aorist is used 'for a single specific action in a particular situation', and 'not intended to govern behaviour more broadly' (p. 334). In prohibitions the traditional rule of thumb works only for specific commands: the present for 'stop doing [this action presently occurring]' and the aorist for 'do not do [this imminent act]'. However, in general precepts the present is used in the sense 'make it your practice not to', while the aorist is used to mean, 'never do' (p. 337). Furthermore there are idiomatic exceptions to these patterns, where specific verbs are used mostly in only one or the other aspect.

Aspect usage in the other modes, infinitive, subjunctive and optative, is presented together more briefly in the final chapter. Viewpoint is again basic to the meaning of aspect; 'present focuses on the internal make-up of the occurrence', while 'aorist views the occurrence as a whole'. The combinatory features yield further distinctions, such as 'ingressive vs. consummative sense, general vs. specific reference, single vs. multiple occurrence' (p. 390). In the participle Fanning validates as a secondary feature in most instances the relative temporal meanings of simultaneous for the present participle and antecedent for the aorist (p. 407).

Fanning's conclusion emphasizes the complexity he sees in verbal aspect: 'understanding verbal aspect requires a grasp of both the basic meanings of the aspects themselves and their function in combination with other linguistic and contextual features'. This semantic complexity involves several levels of meaning, which can be accounted for only by analyzing aspect at the levels of both definition and function (p. 420).

Since Fanning is attempting to analyze all the uses of the aspects, it would be unfair to criticize him for not having analyzed aspect even more extensively. While some readers will value the careful treatment given to classical crux texts, apparent 'exceptions', or very small sub-categories, there are other readers who would have preferred fresh treatment of longer texts to illustrate the use of aspects in relationship to each other. Nonetheless, there is much valuable substance to mine from this book.

Porter's work on verbal aspect is even more overwhelming to the reader. Porter has amassed a staggering amount of material, and much of it is printed in reduced type. This is not a book one sits down and merely reads. Rather, individual sections must be carefully scrutinized, both for the general approach espoused and for the detailed examples given.

As Porter's title indicates, he also addresses tense and mood, giving the reader even more to deal with. Furthermore, Porter tends to treat corollary issues in extended asides, footnotes, or appendices. Whole chapters are devoted to matters that Fanning treats mostly in summary fashion: influence of Semitic languages, conditional statements, future forms and periphrastics. While each of these features contains a wealth of information, they also prevent the kind of focus that the reader appreciates in Fanning. Both of them treat non-indicative forms, but Fanning looks at them strictly in terms of how aspect is used, while Porter first proposes a systemic schema to account for the features of modality that are grammaticalized in each form.

One of Porter's more commendable features is that he does not treat the New Testament as an inherently isolatable corpus, but rather includes an extensive number of 'extra-biblical' references (see index, pp. 567-80)—though the focus is not synchronically on Hellenistic Greek, as the full page of references to Homer in the index indicates.

A second notable feature of Porter's book is his more explicit linguistic framework as suggested in the opening statement of his preface (p. xi):

> The major assertion of this work in biblical Greek linguistics is that the category of synthetic verbal aspect—a morphologically-based semantic category which grammaticalizes the author/speaker's reasoned subjective choice of conception of a process—provides a suggestive and workable linguistic model for explaining the range of uses of the tense forms in Greek.

The model that Porter utilizes to demonstrate this assertion is systemic linguistics, which developed out of the linguistics framework of J.R. Firth, especially formulated by M.A.K. Halliday.[1] It is a

1.   J.R. Firth, *Selected Papers of J.R. Firth 1952–59* (ed. F.R. Palmer; London:

functional linguistic model that seeks 'to establish a network of systems of relationships...which will account for all the semantically relevant choices in the language as a whole'.[1] In utilizing this model, Porter accepts the same criticisms of Comrie by Bache that Fanning builds on. As Porter develops that independently from Fanning within his own explicit linguistic framework, he too argues that aspect represents the speaker's subjective viewpoint of a process. Thus the general definitional perspective of these two scholars is quite similar. Furthermore, they both use the linguistic convention of equipollent binary oppositions to formalize the relationship of their aspectual categories.

Porter's schema for aspect is to use the linguistic contrast between '+ perfective' and '– perfective'. The perfective in Greek is realized in the aorist, and the non-perfective has two realizations: imperfective, in the present and imperfect, and stative, in the perfect tense forms (pp. 89-90, 109). Here the reader who has just read Fanning misses a more extended discussion on the nuances of meaning associated with these labels.

The most distinctive feature of Porter's work is his strong insistence that disassociating aspect from tense completely removes the appropriateness of any temporal dimension to verb morphology. Thus tense itself has no temporal dimension.

Porter begins his systemic analysis of Greek verbal aspect by first demonstrating that 'Greek does not grammaticalize *absolute* tense with the Present' (p. 77, emphasis added). He cites the historic present, such as in Mk 11.27, as 'the most convincing example'. With analogous examples of the aorist and the perfect, Porter concludes that 'Greek does not grammaticalize tense in any of the three major tense categories' (p. 78). The latter, more general statement has dropped the qualifying 'absolute' from his earlier statement. This seems to make it an over-generalization that is more difficult to support.

The more accurate claim would appear to be: tense forms in the indicative do not grammaticalize *absolute time*, any more than they grammaticalize *absolute* aspect. But this is far short of demonstrating

Longmans, 1968); M.A.K. Halliday, *Halliday: System and Function in Language* (ed. G.R. Kress; Oxford: Oxford University Press, 1976).

1.   D. Crystal, *A Dictionary of Linguistics and Phonetics* (Oxford: Basil Blackwell, 2nd edn, 1985), p. 320.

that tense in the indicative has no temporal dimension. An analysis of tense along similar lines as the analysis of aspect would suggest that tense is likewise related to the speaker's subjective choice. Thus translating the historic present as a past in English tells us nothing about narrative style in Mark, only about one kind of narrative style in English.

Porter proposes in place of any temporal dimension a feature marked for more or less 'remoteness', so that what distinguishes the imperfect from the present is its use in contexts where it grammaticalizes the feature '+ remoteness' in relation to the non-remote present (p. 207). It is difficult to see how this could include the usage that is traditionally said to portray 'vividness' in narrative. However, little attention is paid to the actual usages of the imperfect, since it has neither distinctive aspect nor tense.

Porter's proposal in effect turns on its head the traditional approach, which has devoted so much attention to accounting for the aorist and imperfect indicatives that cannot easily be understood as past-time referring, and the present indicatives that cannot easily be understood as non-past-time referring. His systemic approach seeks a generalization that will account for all extant usages without exception. The heavy price to be paid for such a powerful theory is the complete disregard of the augment as morphologically significant.

Porter's proposal does not account for the stylistic choices the author of Mark made in the use of present and imperfect tenses. If there are no temporal considerations involved, then how does this take account of the care taken by both Matthew and Luke in 'correcting' Mark's tenses? One example cited by Porter is Mk 5.22-24, which begins with three present indicative verbs, all translated by Porter as simple pasts (p. 208). A comparison with Luke indicates that Porter's translation is better suited for Luke's version with two aorists and an imperfect.

Since there are no temporal dimensions to tense, that removes the need to treat the perfect tense as more complex, in Fanning's approach, and it becomes the 'stative aspect' (p. 257). The notion 'stative' has become rather commonplace in *Aktionsart* discussions. By insisting that the 'stative' perfect is a third aspect, Porter is in a sense more traditional in his approach than is Fanning. However, Brinton's recent work in English also argues for the perfect aspect.

Porter's treatment of non-indicative forms is again much more extensive than Fanning's. Here they demonstrate opposite faults: Fanning provides mere lists of examples without translation or comment, while Porter engages in a running commentary of texts, mostly cited complete with literal English glosses. The forced use of 'might' as the gloss for the subjunctive, even for indirect commands such as Mk 6.8 (p. 326), draws attention away from the focus on aspect. In the participle Porter acknowledges the relative temporal relation that can often be found, but typically the exceptions to the pattern are cited as reason to associate these features only with context, not with verbal aspect.

The wealth of detail amassed by Porter, far in excess of Fanning, prevents more than a cursory comparison of the two. They take two rather different approaches. But that makes it all the more important where they converge. It would be a significant combined contribution to the study of Greek grammar if the clear distinction between aspect and *Aktionsart* could now be accepted as clearly established, and furthermore, that the core of aspect is the contrast between present and aorist. The issues involve viewing a situation as a whole and viewing it partially. If partial, then the focus can be on the beginning, or end, or continuing, or merely ongoing, or repeating. These sub-categories are often grammaticalized as chaining verbs or 'aspectualizers'.[1]

One caution must be expressed about this focus on viewpoint as the speaker's conscious choice. Porter in particular seems inclined to over-emphasize it. For example, on p. 355 alone Porter has both: the choice of present and perfect imperative in Mk 4.39 'appears self-conscious' (also p. 325), and in Lk. 3.11 he talks about 'the progression in the author's mind'. Porter is aware that, by its very nature, subjective choice is something we cannot always explain (p. 335). In fact, in working with an ad hoc corpus from a dead language, there likely would be many instances when no apparent explanation would be forthcoming for such choices.

In general, there is need for greater sensitivity to the nature of narrative, for example, regarding the use of the indicative for 'non-factual' statements. Porter cites Mk 3.22 'he has Beelzebul' and 5.35 'your daughter is dead'. Here we need to be explicit: the author's choice is that the characters in the narrative express their viewpoint in the indicative, because the narrative plot requires that these statements be treated as 'true'. Labelling them as 'non-factual' is an unwarranted non-narrative judgment that would preclude the use of irony.

The divergent practice on the use of translation in these two volumes requires a final note. Fanning does not provide any translation for the samples he uses. This is mostly workable, because his examples are grouped into explicit categories, and the reader is expected to read Greek well enough to understand how they can function this way. However, at times the reader is left unsure quite how all the examples cited illustrate the same point.

Porter, on the other hand, does follow the convention in linguistic scholarship of giving a translation, or better, an English gloss, for his Greek examples. However, the glosses become problematic when they highlight features in categories other than the one being discussed. For example, Porter cites in his discussion of subjunctives Mk 6.12, with the gloss: 'so that they might repent' (ἵνα μετανοῶσιν), and a comment labelling it 'purpose' (p. 326). The gloss does not help to illustrate Porter's point about the shift from aorist to present aspect, but rather confuses the reader by using 'might' for a ἵνα- construction that embeds a type of indirect command which has been consistently translated as 'should' ever since Tyndale.[1]

The vast amount of data in these two volumes will require much close scrutiny. While the cost of each is rather prohibitive, they must be seen more as reference volumes. Porter's especially warrants extended reference use, limited only by its lack of a subject index. Together they will shape all future discussion of verbal aspect in Greek.

---

1. For a treatment of such embeds, see D.D. Schmidt, *Hellenistic Greek Grammar and Noam Chomsky: Nominalizing Transformations* (SBLDS, 62; Chico, CA: Scholars Press, 1981), pp. 55-59.

A RESPONSE TO FANNING AND PORTER ON VERBAL ASPECT

Moisés Silva

Few grammatical questions are more puzzling than those surrounding the aspectual functions of verbs. At the same time, these functions are singularly seductive for students hoping to find 'rich exegetical nuggets' in the Greek text of the New Testament. Given those two factors, the results are almost predictable. The Greek aorist in particular has been badly bruised in the process, but the present and the perfect have hardly escaped exegetical (let alone homiletical) misuse. More fundamentally, New Testament students, and even New Testament grammarians, have failed to come up with a coherent description of verbal aspect. None of our standard New Testament Greek grammars takes into account the significant advances made by general linguistic theory in this area, while most commentaries are simply unreliable when they attempt explanations of aspectual choices. Aside from scattered articles and books, we have had very little guidance indeed.

Because I have been concerned about these problems for twenty-some years,[1] the appearance of two substantive works on Greek verbal aspect has had more than passing interest for me. And reading what Fanning and Porter actually have to say is something that I have found most encouraging and gratifying. While their works are very different in temperament, they coincide in some crucial and fundamental areas, such as the recognition that our standard grammatical descriptions are not satisfactory, the commitment to examine the data in the light of general linguistic principles, the concern for methodological self-consciousness, the attempt to distinguish what has often

---

1. Unfortunately, I have written very little about it: a few scattered remarks in my commentary on *Philippians* (Chicago: Moody, 1988), e.g., pp. 13, 82-83 and *passim*, and a brief discussion in *God, Language, and Scripture: Reading the Bible in the Light of General Linguistics* (Grand Rapids: Zondervan, 1990), pp. 111-18.

been confused in the past, the appreciation that aspect does not by itself say anything about objective reality, and so on. It is only a mild exaggeration to say that, with the almost simultaneous publication of these volumes, our knowledge and understanding of the Greek verbal system has taken a quantum leap forward.

Porter's work takes one's breath away.[1] Most of the book is printed with a very small typeface, and so its 'real' length must approach 1000 pages. The fifty-page bibliography lists approximately 1500 titles in half a dozen modern languages, and even a cursory look at the text makes clear that those titles are not there just for show. Porter has left no stone unturned in his search for any material that might conceivably strengthen his descriptions. It is a total mystery to me how this work could have been produced by such a young scholar.

Fanning's volume, for its part, is a thing of beauty.[2] Some might be tempted to say it is too neat, as though some artificial scheme had been imposed on the material. Such a judgment would be a mistake. Fanning's control over the data, as well as his respect for those data, is unquestionable. Moreover, his success in distilling what is most valuable in the technical literature and presenting it in a sparklingly clear and accessible fashion is a wonderful boon for students of New Testament Greek grammar.

Any attempt to critique these works must take into account their quasi-pioneering character. The serious study of verbal aspect in *any* language is a relatively young science—much more so its specific application to New Testament Greek. The inevitable rough edges are only natural. Furthermore, we need to be as clear as possible about the character and purpose of the books we are evaluating. I would therefore like to begin by making certain distinctions about how one approaches the study of verbal aspect.

In the first place, one's approach may be strictly *linguistic*. By that I mean that a scholar may wish to provide, on the basis of a valid theoretical model, a scientific description and explanation of verbal aspect. Such a work tends to be technical and abstract, not encumbered by pragmatic considerations. It addresses the linguistic scholarly com-

1. S.E. Porter, *Verbal Aspect in the Greek of the New Testament, with Reference to Tense and Mood* (New York: Peter Lang, 1989).
2. B.M. Fanning, *Verbal Aspect in New Testament Greek* (Oxford: Clarendon Press, 1990).

munity rather than the 'practitioners'.[1] Secondly, the approach may be pedagogical, in which case the work belongs rather in the field of *applied* linguistics (assuming that linguistics is used at all, which often it is not). What I have in view here, of course, are elementary and intermediate textbooks. In the third place, one's goal may be to provide guidance in the *translation* of aspectual uses from one language to another. Finally, one may really be interested in *interpretation*. What difference does it all make when trying to identify the meaning of a particular proposition?

I do not need to emphasize that these four approaches (and there are probably others) are very closely related, and in practice it is almost impossible to separate them. But *distinguish* them we must. Ideally, for example, an elementary textbook ought to be built on a rigorous theoretical understanding, but the truth of the matter is that some of the best and most successful teachers of language are surprisingly ignorant of linguistic principles, at least in any self-conscious way (conversely, some people who have a profound linguistic background can prove to be a total disaster in teaching a language or writing a textbook). Or take another example. We have traditionally assumed that learning Greek means being able to translate, but that is really mixing apples and oranges. If you want to become proficient in Italian, you go to Italy, hear and imitate the spoken language even as you learn to read it, and never once produce a written English translation of anything. Of course, since Greek is an ancient language, we are virtually obligated to rely on translation, but it remains true that being able to translate is a very distinct skill from learning a language.

The reason I have mentioned these things is that neither Porter nor Fanning, in my opinion, sufficiently distinguishes among them: all four of the approaches listed above surface frequently in both works. Here and there, to be sure, they show some sensitivity to the problem, and they certainly know what their primary aims are (Porter's emphasis is linguistic while Fanning's is interpretative). But that is not enough. I believe that a more formal description (and justification) of what lies within and without their province would have enhanced their treatment. More important, in the actual treatment of the material these various concerns get mixed up and the reader is seldom warned about what is taking place.

I suppose that this problem lies behind a curious thing. In general terms, I found Porter's *theoretical* framework more convincing than Fanning's.[1] Fanning is, I think, much too generous in his attempt to salvage what he can out of the traditional grammars; while I commend him in the attempt (it needs to be done), the result is a certain instability. On the other hand, when it came to looking at their *implementation* of the principles, I had many more problems with Porter than with Fanning: time and time again I failed to see either the logic or the evidence for his interpretations. I am not ready to suggest that we adopt Porter's explanation of the linguistic system and Fanning's interpretation of actual occurrences.[2] My point is only that some

1. Porter approaches his subject as a linguist and adopts so-called *systemic linguistics* as his model (an approach based on the fruitful and pioneering work of J.R. Firth and developed by a number of recent British scholars). That decision affects certain features of his method and presentation but it does not by itself determine Porter's actual interpretation of the data. In line with generally accepted conclusions, Porter draws a clear distinction between aspect and time, with the latter category being played down. He goes well beyond this consensus, however, when he argues that even in the indicative mood 'Greek does not grammaticalize temporal reference' (p. 81; on p. 98 he states that the Greek tenses 'do not refer to any specific absolute time'). Indeed, Porter's analysis is particularly vulnerable in its reluctance to distinguish more sharply between the indicative and the non-indicative moods. I find it perplexing that Porter can so easily dismiss the significance of the augment for this issue (his extremely brief discussion of the augment, on pp. 208-209, focuses on Homer and is almost totally diachronic in perspective). Nor does his analysis explain why, for example, the subjunctive and imperative moods are limited to a simple binary opposition between aorist and present (the perfect is rare), whereas the indicative mood sports half a dozen different forms.

2. I do not want to be guilty of exaggerating the differences between these two authors. I am very comfortable with Fanning's primary definition of the aorist ('presents an occurrence *in summary, viewed as a whole from the outside, without regard for the internal make-up of the occurrence*', p. 97) and present ('reflects an *internal* viewpoint concerning the occurrence which *focuses on its development or progress* and sees the occurrence *in regard to its internal make-up, without beginning or end in view*', p. 103). The affinities between this approach and that of B. Comrie (*Aspect: An Introduction to the Study of Verbal Aspect and Related Problems* [Cambridge Textbooks in Linguistics; Cambridge: Cambridge University Press,

important inconsistencies remain in the field as a whole, and that we all need to clarify more precisely what we are trying to do. So much for generalities. A few specifics may help to focus my concerns.

1. In the first place, one could wish both authors had given their readers a clearer perspective on the relationship between a scientifically precise analysis of aspect and the work of exegesis. In our attempt to understand what a biblical passage means, just how necessary is it that we have 'nailed down' the way aspect functions in a linguistic system? The fact is that even with respect to English—a living language that can be directly analyzed and that in fact has received enormous attention from scholars—there is an astonishing diversity of opinion regarding aspect.[1] This confusion, however, does not prevent anyone from understanding English perfectly well when it is spoken or written.

Unfortunately, many of the actual comments by Porter and Fanning will mislead readers to think otherwise about New Testament Greek, as though the ability to identify the reason for, say, Paul's aspectual choices were a prerequisite for sound exegesis. In fact, I have yet to see one example of good exegesis that *depends* on the interpreter's ability to explain why one aspect rather than another was used. The matter gets complicated by the fact that both authors continue to use expressions like 'the aorist here emphasizes...' or 'the use of the present stresses...' Aspectual distinctions are largely determined by the context (see below), and when a choice is involved, it is not likely to be a conscious one; therefore it is most doubtful that a speaker or writer would make use of this syntactical subtlety to stress any point.

2. The desire to come up with a clear cut, comprehensive definition of aspect is certainly understandable, but I have to wonder whether it is misguided. In Porter's case, the problem comes to expression by his

1976]) are evident; moreover, it is broadly compatible with much of Porter's work.

1. G. Rojo ('Relaciones entre temporalidad y aspecto en el verbo español', in *Tiempo y aspecto en español* [ed. Ignacio Bosque; Madrid: Cátedra, 1990], pp. 17-44) comments on the general discrepancy among scholars on the category itself: 'No es fácil encontrar una categoría gramatical en que las discrepancias entre los lingüistas sean tan llamativas como las que es posible hallar en el caso de aspecto. En efecto, hay fuertes divergencias en la definición de la categoría...' (p. 31). Fanning (on p. 81 n. 209) refers to R. Chatterjee's pessimism about the likelihood of success in defining the category.

unwillingness to admit exceptions: proposal after proposal is rejected on the grounds that it does not explain every instance. Fanning, for his part, often speaks about the need to identify an 'invariant' meaning for the various aspects. Given the fluidity of language, however, the goal seems unrealistic. With regard to vocabulary, the desire to tie the meaning of individual words to one 'basic' idea has rightly been abandoned by most scholars. As for syntax, the attempt to identify the one unifying meaning of, say, the genitive case misled a previous generation of grammarians (notably A.T. Robertson) to describe Greek on the basis of Sanskrit. If we recognize that the semantic information conveyed by the cases can be strikingly diverse, can we expect to come up with a definition of verbal aspect that is invariant or unexceptionable?

3. Neither Fanning nor Porter takes sufficient account of the fact that, quite frequently, aspectual choices may be greatly restricted by a variety of factors, such as the grammatical system itself.[1] If I say, 'When Mary got home, her husband was reading a book', the use of the verbal form 'was reading' (as opposed to the simple past 'read') is almost completely determined for me by the grammatical rules of the language. It may indeed be accurate to point out, with Fanning, that the act of reading is presented as a process without reference to its beginning or end. The point, however, is that there is no deliberate choice involved on my part. In short, that's just the way we say it— and it would be of no real help to a foreigner seeking to understand English syntax if he or she were given a description of the aspectual function.

4. Another restriction to which more attention needs to be given is that of individual preferences (idiolect). Porter places a good bit of emphasis on the present as the marked aspect, especially in the subjunctive and imperative moods. Part of the argument is that the aorist is more frequent than the present (p. 323). But this distribution is not consistent among the various authors. The present imperative in Paul, for example, is at least three times more frequent than the aorist (the difference is considerably greater if we leave out of account the more than 20 instances of ἀσπάσασθε, most of which occur in Rom. 16).

---

1. Fanning explicitly acknowledges the problem on p. 34. Note also his recognition that aspect, like other grammatical features, is 'maximally redundant in context' (p. 82).

5. Especially interesting is the fact that some specific verbs are characteristically used in one rather than another aspectual form. To the extent that this may be the case, the significance of such a use diminishes significantly. Here is where most of my disagreements with Porter's interpretations surface. For example, in connection with his thesis that the present is the marked aspect, Porter deduces that this aspect is often used to emphasize a point.[1] Many of his references, it turns out, have the verbs ἔρχομαι, ὑπάγω, and πορεύομαι. A quick look at the concordance, however, makes clear that these verbs of motion in the imperative characteristically occur in the present.[2] As far as the imperative of these verbs is concerned, attaching *any* significance at all to the 'choice' of the present aspect seems precarious in the extreme. Fanning is much more sensitive to this phenomenon, but I suspect even he has only scratched the surface.

Consider some additional data. I noticed that the imperative of γίνομαι often occurs in the present, so I checked the statistics and found that, indeed, Paul uses the present 22 times, but the aorist only twice. In the subjunctive, however, the proportions are almost exactly reversed: the present subjunctive of γίνομαι occurs twice, while the aorist 23 times. I was curious about this matter and decided to check Epictetus.[3] The proportions were remarkably similar. Present imperative 13 times, aorist 2 times; present subjunctive 3 times, aorist 35 times. Now there is probably an explanation—maybe even a semantic explanation—for these figures (I have some ideas of my own). But the point is that these are significant patterns of usage that

1. He argues, for example, that ἔρχου in Rev. 22.20 expresses John's 'keen desire' (p. 350). With regard to πορεύεσθε in Mt. 25.9 he makes the remarkable comment: 'The Present Imperative may be used to stress the urgency of the situation or the hardship the maidens face by being compelled to go, or, with a twist of irony, to draw attention to the wise maidens' knowledge that to leave is to risk the bridegroom coming' (p. 352).

2. A GRAMCORD search produced 75 instances of the present and only 9 of the aorist: 4 in Matthew, 4 in Luke–Acts, 1 in John. In particular, the verb ὑπάγω, which occurs almost 40 times in the present, does not occur once in the aorist.

3. Since there is no 'GRAMCORD' for Epictetus, I used the Ibycus computer to search the TLG data for specific forms. The results may not be completely accurate. Incidentally, note that the literature in question (what survives of the *Discourses* and *Enchiridion*) is approximately two and one half times longer than the total Pauline Corpus.

may be far more determinative than the desire to convey a semantic point.

6. Finally, both authors fail to address directly and solve the biggest conundrum of all: how does one distinguish between the information conveyed by the aspect itself and the information conveyed by the context as a whole? In a way, this criticism is somewhat unfair, since it applies to almost everything we do related to language. Take the vocabulary: we depend on the context to figure out the meanings of words; if so, have we identified the meaning of the word or only of the context? A good example of this problem is the question whether the present by itself indicates habitual action. Responding to the argument that this habitual meaning is found only when other words in the text make it explicit, Fanning acknowledges that there is some merit to this point, but adds: 'There are numerous presents in the NT denoting a custom or habit *without* other explicit indicators. The sense of the context indicates the customary or habitual nature of the occurrence' (p. 215). But if the context is sufficient indication of this habitual action, have we established that the aspect itself indicates the same thing? (And even if it does, one wonders how much significance should be attached to that fact, since it was the context that gave us the information.)

I suspect that this methodological problem may be the reason for the many differences of interpretation between Fanning and Porter. Particularly striking is their view of commands and prohibitions. According to Fanning, the aorist may be used to enhance the urgency of a command,[1] while Porter attributes the high incidence of the present subjunctive in 1 Thessalonians and Philemon to 'the practical moral urgency of the epistles' (p. 332). Obviously, something is rotten in the state of Denmark if two fine scholars, after their thorough and well-informed research, come to such diametrically opposed conclusions. I for one am not at all persuaded by either of them. At any rate, this difference of opinion gives the strongest

---

1. This supposedly applies to aorists used in general precepts. In the case of consummative aorists, the aspect 'is used to emphasize the accomplishment or fulfilment of an effort: a command not merely to work at or attempt the action, as the present may imply, but to do it successfully or actually'. In the case of constative aorists, the significance is 'to underline the *urgency* of the command calling for some customary or general occurrence' (p. 369). To my mind, the supporting examples given are, at best, ambiguous.

support to the view that exegetes and pastors are well advised to say as little as possible about aspect.

It would be a grave mistake to infer, however, that these volumes are irrelevant. I strongly recommend that students of New Testament Greek read carefully chapter 1 of Fanning's work or chapter 2 of Porter's; these introductory materials go a long way in providing a sensible, refreshing appreciation of the Greek verbal structure in the light of general language study. More important, however, the grammar books of the future will be able to present, in a way that was never possible before, a truly defensible description of aspectual functions. We are greatly indebted to both of these scholars for their wonderful contribution to New Testament scholarship.[1]

---

1. Much of the material in this paper appears as a review in *WTJ* 54.1 (1992), pp. 179-83, and is used by kind permission of the editor.

Part II
OTHER TOPICS

An Introduction to Other Topics in Biblical Greek Language and Linguistics

Stanley E. Porter

If one consulted the major sources in Greek grammar fifty years ago and earlier, in the overwhelming majority one would have found common-sensical grammatical discussions of the Greek language. In many places such traditional discussions continue to be carried on, without apparent recognition that the principles by which language is examined have been reassessed with the advent of modern linguistics. The fact that such work was being done fifty years ago is excusable on the grounds that the principles of modern linguistics had yet to be applied in any systematic way to the study of ancient languages. That such methodology is still so easily found is far less readily understandable. It would be unkind to mention by name the authors and works that continue to exemplify such practices, but these kinds of studies are familiar. For example, many of these studies are characterized by a methodology that assesses the meaning and significance of a grammatical phenomenon on the basis of its translation. Thus, one might find statements to the effect that the Greek historic present, aorist and imperfect are equivalent because they can be translated by similar past tenses in the receptor language. Some studies have been as basic as debating whether and when the Greek aorist should be rendered by the English simple past or past perfect, as if these renderings shed light on the Greek language. Or one might find a discussion of the cases or the prepositions that argues that one case or preposition is equivalent to another because the same English words can be used in an English rendering. Other studies of this kind are characterized by simple descriptions or catalogues of the data available in the Greek of the New Testament. It is almost as if there is the unstated belief that the data speak for themselves, when there is in fact a masked pre-understanding of the linguistic phenomenon at issue. And still other studies are efforts in theology in the guise of grammatical study. One does not need to look too far to find theological over-readings of the significance of the aorist tense and of the prepositions, even in some very recent commentaries.

Most of these studies, it seems to me, are characterized by several general shortcomings that modern linguistics helps us to see more clearly. One of these is an atomistic approach to language. This means that single items of significant linguistic interest are selected and subjected to analysis apart from their larger linguistic contexts. For example, one of the Greek cases is described in detail but without regard for the other cases with which it is used, or the future form is discussed in isolation from the entire verbal paradigm of the future form or the other verbs in the Greek language system, or a single conjunction is examined without regard for other words that might do similar or different things. Another shortcoming is the mistaken belief that to translate the language in some way demonstrates a more thorough grasp of the language than do other ways of discussing it. The item of discussion is often reduced to its English-language equivalent and this equivalent is then subjected to analysis. One often learns more about English than one does about Greek through this method. And the third and most serious shortcoming is a methodological naivety. Many of those who have undertaken to analyse various languages have failed to take into account that they see the phenomena of the language through the spectacles of a particular linguistic model. This has usually been the model utilized by the Greek-language tools available to the interpreter, including elementary textbooks and standard reference grammars. Whatever their many good features, elementary textbooks contain simplified (or even simplistic) analyses of the language, synthesized in such a way as to make better teaching tools. They cannot be relied upon as reference grammars. Unfortunately, the reference grammars themselves are dominated by nineteenth-century methodology, given over to a comparative and historical approach to language. If modern linguistics has accomplished anything in its brief tenure in this century, it has made those who discuss language aware of the facts that a language must first of all be understood on its own terms, without recourse to any other language, no matter how closely related; and that for understanding language usage synchronic analysis, that is, analysis of the language as it is used at a given time, must take precedence over the historical development of a language.

When the co-chairpersons of the Consultation on Biblical Greek Language and Linguistics first advertised for papers, there was some apprehension that the Consultation might receive numerous applications for language studies of the older style. It was not that we would automatically reject such studies, but we were hoping for papers that would approach a traditional corpus from modern and new angles, if for no other reason than to test if these modern linguistic models had anything to offer. As the four essays published here reveal, we were not disappointed. Although each of the papers below demonstrates a different methodological approach to the study of the Greek of the New Testament, each is methodologically aware and explicit in its assumptions. The result is a satisfying and varied collection. This is not the place to offer anything like a full appraisal of each essay, so I offer a brief summary and some indication of the significance of each.

In the first essay, Jeffrey T. Reed brings recent work in discourse analysis to bear upon an entire biblical book, 1 Timothy. Finding that many scholars who have analysed the Pastoral Epistles uncritically accept conclusions about its intended recipients, Reed analyses 1 Timothy using one form of discourse analysis. For many biblical scholars discourse analysis is a new method for treating the biblical text. As Reed makes clear, however, the field of discourse analysis itself is diverse. He utilizes a method that focuses upon micro- and macrostructures. That is, he breaks a complete discourse down into its increasingly smaller component parts and analyses their interrelations, rather than treating only one level of unit, such as a sentence. On the basis of his method Reed finds that virtually all of the macrostructural linguistic indicators, including the epistolary opening and closing (including 1 Tim. 6.21), the participant structure, the lexical choices, the references to grammatical person, and the event structure all point to 'Timothy' as the letter's intended recipient (of course, this is the Timothy embodied in the text, without necessarily answering the question of what this 'person's' relation is to a historical personage). With this framework in mind, Reed then applies this to microstructural analysis of a difficult passage, 1 Tim. 3.14-15, where he finds that this structure is to be interpreted as an encouragement for Timothy to behave properly as the leader of the Ephesian church. The strengths of this essay, which was presented in 1991 in Kansas City,

Missouri, are several. First, it provides a workable methodology that can be applied to the analysis of discourse. Reed's method is clearly defined and he illustrates the process at both macro- and microstructural levels. Secondly, and perhaps as importantly, Reed says something significant about 1 Timothy, both in the light of previous interpretation of this problematic book and in the light of larger interpretative questions regarding audience and even theology.

In the second essay, Paul Danove introduces biblical scholars for the first time to a new model of linguistic description, Construction Grammar, currently being developed by the linguist Charles Fillmore. It is entirely appropriate in the light of its recent development that Danove begins by detailing the presuppositions of Construction Grammar. He describes this grammar as a 'descriptive, non-transformational grammar which renders the locutions of a language systematically according to their syntactic and semantic properties'. Building upon Fillmore's previous work with case grammar, the model makes significant use of deep cases but they are analysed in terms of semantic frames, in other words, frameworks that contain the cognitive knowledge of the language user. If this all sounds a bit abstract, along the way Danove provides several germane examples, as well as setting forth a graphic diagram, a Valence Description, which is used to display grammatical constructions. With his method firmly in place, Danove makes two specific applications. The first is to the transitive use of the verb ἀκούω. After a thorough analysis, Danove presents some new conclusions regarding the use of this verb with genitive and accusative objects, introducing the concepts of speaker involvement and of the indicated impact of what is heard. Danove also utilizes Construction Grammar to analyse the textual variant at 1 Jn 2.20, where he concludes that πάντες is the best reading on the basis of the number of complements taken by the verb οἶδα. This essay, which was presented in 1990 in New Orleans, Louisiana, may prove challenging to those new to the terminology and methodology of modern linguistics, but the rewards are certainly worth the effort. First, this essay puts biblical scholars at the forefront in being exposed to a linguistic method as it is being developed. Although not all will find Construction Grammar as compelling as Danove does, there are several concepts that biblical scholars can benefit from, including its use of the semantic frame and its explicit attention to syntax. Secondly, for those who demand a payoff for their methodological endeavours, there could be fewer rewards more welcome than insight into the perpetual problem of how to understand the genitive and accusative objects of ἀκούω. Danove's conclusions may well need refinement, but they illustrate that new methods can prove useful in getting new perspectives on difficult grammatical phenomena.

In the third essay, Micheal W. Palmer raises the vital question of the proper procedures to be employed when describing an ancient or dead language. The concept of the 'native informant' cannot be used in the same way as with modern languages, since all of the language's users are by definition deceased. There are other problems for studying an ancient language as well, including the scope for formulating hypotheses and the limitations on available data. Along the way, Palmer explores the use of diachronic linguistic data, within the larger framework of synchronic criteria. He also discusses the use of computer databases in the analysis of the text of the New Testament. To overcome what he sees as manifest procedural shortcomings, Palmer draws upon syntactic tests as a means of assessing the validity of any linguistic hypothesis. In this instance, he tests the viability of a phrase-level constituent by means of two kinds of evidence: semantic and syntactic. Semantic evidence includes analysis of structural ambiguity, in which a phrasal unit may be posited as a means of clarifying potentially ambiguous syntax. Syntactic evidence includes tests regarding the distribution of phrasal units, the occurrence of sentence fragments, the presence of pronominalization, and coordination. He finishes with discussion of the word as a phrase-level constituent. Palmer's essay, which was presented in 1990 in New Orleans, Louisiana, raises at least two major issues. The first is of a procedural nature. Palmer asks legitimate questions about not only which models may be appropriate to analysing an ancient language, but which procedures should be used in the light of the limitations and restrictions attendant upon such languages. Secondly, although this treatment of Greek has a distinctly Chomskian look and feel about it, Palmer utilizes generative grammar fully cognizant of its limitations and restricted to a clearly defined problem, to which he brings some useful insights regarding the phrase as a constituent. His development of tests to determine the viability of the phrase as a constituent structure has implications for developing appropriate procedures in other areas of linguistic investigation.

In the fourth essay, Mark S. Krause assesses the New Testament Greek grammatical construction of the finite verb and cognate participle as a possible indication of Semitic influence upon the Greek of the New Testament. Although investigation of possible Semitic influence on New Testament Greek has been a long-standing endeavour, Krause shows that there is frequently room for re-examination of some tried and trusted conclusions. Krause begins with investigation of the Hebrew finite verb with infinitive absolute, and finds that this is used with emphatic or intensive force in the Hebrew Scriptures. In the LXX, this Hebrew structure is rendered several different ways, including by Krause's target construction, the Greek finite verb and cognate participle. In many instances he sees a similar intensive force. However, in virtually all of the few examples of this construction in non-biblical Greek, Krause contends that the emphatic force is missing. In the New Testament, Krause finds that the Greek finite verb and cognate participle occurs seven times, each instance a translation or rendering of an Old Testament passage with the requisite emphatic or intensive force. He concludes that this syntactical pattern reflects translation of a Hebrew syntactical construction, and its full force should be reflected in modern translations. Krause's essay, which was presented in 1991 in Kansas City, Missouri, has perhaps the most traditional feel about it of all the essays in this volume. But this must not detract from its useful approach and findings. First, Krause takes his readers back to a traditional grammatical problem and, using a computer database, has exhaustively searched the New Testament for this syntactical pattern. Future investigators can thus know the limits of the corpus. Secondly, Krause has his linguistic priorities straight. Although some may well look for a more refined method in determining the presence or absence of emphasis or intensity, Krause makes every effort to analyse the linguistic phenomenon before assessing how it should be translated.

TO TIMOTHY OR NOT?
A DISCOURSE ANALYSIS OF 1 TIMOTHY

Jeffrey T. Reed

Three New Testament letters, 1 Timothy, 2 Timothy and Titus, christened the 'Pastoral Epistles' (PE) by Aquinas in the thirteenth century and similarly by the German scholar, Anton, in the eighteenth century, have evaded the critical attention of many New Testament scholars. Such ill-fated neglect stems in part from the dubious position, according to most scholars, which these letters have in the Pauline corpus. The PE reveal a developed, institutionalized ecclesiology presumably found in early Catholicism (*Frühkatholizismus*), that is, a post-Pauline era.[1] Supposedly, 1 Timothy reveals this church structure the most. For example, in contrast to 2 Timothy where 'the personal element is strongly emphasized, and. . . the exhortations in the epistle really apply to the addressee and therefore can well be accounted "correspondence"', M. Dibelius and H. Conzelmann claim that in 1 Timothy 'personal elements fade into the background, and the letter's primary purpose is to transmit regulations (see 1 Tim. 2, 3, and 5)'.[2] In this schema, the personal elements are limited to an

---

1. See W.G. Kümmel, *Introduction to the New Testament* (trans. H.C. Kee; Nashville: Abingdon Press, 17th edn, 1975), pp. 380-82; C.J. Roetzel, *The Letters of Paul: Conversations in Context* (Atlanta: John Knox, 2nd edn, 1982), p. 111; and C.F.D. Moule, *The Birth of the New Testament* (San Francisco: Harper & Row, 3rd edn, 1982), pp. 197-200. J.D.G. Dunn (*Unity and Diversity in the New Testament: An Inquiry into the Character of Earliest Christianity* [London: SCM Press, 2nd edn, 1990], p. 351) argues that 'increasing institutionalization is the clearest mark of early catholicism' and is clearly noticeable in the PE.

2. M. Dibelius and H. Conzelmann, *The Pastoral Epistles: A Commentary on the Pastoral Epistles* (Hermeneia; Philadelphia: Fortress Press, 1972), p. 1. Even Titus is more apt to be considered authentic Pauline correspondence because 'the fact that the regulations are addressed to the apostle's disciple seems more justified in this case, since in Crete the foundation for church organization had yet to be laid'.

authenticating function, that is 'to demonstrate the authorship of Paul.
What the author himself wanted to say is to be inferred first of all
from passages with a different content.'[1] Consequently, the persona of
Timothy has little import for the interpretation of the letter, and the
Ephesian church is assumed to be the real, intended recipient of the
letter.[2]

Contributing to many scholars' snub of the PE is the equally abusive
estimation that the PE are, to put it bluntly, incoherent. 'The
Pastorals', asserts A.T. Hanson, 'are made up of a miscellaneous collection of material. They have no unifying theme; there is no
development of thought.'[3] A recent response from several scholars,
representing a renewed interest in these letters, has objected to this
assessment. They argue for a coherent understanding of the PE.[4] The

1. Dibelius and Conzelmann, *The Pastoral Epistles*, p. 5. Cf. J.L. Houlden,
The Pastoral Epistles (repr.; Trinity Press International New Testament
Commentaries; London: SCM Press, 1976), p. 34. According to this logic, if the
personal elements do not count as criteria for authorship (which, if they did, would
argue for the Pauline authorship of 2 Timothy), then the only way to deal with them
is to avoid them. Others on both sides of the authenticity issue have not been so
skeptical of the personal elements, e.g. B. Fiore, *The Function of Personal Example
in the Socratic and Pastoral Epistles* (AnBib, 105; Rome: Biblical Institute Press,
1986), pp. 209-11, and M. Prior, *Paul the Letter-Writer and the Second Letter to
Timothy* (JSNTSup, 23; Sheffield: JSOT Press, 1989), pp. 50-59. I remain uncon-
vinced by the 'fragmentary' hypothesis which explains the personal elements as
authentic insertions from Pauline letters. For arguments against such a hypothesis,
see Kümmel, *Introduction*, p. 385, and the decisive argument of D. Cook, 'The
Pastoral Fragments Reconsidered', *JTS* NS 35 (1984), pp. 120-31. A pressing
question then remains: why are there personal elements in a pseudepigraphical letter?

2. See, e.g., C.K. Barrett, *The Pastoral Epistles* (New Clarendon Bible;
Oxford: Clarendon Press, 1963), p. 90; A.T. Hanson, *The Pastoral Epistles* (NCB;
Grand Rapids: Eerdmans, 1982), p. 116; N. Brox, *Die Pastoralbriefe* (RNT;
Regensburg: Pustet, 4th rev. edn, 1969), p. 222; C. Spicq, *Saint Paul: Les épîtres
pastorales* (EBib; 2 vols.; Paris: Gabalda, 4th rev. edn, 1969), pp. xxi-xxxi.

3. Hanson, *The Pastoral Epistles*, p. 42. Along similar lines, D. Guthrie (*The
Pastoral Epistles: An Introduction and Commentary* [TNTC; Grand Rapids:
Eerdmans, 1957], p. 12) remarks, 'There is a lack of studied order, some subjects
being treated more than once in the same letter without apparent premeditation'.

4. See, e.g., L.R. Donelson, 'The Structure of Ethical Argument in the
Pastorals', *BTB* 18 (1988), p. 108, who disputes Hanson's view:

Recently, however, there have been a number of attempts to trace the flow of argument
in these letters and to discover logical connections among the various literary types

purpose of this study is to press forward recent discussions regarding the coherence of the PE, focusing on the most criticized of the three, 1 Timothy. Central to an understanding of the letter's coherence is the question of the letter's intended recipient. The modern linguistic field of discourse analysis supplies a working methodology, which is briefly introduced below. For the purpose of simplicity, the names of 'Paul', 'Timothy', and the 'Ephesian Church' are used throughout this study, but without implying that the names refer to any corresponding historical persons.

1. *Discourse Analysis as an Interpretative Model*

Questions regarding textual coherence have been the focus of a recently developing field of study within modern linguistics, discourse analysis (sometimes labeled 'text linguistics' = *Textwissenschaft*).[1] Broadly defined, discourse analysis is founded on two fundamental assumptions.[2] First, analysis of language, especially of discourse

---

(Donelson; Fiore; Karris; Verner). It is being argued that the Pastorals are not a mindless combination of incompatible materials but are the result of a coherent and consistent view of the Christian life.

See L.R. Donelson, *Pseudepigraphy and Ethical Argument in the Pastoral Epistles* (Hermeneutische Untersuchungen zur Theologie, 22; Tübingen: Mohr [Paul Siebeck], 1986); Fiore, *The Function of Personal Example*; R.J. Karris, *The Pastoral Epistles* (New Testament Message, 17; Wilmington, DE: Michael Glazier, 1979); D.C. Verner, *The Household of God: The Social World of the Pastoral Epistles* (SBLDS, 71; Chico, CA: Scholars Press, 1983). Cf. also P. Bush, 'A Note on the Structure of 1 Timothy', *NTS* 36 (1990), p. 152, who contends that the continuing debate over authorship has hindered fruitful discussion and 'resulted in the artistry of the individual letters being ignored'.

1. See P. Cotterell and M. Turner, *Linguistics and Biblical Interpretation* (Downers Grove, IL: IVP, 1989), pp. 230-31. The term 'discourse analysis' is generally used to refer to analysis of either spoken or written communication, with the terms 'text linguistics' or 'text grammar' reserved for the written use of language. Some linguists, however, do not maintain this distinction and may use the terms interchangeably or they may reserve 'discourse' solely for speech and 'text' for the written use of language. In this essay 'discourse analysis' and 'discourse' are used comprehensively, with reference to either written or spoken text.

2. The following are helpful introductions to discourse analysis: W. Dressler, *Einführung in die Textlinguistik* (Tübingen: Niemeyer, 1972); R. de Beaugrande and W. Dressler, *Introduction to Text Linguistics* (London: Longman, 1980); G. Brown

(whether it be written or spoken), must take into consideration the *functional* nature of language. Humans principally use language in a cultural context, observing appropriate social norms and mores. These values must be factored into any analysis of the use of language. The linguistic data under inspection should consist of actual instances of language used in socio-cultural contexts (fictitious or non-fictitious). Secondly, analysis of language must be performed from the vista of complete discourses, as opposed to single sentences, clauses, or words. Words obtain meaning only when used in a broader linguistic context. The larger discourse structure, then, must influence the interpretation of words, clauses, and even pericopes. As Talmy Givón remarks,

> It has become obvious to a growing number of linguists that the study of the syntax of isolated sentences, extracted, without natural context from the purposeful constructions of speakers is a methodology that has out-lived its usefulness.[1]

This is not to say that discourse analysts neglect clausal or lexical levels of interpretation; rather, they advocate a more holistic approach. Discourse is to be analyzed from the 'top-down' *and* 'bottom-up', that is beginning with larger *macrostructural* themes (e.g. the discourse) and working down through linguistic *microstructures* (e.g. pericopes, clauses, phrases and individual words) and then back up.[2] Focus on the larger discourse unit does not

---

and G. Yule, *Discourse Analysis* (Cambridge Textbooks in Linguistics; Cambridge: Cambridge University Press, 1983); and M. Coulthard, *An Introduction to Discourse Analysis* (London: Longman, 2nd edn, 1985); and for the more intrepid: J.E. Grimes, *The Thread of Discourse* (Janua Linguarum Series Minor, 207; Berlin: Mouton, 1976), and R.E. Longacre, *The Grammar of Discourse* (New York: Plenum, 1983).

1. T. Givón, 'Preface', in T. Givón (ed.), *Syntax and Semantics*. XII. *Discourse and Syntax* (New York: Academic Press, 1979), p. xiii.

2. On 'bottom-up' and 'top-down' analysis of texts, see Brown and Yule, *Discourse Analysis*, pp. 234-36; cf. R.E. Longacre, 'The Paragraph as a Grammatical Unit', in Givón (ed.), *Syntax and Semantics*. XII. *Discourse and Syntax*, p. 116; R. de Beaugrande, *Text, Discourse, and Process: Toward a Multidisciplinary Science of Texts* (Norwood, NJ: Ablex, 1980), pp. 26-27. In brief, macrostructures refer to overarching topics of discourse (i.e. themes, plots) which dominate the composition and structure of texts. Macrostructures are then said to be composed of smaller, sequenced microstructures (e.g. words, phrases, cola, sentences, pericopes). For further detailed treatment of these concepts, see the three

94   *Biblical Greek Language and Linguistics*

eliminate the need for scrutinizing smaller linguistic units. Analysis of words and clauses is important, but only within the perspective of the larger discourse.[1]

The second tenet of discourse analysis—it must be performed on complete discourses—forms the primary methodology of this examination of 1 Timothy.[2] First, the macrostructure of 1 Timothy is treated. The question asked is: what thread of the discourse binds the letter into a cohesive whole? Secondly, macrostructural conclusions are applied to an ambiguous microstructure, 1 Tim. 3.14-15, resulting in an interpretation that runs against the majority of commentators.

works of T.A. van Dijk: *Some Aspects of Text Grammars* (The Hague: Mouton, 1972), pp. 6-7, 34-129, 130-62; *Text and Context: Explorations in the Semantics and Pragmatics of Discourse* (London: Longman, 1977), pp. 130-63; and *Macrostructures: An Interdisciplinary Study of Global Structures in Discourse, Interaction, and Cognition* (Hillsdale, NJ: Lawrence Erlbaum, 1980).

1.   Although scholars applying discourse analysis to the New Testament have assumed this methodology, J.P. Louw's definition of the pericope as 'the largest readily perceptible whole... having some autonomy of its own and exhibiting its own peculiar structural pattern' has resulted in New Testament applications of discourse analysis which often restrict the scope of investigation to the pericope rather than to the whole text ('Discourse Analysis and the Greek New Testament', *BT* 24 [1973], p. 103). Louw's own recent *A Semantic Discourse Analysis of Romans* (2 vols.; Pretoria: Department of Greek, University of Pretoria, 1979) is a fortunate exception to this trend.

2.   For other applications of discourse analysis to the New Testament, see Louw, 'Discourse Analysis', pp. 101-18; A.B. du Toit, 'The Significance of Discourse Analysis for New Testament Interpretation and Translation: Introductory Remarks with Special Reference to 1 Pet 1.3-13', *Neot* 8 (1974), pp. 54-79; W. Schenk, 'Textlinguistische Aspekte der Strukturanalyse, dargestellt am Beispiel von 1 Kor 15.1-11', *NTS* 23 (1977), pp. 469-77; *idem*, 'Hebräerbrief 4.14-16: Textlinguistik als Kommentierungsprinzip', *NTS* 26 (1980), pp. 242-52; *idem, Die Philipperbrief des Paulus* (Stuttgart: Kohlhammer, 1984), esp. pp. 13-28; J.R. Werner, 'Discourse Analysis of the Greek New Testament', in J.H. Skilton and C.A. Ladley (eds.), *The New Testament Student and his Field* (Phillipsburg, NJ: Presbyterian and Reformed, 1982), pp. 213-33; E.A. Nida, J.P. Louw, A.H. Snyman, J.v.W. Cronje, *Style and Discourse, with Special Reference to the Text of the Greek New Testament* (Roggebaai, South Africa: Bible Society, 1983); D.A. Black, 'Hebrews 1.1-4: A Study of Discourse Analysis', *WTJ* 49 (1987), pp. 175-94; Cotterell and Turner, *Linguistics and Biblical Interpretation*, esp. pp. 238-92; and S.E. Porter and J.T. Reed, 'Greek Grammar since BDF: A Retrospective and Prospective Analysis', *FN* 4 (1991), pp. 143-64.

This interpretation of 1 Timothy, furthermore, suggests that the intended recipient of the letter is 'Timothy', whether he be a pseude-pigraphical creation or not.

2. *The Intended Recipient(s) of 1 Timothy: A Macrostructural Inquiry*

Analyzing the epistolary genre and the participant/event structure of 1 Timothy serves well the task of determining the letter's macrostructure. Both of these aspects of the macrostructure are directly relevant to the larger question: who is the intended recipient of the letter?

a. *The Epistolary Setting*

John L. White convincingly argues that Graeco-Roman letters served three essential functions: 'the maintenance of contact, the communication of information, and the statement of request or command'.[1] He also attempts to explicate how these three functions are grammaticalized in textual features. For example, in the opening and closing sections of the letter 'the writer's presence and disposition in writing is conveyed to the recipient(s)'.[2] The letter's opening superscription (i.e. from whom) and adscription (i.e. to whom) take on special significance, since the epistolary genre is used in contexts where one or more individuals, separated by distance, wish to communicate with others.[3] If this working definition of the epistolary genre is adopted,

---

1. J.L. White, *Light from Ancient Letters* (Foundations and Facets; Philadelphia: Fortress Press, 1986), pp. 218-19.
2. White, *Light from Ancient Letters*, p. 219. The functions of making requests/commands and giving information are generally formalized in the body.
3. Cf. the letter definitions of G.J. Bahr, 'The Subscriptions in the Pauline Letters', *JBL* 87 (1968), p. 27; J.L. White, 'The Greek Documentary Letter Tradition Third Century BCE to Third Century CE', *Semeia* 22 (1981), p. 91; and W.G. Doty, 'The Classification of Epistolary Literature', *CBQ* 31 (1969), p. 198, who rightly concludes that an inclusive definition (with reference to his own) 'will permit us to be informed by the genre as a whole, while allowing more specific qualifications to distinguish within each group'. Some may argue that pseudepigraphical letters, as 1 Timothy may well be, do not necessarily fulfill the function of 'spatially separated communication' since the real author and audience may very well dwell in the same locale. However, a better approach to the pseudepi-graphical letter is that, although the real sender and recipient may be in the same locale, the 'real' author creates 'pseudo' senders and recipients in his letter who are

then the superscription and adscription of 1 Timothy should say much about the intended recipient of the letter, or any letter.

1. *The epistolary opening.* The epistolary opening sets the social and interpersonal communicative context of a letter.[1] Elements commonly found in this section are the superscription (sender), adscription (addressee), and salutation/greeting. These are commonly expressed by forms such as (1) *X* (nominative) to *Y* (dative), *greetings* (e.g. χαίρειν) or (2) to *Y* (dative) from *X* (nominative or prepositional phrase), omitting the greeting.[2] The only obligatory elements in the epistolary opening are the superscription and adscription, which are necessary because of the spatial distance separating the individuals. These elements set the interpersonal context of the letter, whether it be from a king to a city or from a boy to his father. The superscription and adscription are often expanded through the addition of epithets, titles, terms of relationship or endearment, and

figuratively, if not spatially, separated. In his typology of pseudepigraphical letters, R. Bauckham ('Pseudo-Apostolic Letters', *JBL* 107 [1988], p. 475) claims that, except for testamentary letters in which the supposed author could directly address the setting of the 'real' audience, 'the readers [the "real" readers] of a pseudepigraphical letter cannot read it as though they were being directly addressed either by the supposed author or by the real author... 'they must read it as a letter written to *other* people, in the past'. In this definition of pseudepigraphy, the contrived context of situation in which the pseudepigraphical letter is written *is* the situational context which the exegete must interpret. Cf. Doty, 'Classification', pp. 196-97, who correctly categorizes 'non-real' pseudonymous or imaginary letters as types of letters rather than denying their 'letterness'. The tendency to imitate *real* letters would especially be the case for Christians looking back on the Pauline epistolary tradition (see J.L. White, 'Saint Paul and the Apostolic Letter Tradition', *CBQ* 45 [1983], p. 444).

1. Cf. Julius Victor, *Ars Rhetorica* 27 (*De Epistolis*), who teaches that epistolary openings and closings should concur with the degree of friendship between the sender and recipient: 'Praefationes ac subscriptiones litterarum computandae sunt pro discrimine amicitiae aut dignitatis' (cited in A.J. Malherbe [ed.], *Ancient Epistolary Theorists* [SBLSBS; Atlanta: Scholars Press], p. 65).

2. The omission of the opening greeting is often found in more formal registers (e.g. petitions, complaints); see J.L. White, 'Epistolary Formulas and Cliches in Greek Papyrus Letters', in *SBLSP*, 1978, II, p. 292. Examples of letters omitting the greeting include: *P.Oxy.* IX, 1188 (13 CE); *P.Ryl.* 166 (26 CE); *P.Ryl.* 167 (39 CE); *P.Ryl.* 171 (56-57 CE); and *P.Hamb.* 5 (89 CE).

geographical locations.[1] Such additions provide vital clues to the social relationships between the sender and recipient of the letter.

1 Timothy follows this typical epistolary pattern. In 1.1, 2, Paul (Παῦλος) writes to Timothy (Τιμοθέῳ). The expansions are brief but enlightening. Paul is an apostle of Christ Jesus (ἀπόστολος Χριστοῦ Ἰησοῦ; v. 1). His apostleship, no doubt, invokes the role's attendant responsibilities and authority. This authority was established by the command of God and of Christ Jesus (κατ᾽ ἐπιταγὴν θεοῦ σωτῆρος ἡμῶν καὶ Χριστοῦ Ἰησοῦ τῆς ἐλπίδος ἡμῶν; v. 1). The additional descriptions of Timothy are also insightful. Paul addresses him as a legitimate child in faith (γνησίῳ τέκνῳ ἐν πίστει; v. 2). πίστις, which Paul ascribes to Timothy, denotes an important virtue of the believer in 1 Timothy. It came to Paul in his calling (1.14); it comprises part of his message to the nations (2.7); and it is to be pursued (6.11). In contrast, some have left the faith (1.19) and others may deny it by their actions, becoming like 'unbelievers' (ἄπιστος; 5.8).

In this brief verbless clause of 1 Tim. 1.1-2, Paul introduces the main characters of his communication—viz. Paul and Timothy—and their standing within the believing community. Paul consistently maintains this participant macrostructure throughout the letter. To assert that the letter is primarily addressed to the wider church goes against these explicit statements in the opening formula. Although such a claim is possible, one would like to find linguistic evidence in the text on its behalf. At first glance, the epistolary closing provides just such evidence.

2. The epistolary closing. Ancient letters developed common formulas for concluding the communicative process. Although ἔρρωσο or ἐρρῶσθαι and εὐτύχει or the combination ἐρρῶσθαι σε εὔχομαι are often found at the close of ancient letters, the closing is at times dropped from the letter. Most discourse requires some sort of 'close' or 'wrap-up' to the communicative event, and Hellenistic letters are no exception to this general pattern. What occupies this epistolary slot, however, is open to variation. Whereas Pauline letters usually have

---

1. See, e.g., *BGU* III, 846 (II CE): Ἀντῶνις Λόγγος Νειλοῦτι τῇ μητρὶ πλῖστα χαίρειν; *P.Ryl.* II, 231 (40 CE): Ἀμμώνιος Ἀφροδισίωι τῷ φιλτάτῳ χαίρειν; *Sel. Pap.* I, 104 (I BCE): Ἀθηναγόρας ὁ ἀρχίατρος τοῖς ἱερεῦσι τῶν ἐν τῶι Λαβυρίνθωι στολιστῶν καὶ τοῖς στολισταῖς χαίρειν.

additional elements which signal movement towards the end of communication (e.g. notification of a visit, greetings), 1 Timothy abruptly
ends with ἡ χάρις μεθ᾽ ὑμῶν ('grace be with you'; 6.21). This formula, at times slightly adapted, is not only characteristic of the PE but
is found at or near the end of all Pauline letters.[1] In 2 Tim. 4.19-21
and Tit. 3.15, closing greetings (ἀσπάσασθαι) are included as tran-
sition points to the grace formula.[2]

The *crux interpretum* of 1 Tim. 6.21 concerns the sole use of
second person plural language in the entire letter, the pronoun ὑμῶν.
Those who advocate a view of 1 Timothy as being addressed to a
wider audience point to this verbless clause as approbative evidence.
Dibelius and Conzelmann contend, 'The plural "with you" (ὑμῶν)
reflects the acknowledgement that a writing with this particular content is *directed to a wider circle*, despite the address' (emphasis
added).[3] Similarly, Brox maintains,

> The plural of the short closing greeting ('with you' [pl.]) unexpectedly
> indicates what the entire letter shows: it was written not only for an
> individual recipient but for the leader of the community and his particular
> church.[4]

This is difficult to imagine since upon reaching the closing, to quote
Kelly, 'we are left wondering why the author should have decided to
drop his skillfully contrived illusion at the last moment',[5] especially in

1. See Rom. 16.20; 1 Cor. 16.23; 2 Cor. 13.13; Gal. 6.18; Eph. 6.24; Phil.
4.23; Col. 4.18; 1 Thess. 5.28; 2 Thess. 3.18; 2 Tim. 4.22; Tit. 3.15; Phlm. 25. A
cursory glance at several of these passages reveals their somewhat uncertain textual
history. This should at least be considered when accounting for the reading of ὑμῶν
in 1 Tim. 6.21.

2. This raises a problem for the view which understands 1 Timothy as a letter
intended for a wider audience: why would the author of the PE include greetings to a
larger audience in the more personal 2 Timothy, and yet omit them from 1 Timothy
which is really intended for a wider audience? That 1 Timothy lacks closing greetings
perhaps suggests that Paul is not as concerned with directly addressing those in the
church as some have maintained.

3. Dibelius and Conzelmann, *The Pastoral Epistles*, p. 93; cf. Hanson, *The
Pastoral Epistles*, p. 116; Barrett, *The Pastoral Epistles*, p. 90; E.K. Simpson, *The
Pastoral Epistles: The Greek Text with Introduction and Commentary* (Grand Rapids:
Eerdmans, 1954), p. 93.

4. Brox, *Die Pastoralbriefe*, p. 222.

5. J.N.D. Kelly, *The Pastoral Epistles* (repr.; Grand Rapids: Baker, 1963),
p. 152.

view of the vocative address (ὦ Τιμόθεε) in the preceding verse
(v. 20).

Several possibilities may explain the presence of the plural pronoun
in a letter addressed to an individual, reducing the force of overstated
claims regarding the meaning of this verse. First, all three endings of
the PE contain textual variants, with 1 Tim. 6.21 receiving a C rating
in the *UBSGNT*[3] text. Several textual variants contain μετὰ σοῦ.[1] To
dismiss the singular reading (as Dibelius and Conzelmann do) with the
explanation that the scribe has altered it to fit the context of the letter,[2]
however, forgets that it would be equally likely for a scribe to change
the singular pronoun to the plural in light of the normative Pauline
plural phrase.[3] Or perhaps W. Lock's explanation is adequate: 'A
change to the plural would have been natural when the Epistle was
treated as canonical and as affecting the whole Church'.[4] This
argument is strengthened by the conspicuous scribal tampering with
several Pauline epistolary closings.[5] If the option of the singular
textual variant still seems implausible, another recourse remains. In a
study of Greek papyri, J.H. Moulton concludes that 'singular and
plural alternated in the same document with apparently no distinction
of meaning'.[6] Although Moulton is specifically discussing first person
plural forms, he is tangentially concerned with denouncing Van

1. The singular is also evidenced in D[c] E K L Ψ etc. See J.K. Elliott, *The
Greek Text of the Epistle to Timothy and Titus* (Studies and Documents, 36;
Salt Lake City: University of Utah Press, 1968), p. 115, who accepts the singular
reading.

2. Cf. G. Holtz, *Die Pastoralbriefe* (THKNT, 13; Berlin: Evangelische
Verlagsanstalt, 1965), p. 148.

3. Elliott (*The Greek Text*, p. 110) similarly notes, 'It is likely that μετὰ σοῦ is
original here. It was altered to the plural when the epistle became common and was
read in the church.' J.D. Quinn notes the possibility that 6.21b never existed at all in
the original text (*The Letter to Titus* [AB; New York: Doubleday, 1990], p. 10).

4. W. Lock, *A Critical and Exegetical Commentary on the Pastoral Epistles*
(ICC; Edinburgh: T. & T. Clark, 1924), p. xxxvii.

5. See Rom. 16.20; Phil. 4.23; Col. 4.18; 1 Thess. 5.28; 2 Thess. 3.18; Phlm.
25.

6. J.H. Moulton, 'Notes from the Papyri', *Expositor*, 6th series, 7 (1903),
p. 107; followed by Guthrie, *The Pastoral Epistles*, p. 119. His papyrus examples
are: *P.Tebt.* 55, 58; *P.Amh.* 37, 144; *P.Fay.* 117. N. Turner (*A Grammar of New
Testament Greek*. IV. *Style* [Edinburgh: T. & T. Clark, 1976], p. 28) states, 'Sing.
and Plur. alternate as capriciously in Paul as in contemporary letters'.

Manen, who denies the authenticity of Philemon because of the '"surprising" mixture of singular and plural both in the persons speaking and in the persons addressed'.[1] Pursuing Moulton's reasoning, the implication may be that the semantically insignificant shifts from *first* person singular to plural may also apply to shifts from *second* person singular to plural.[2] In other words, shifts between grammatical person are semantically significant but shifts between grammatical number of the same grammatical person may be semantically vague.

One final explanation of the plural pronoun remains: although Paul may have had a larger group in mind when employing ὑμῶν, he may have done so only as an ancillary address and without specifically intending the letter to be read by them. For example, in Paul's letter to Philemon, although the opening in v. 3 (χάρις ὑμῖν) and the closing in v. 25 (ἡ χάρις τοῦ κυρίου Ἰησοῦ Χριστοῦ μετὰ τοῦ πνεύματος ὑμῶν) are addressed to plural recipients (see also v. 22), the rest of the letter is addressed specifically to Philemon.[3] A recent letter addressed to me and sent from a friend concluded with a familiar American formula: 'See you both soon', signed 'Tom'. 'Both' clearly refers to my wife and me. However, although certain aspects of the letter involved my wife (e.g. 'Tell Jamie "Thanks" for the phone call'), it is evident that the letter was specifically intended for my eyes, and that it was written with the realization that my wife may neither see nor read it. Perhaps 1 Timothy is not far from this modern epistle. Paul writes to his colleague, Timothy, about people and events in the latter's social sphere. That Timothy is commanded to entrust Paul's instructions to the brethren (4.6) implies that they will

---

1. Moulton, 'Notes', p. 107.
2. See, e.g., *P.Oxy.* II, 300 (late I CE) where Indike writes to her lady Thaisous (Ἰνδικὴ Θαεισοῦτι τῇ κυρίᾳ) but closes the letter with a greeting from Longinus to the plural ὑμᾶς (ἀσπάζεται ὑμᾶς Λογγεῖνος). The use of the plural occurs because other people are referred to in the letter, but it is clear that the message of the letter was directed primarily to Indike. C.R. Erdman (*The Pastoral Epistles of Paul* [Philadelphia: Westminster Press, 1923], p. 81) notes similar uses in papyri, yet concedes to the prevailing interpretation of 1 Tim. 6.21: 'While in Greek correspondence this [plural pronoun] was often used in reference to an individual, it is commonly supposed that Paul had in mind here the whole church at Ephesus'.
3. This is not to suggest that others may not have read the letter; however, its contents are specifically directed to the individual Philemon.

hear about them. It does not, however, imply that they must read them,[1] or that the letter primarily addresses them.

These alternative explanations of ὑμῶν suggest that the author is not necessarily moving the 'direct' scope of his communication beyond that of Timothy. At the least, then, the three alternatives suggest the plausibility of a singular understanding (explicit or implicit) of the epistolary closing. Therefore, the closing does not supply incontrovertible evidence for the view that 1 Timothy is addressed and written to a wider church audience.

b. *The Linguistic Composition of 1 Timothy*
Although the epistolary opening and closing supply important evidence for the question of the intended recipient of 1 Timothy, there is much more linguistic information in the discourse. The following macrostructural investigation centers around the participant and event structure of the letter, with remarks on their bearing for the question of the letter's intended recipient.

1. *Participant structure.* Participant structure can be fairly complex in discourse, and 1 Timothy is no exception. Participants of discourse regularly involve a *spokesperson* and a *recipient*.[2] This is straightforward enough. However, the spokesperson can be distinguished from the *source* of an utterance. Although Paul is the spokesperson/speaker in 1 Timothy, the source of the message is likely considered to be God, at least in Paul's mind (cf. 1 Tim. 2.7). Furthermore, the recipient need not be the *target* of the address. As illustrated above, several scholars contend that the target recipient of 1 Timothy involves the wider church membership at Ephesus. Further

---

1. Kelly's suggestion that Paul uses the plural pronoun here because he intends the letter to be read in the assembly is conceivable (*The Pastoral Epistles*, pp. 2, 152; cf. G.D. Fee, *1 and 2 Timothy, Titus* [New International Bible Commentary; Peabody, MA: Hendrickson, 1984], p. 162). If granted, however, this does not invalidate the first stage in the communicative process: Timothy reads the letter himself.

2. The following discussion takes much of its impetus from S.C. Levinson, *Pragmatics* (Cambridge Textbooks in Linguistics; Cambridge: Cambridge University Press, 1983), pp. 68-73; Grimes, *Thread of Discourse*, esp. pp. 33-50; and K. Callow, *Discourse Considerations in Translating the Word of God* (Grand Rapids: Zondervan, 1975), esp. pp. 32-48.

distinctions regarding recipients can be made. If in 1 Tim. 4.13 Paul
expects his letter to be read to the larger church, he may only want
part of the church body to hear the letter. In other words, there may
be *ratified* and *unratified* recipients of the message. The church
leaders may be ratified to read the letter. These leaders (including
Timothy) are then expected to transmit Paul's message to the church
members, who, however, are unratified recipients. The contention
here is that Timothy is the only entirely ratified recipient to whom the
whole letter would apply. It is necessary, however, to deal with the
reality of the multi-faceted participant structure in 1 Timothy. Two
linguistic phenomena contribute to an understanding of this aspect of
discourse: lexical choices and person deixis.

a. *Lexical choices.* Lexical items representing the textual participants
of 1 Timothy can be divided into two spheres: supernatural beings and
humans. Each of these can be further subdivided into positive and
negative roles (i.e. antonymous functions). Advantageous supernatural
beings (with reference to the Christian community) include God (1.1),
Christ (1.1), angels (3.16), and the spirit/Spirit(?) (4.1). These are
opposed by injurious supernatural beings such as Satan/Devil (3.6),
deceptive spirits (4.1), and demons (4.1). These groups of
supernatural beings, although respectively symbolizing the ultimate
source of any trustworthy or errant teaching, are not the primary
participants of the discourse; rather, they play a secondary role.

Human participants are not as meticulously divided into dichoto-
mous groups. Regarding 'Christians', some believers have totally left
the faith (1.19), others are standing strong (e.g. Timothy),[1] others are
recent converts and are thus subject to suspicion (3.6), and others have
yet to believe (1.16). Put another way, there is a continuum on which
at one end are believers secure in the faith and at the other are
apostate believers. With this complexity in mind, those who are at
least on the continuum of 'church' people (i.e. those within the believing community) include Paul (1.1), Timothy (1.2), those coming to
believe (1.16), overseers (3.1), recent converts (3.6), deacons (3.8),
deacon's wives/deaconesses (?) (3.11), believers (4.10), fathers (5.1),
brothers (5.1), old men (5.1), young men (5.1), mothers (5.2), sisters

1. But even Timothy is pictured as one who has not yet completed all of his
immediate duties, implying possible failure (see 1.18-19; 4.6).

(5.2), old women (5.2), young ladies (5.2), older widows (5.3), grandchildren (5.4), parents (5.4), grandparents (5.4), young widows (5.11), presbyters (5.17), slaves (6.1), believing masters (6.1), beloved ones (6.2), brothers (6.3), and those believers who are wealthy (6.9). These terms are in a hyponymous relationship to the word ἐκκλησία and the phrase οἶκος θεοῦ (3.15), that is they represent subcategories of the more inclusive terms. Additional terms are also used to distinguish this group: πιστοί (4.10; 6.2); ἀδελφοί (6.2); ἀγαπητοί (6.2).

Besides those within (or at least at one time within) the believing community, some human participants stand outside of the household of God. But even here there is a complexity to the participant structure. On the one hand, there are those outside of the church who religiously oppose the church. These are not simply so-called 'ex-believers' but they are insurgents who never followed Christ and who promote teachings and lifestyles opposed to the gospel proclaimed by Paul (e.g. 1.10-11). Paul himself is an illustration of one who once opposed the Christian community (1.12-17). In contrast to these religious opponents outside of the church, there are those outside of the church with whom the church should have favorable relationships. These groups include political leaders (2.2) and those in the general populace (τῶν ἔξωθεν; 3.7). The participant structure symbolizing unbelievers, like the participant structure of believers, forms a continuum of good and bad—some are in clear opposition to the church and some are vital to the church's existence.

This brief survey of the lexical choices exposes a complex matrix of participants in the letter. This complex participant structure produces diverse discussions on such topics as widows, bishops, slaves and women, which no doubt produces a jagged effect on the flow of the discourse. As one participant is introduced, contrastive participants often come to bear on the discussion.[1] From this perspective the discourse often appears incohesive. Nevertheless, the various participants have one unifying thread or macrostructure: they all concern Timothy, Paul's co-worker, as he attempts to address the problem of the 'heretics' and to establish the church of God. This thread of the

1. See, e.g., 5.3-16, which is a discussion of widows but involves other participants as well: family members, immoral widows, and young widows.

discourse is most evident from the use of grammatical person in the letter.

b. *Person deixis*. Because Greek is a monolectic language, grammatical person is expressed in a verbal form. Thus an understanding of the participant structure in Greek discourse must include investigation of grammaticalized person, since participants need not always be grammaticalized in lexical items but can be expressed by the verb alone. The following discussion of grammatical person as an indicator of macrostructure is divided into six categories according to grammatical person and number.

First person singular usage is straightforward in 1 Timothy, with all verbal forms having Paul as the grammatical subject.[1] Second person singular verbal usage is limited to Timothy as the grammatical subject, being found in an abundant number of passages but concentrated in chs. 4–6.[2] Third person singular verbal usage complicates analysis of grammatical person, since this form 'does not correspond to any specific participant-role in the speech event'.[3] In other words, the author can speak of various persons or entities, without including them as main participants in the discourse. A wide variety of subjects and corresponding topics can enter the discussion of the discourse, without being linked to the sender and recipient of the letter.[4] Such is the case in 1 Timothy, which contains several third person topics (e.g. supernatural beings, church members, those outside of the church, and peripheral figures such as Adam and Eve).[5]

First person plural verbal usage raises an interesting exegetical problem: who does the author of 1 Timothy have in view when using

---

1.   See 1 Tim. 1.3, 11, 12, 13 (2×), 15, 16, 18, 20; 2.1, 2, 7 (3×), 8, 12; 3.14; 4.13; 5.14, 21; 6.13.

2.   See 1 Tim. 1.3, 18; 3.14; 4.6 (2×), 7, 11 (2×), 12, 13, 14, 15 (2×), 16 (3×); 5.1 (2×), 3, 7, 11, 19, 20, 21, 22 (3×), 23 (2×); 6.2 (2×), 11 (2×), 12 (4×), 17, 20.

3.   Levinson, *Pragmatics*, p. 69.

4.   Componentially, use of third person is understood as excluding both speaker [– speaker] and addressee [– addressee].

5.   See 1 Tim. 1.5, 8, 9, 10, 12, 14, 15, 16, 20; 2.4, 10, 11, 13, 14 (2×), 15; 3.1 (2×), 2, 5 (2×), 6, 7 (2×), 15 (2×), 16 (7×); 4.1, 3, 5, 8, 10, 12, 14, 15; 5.4 (3×), 5 (2×), 6, 8 (3×), 9, 10 (5×), 16 (4×), 18; 6.1, 3 (2×), 4 (2×), 6, 15, 16 (2×).

first person plural forms?[1] Five understandings are possible: (1) Paul
and Timothy; (2) Paul and any fellow workers (or believers) present
with him; (3) Paul and the believers at Ephesus; (4) the universal
church; or (5) universal humanity. If possibility 3 is the author's
intent, does this further evidence the view that the larger church is the
intended audience of 1 Timothy? A cursory glance at 1.8 and 4.10
suggests that Paul limits the semantic scope of his grammar to the
Christian community,[2] with 4.10 possibly referring more specifically
to God's laborers, which is a specialized role for only some
believers.[3] However, 6.7-8 is clearly a timeless maxim and universal
in scope. Furthermore, 2.2 most likely refers to a life of peace and
godliness universally experienced (at least for the religiously
orientated), since the idea is that good kingly leadership will result in
peace throughout the kingdom for all inhabitants. Usage of third
person plural *pronouns* adds further insight into the author's use of
first person plural verbal forms.[4] 1 Tim. 1.1a contains the statement,
'God, the savior of *us*' (θεοῦ σωτῆρος ἡμῶν). The pronoun probably
includes unbelievers within its scope, in light of 4.10 which asserts
that God is the savior of all humanity (σωτὴρ πάντων ἀνθρώπων)
even though believers are given special prominence (μάλιστα
πιστῶν). But in 1.1b (Χριστοῦ Ἰησοῦ τῆς ἐλπίδος ἡμῶν) it is
doubtful that the author understands unbelievers as having Christ as
their hope,[5] especially since elsewhere only mature believers are
portrayed as having hope in God.[6] Therefore, if semantic consistency
is to be preferred here, 1.1a also probably refers only to the Christian
community. Likewise, in 1.2 (Χριστοῦ Ἰησοῦ τοῦ κυρίου ἡμῶν),
1.14 (ἡ χάρις τοῦ κυρίου ἡμῶν) and 6.14 (τοῦ κυρίου ἡμῶν

   1.   First person plural verbal forms include: 1 Tim. 1.8; 2.2; 4.10 (3×); 6.7-8
(3×).
   2.   Kelly, *The Pastoral Epistles*, p. 48.
   3.   In view of the use of the word 'hope' to refer to strong believers elsewhere
(see 5.5; 6.17), and the use of 'working' terminology with reference to leaders of the
church (see 1.18; 6.12), 1 Tim. 4.10 appears to refer only to those believers who are
firm in the faith, and possibly only to those believers who are in some form of
leadership.
   4.   See 1 Tim. 1.1 (2×), 2, 14; 6.14, 17.
   5.   Χριστοῦ Ἰησοῦ is probably an objective genitive ('hope in Christ') and
ἡμῶν is a subjective genitive ('we hope in Christ').
   6.   See 1 Tim. 5.5; 6.17.

Ἰησοῦ Χριστοῦ) the first person plural pronoun is probably limited to believers, but not merely to the Ephesian believers. 1 Tim. 6.17 (ἐπὶ θεῷ τῷ παρέχοντι ἡμῖν πάντα πλουσίως εἰς ἀπόλαυσιν) may be universal in scope, but is hardly unambiguous, and thus provides little evidence either way. In summary, Paul uses first person plural verbal forms in a universal sense in 1.1, 2.2, 6.7-8, and possibly 1.1, 2, 14 and 6.14, 17, whereas in the other cases 'Christians' are the particular focus. Paul does not limit first person plural usage to the Ephesian church; rather, the forms are used comprehensively, either of all humanity (believers and non-believers), all believers, or all mature believers. Within this framework the author surely has in view the immediate church at Ephesus, but it cannot be inferred from the first person plural linguistic evidence that he is exclusively addressing this community.

No instances of second person plural verbal forms occur in the text of 1 Timothy. The *prima facie* evidence, then, suggests that Timothy is the only addressee of the letter, for he is the only referent when second person verbal forms are used.[1] If the author wanted to involve a wider audience as his addressees, one would expect second person forms used with reference to someone other than Timothy (especially plural forms used in reference to the church). In this case, an argument from silence (that is, no second person plural verbal forms are used) carries significant weight. Furthermore, all uses of second person personal pronouns are singular, apart from one plural pronoun in 6.21, which is satisfactorily explained above.

Third person plural verbal usage in 1 Timothy, like third person singular, allows the author to include a vast array of topics in his discussion.[2] In every passage except 5.24 and 6.9 (the relative pronoun αἵτινες refers back to 'desires', ἐπιθυμίας) the subjects are humans.

The evidence of the system of grammatical person in 1 Timothy indicates that Paul is the letter's sender, and Timothy, not the wider circle of the church, is the intended recipient. The particular actions

---

1. Regarding the linguistic function of second person forms J. Lyons's componential analysis of grammatical person is helpful here, in which he categorizes second person forms as [+ addressee – sender] (*Introduction to Theoretical Linguistics* [Cambridge: Cambridge University Press, 1968], pp. 470-81).

2. See 1 Tim. 1.4, 6, 7 (2×), 19, 20; 2.15; 3.10 (2×), 12, 13; 4.1; 5.11 (2×), 12, 13, 15, 17, 20, 24 (2×), 25; 6.1 (2×), 2 (4×), 9 (2×), 10 (2×), 19, 21.

carried out by the letter's participants now demand treatment, further verifying the above conclusion.

2. *Event structure*. What recurring actions (i.e., linguistically speaking, *processes* or *events*) appear in 1 Timothy? Are they associated with particular participants?[1] If so, what do these processes say about the sender and recipient of the letter? Answers to these questions form the basis of the following macrostructural analysis and further elucidate why Timothy should be taken as the intended recipient of the letter.

Language of 'instructing' and 'commanding' appears throughout the discourse of 1 Timothy. Paul is 'beseeching' (1.3; 2.1), 'desiring' or 'wishing' (2.8; 5.14), 'giving commands' (1.18; 6.13), 'writing' (3.14), 'saying' (2.7), 'not permitting' (2.12), citing the spirit who 'says' (4.1), and 'testifying' (5.21). In fact, of the seventeen first person singular active verbs involving Paul, eleven denote 'instructional' language.

Timothy also performs actions which are expressed using words from this semantic field. He is to 'command' (1.3; 5.7; 6.17), 'keep' or 'watch over' the command (6.14), 'guard the deposit' (6.20), 'teach' (4.11, 16), 'be an example' (4.11),[2] 'perform the reading' (4.13), 'exhort' (4.13; 6.2), and 'reproach' (5.20). His duties have utilitarian implications. For example, 'the goal of the command is love from a clean heart and a good conscience and an unpretentious faith' (1.5). In other words, 'instructional' language is not endorsed for mere cognitive purposes, but to produce results in the hearers. These hearers apparently include some 'heretical' believers. In other words, the 'goal of the command' in 1.5 is also directed to those who are 'teaching other things' (1.3). Indeed, even Hymenaeus and Alexander, who were at least at one time part of the church community, are given to Satan so that they may be *taught* not to blaspheme (1.20). Furthermore, Timothy's role as a 'teacher' has practical implications

1. I am primarily concerned here with the main participants of the structure: Paul, Timothy, supernatural beings and church members. Peripheral participants are excluded from discussion. The theoretical framework undergirding this analysis is based upon M.A.K. Halliday and R. Hasan, 'Text and Context: Aspects of Language in a Social-Semiotic Perspective', *Sophia Linguistica* 6 (1980), pp. 4-90.
2. Note how two of the five aspects of Timothy's role as an exemplar—love and faith—are two of the three 'goals of instruction' in 1.5.

for himself. If he fulfils this role, he will 'battle the good battle' (1.18) and be 'a good servant of Christ' (4.6). The 'salvation' of Timothy and his hearers hinges upon his faithfulness to the task of teaching (4.16).

The teaching of Paul and the role of Timothy as a mediator of this teaching are often contrasted in 1 Timothy with the teaching of others. They 'have falsely called knowledge' (6.20) which they 'assert' (6.21), 'teach other things' (1.3), 'oppose the healthy teaching' (1.10), have 'turned into vain talking' (1.6), 'blaspheme' (1.20), 'deny the faith' (5.8, 12, 15), 'promote genealogies and myths' (1.4), 'speak things not permitted' (5.13), and 'do not hold to the healthy teaching' (6.3). Many of those involved in the rival teachings are, or at least were, part of the believing community.

The above macrostructural analysis of events in the text unveils Timothy's central role in the letter as the mediator of Paul's instructions. Paul relies upon Timothy as the intended recipient of his letter to confer, communicate, and enforce his message to any relevant church members.

3. *The Purpose of 1 Timothy: A Microstructural Inquiry*

If Timothy is the intended, indeed primary, recipient and audience of the letter, then one might expect that the larger purpose of the letter also directly concerns Timothy. 1 Tim. 3.14-15 provides a litmus test for this conjecture, being an apparently explicit statement regarding the author's purpose for writing some or all of his letter.[1] Paul writes to Timothy (σοι) so that, if he is delayed, Timothy may know (εἰδῇς) the type of conduct which the apostle expects in the household of God.

---

1. Depending on the extent of the reference of ταῦτα, some question remains as to how sweeping this purpose statement is for the letter. At the least, it encompasses the instructions of church leaders in 3.1-13; perhaps, it refers back to 2.1–3.13 (cf. J.H. Bernard, *The Pastoral Epistles* [Cambridge: Cambridge University Press, 1899], p. 60). Lock (*The Pastoral Epistles*, p. 42), however, is probably correct to conclude that the demonstrative refers to chs. 2–3, 'but it also leads onto the warning against false teaching and the advice about Timothy's teaching which follows' (cf. Spicq, *Les épîtres pastorales*, II, pp. 103-105). A similar expansive interpretation applies to Paul's instruction in 1.18 (ταύτην τὴν παραγγελίαν) and the ταῦτα passages in which Paul directs Timothy to command and teach 'these things' (4.11; 5.7).

This passage parallels epistolary 'disclosure formulas' and also corresponds to what has come to be known as Paul's 'apostolic presence'. Most importantly, it is a key interpretative passage for understanding the purpose of the letter.[1]

In stating their rationale for corresponding with the recipient, ancient letter writers often used what modern scholars refer to as disclosure formulas. Formulas disclosing information in ancient epistles often follow one of three conventions: γέγραφα οὖν ὅπως εἰδῇς...(I wrote so that you may know...); γίνωσκε (ἴσθι, μάθε) ὅτι... (know that...); and γινώσκειν σε θέλω ὅτι... (I want you to know that...).[2] All three formulas function to disclose information which, in turn, would often lead to a request. The last two forms are commonly found in 'the introductory part of the body',[3] and the first commonly concludes the body.[4] Although not in the closing section of the body,

1. Several scholars recognize the importance of this passage for the argument of the letter. See, e.g., Dibelius and Conzelmann, *The Pastoral Epistles*, p. 60, followed by Kelly, *The Pastoral Epistles*, p. 86, who notes the transitional nature of 3.14-16 as a bridge between what proceeds and follows; Lock, *The Pastoral Epistles*, p. 42, who labels it the 'heart of the Epistle'; Fee, *1 and 2 Timothy, Titus*, p. 91, who parallels it with 1.3ff. as 'a further statement of its [the letter's] purpose' (cf. C.J. Ellicott, *A Critical and Grammatical Commentary on the Pastoral Epistles* [Andover, MA: Warren F. Draper, 1882], p. xviii); Guthrie, *The Pastoral Epistles*, pp. 86-87, who estimates it as 'the key to the Pastorals'; and Spicq, *Les épîtres pastorales*, II, p. 103, who asserts, 'Nous avons donc ici non seulement le point doctrinal culminant de l'Epître, mais la clef même des Pastorales'. Verner (*The Household of God*, pp. 13-14), however, notes some scholars' discontent with interpreting 1 Tim. 3.14-15 as the real purpose of the letter. He designates it, nevertheless, a key passage for his thesis that the PE depict the church as the household of God. For a survey of the three prevailing views of the purpose of the PE—polemical defense, ecclesiastical discipline, traditional instruction—see Fiore, *The Function of Personal Example*, pp. 1-7.

2. See White, *Light from Ancient Letters*, pp. 207-208. Two characteristic examples include *P.Mich.* VIII, 464 (March 99 CE) and *Sel. Pap.* I, 121 (II CE).

3. White, *Light from Ancient Letters*, p. 207. An interesting closing of a papyrus letter parallels the linguistic elements of 1 Tim. 3.14-15 (*P. Cairo Zen.* V, 59816 [257 BCE]). Artemidoros writes to Panakestor regarding the tillage of Apollonios's land. Due to illness he does not visit Panakestor personally, but sends a letter instead (ἐπεὶ οὖν αὐτὸς οὐ δεδύνημαι παραγενέσθαι διὰ τὸ ἐνωχλῆσθαι, γράψας ἀπέσταλκα πρὸς σέ, ἵνα εἰδῇς καὶ ποιῇς οὕτως).

4. White, *Light from Ancient Letters*, p. 204.

1 Tim. 3.14-15 also appears to be such a formula.[1] It contains the basic formal elements, with a slight adjustment in that the function of the ὅτι clause, whether it be content (recitative) or causal, is now taken by a πῶς clause.[2] And the πῶς clause clearly parallels the disclosure formula's function as the 'explanation of the reason for writing'.[3] Paul explicitly states that he writes[4] 'so that you may know the conduct necessary in the household of God'. The above gloss is purposefully ambiguous in one respect. Who or what is the subject of the infinitive ἀναστρέφεσθαι ('to act, behave, conduct oneself')[5] within the δεῖ clause?[6] One point is clear from the grammar: Paul writes to Timothy (σοι) in order that Timothy may know (εἰδῇς) something. The communicative context, in other words, is between Paul and Timothy. But what exactly is it that Timothy is to know? Various translations divulge the interpretative problem regarding the subject of the infinitive: '...how *one* ought to behave in the household of God' (RSV); '...how *people* ought to conduct *themselves* in the household of God' (NIV); and '...how *thou* oughtest to behave *thyself* in the house

1. See Rom. 1.13; 2 Cor. 1.8; 1 Thess. 2.1; Phil. 1.12; and Gal. 1.11 for examples that are in the opening of the letter, and 1 Cor. 10.1; 11.3; 12.1; 1 Thess. 4.13; and Rom. 11.25 for those outside of the opening.

2. T.Y. Mullins ('Disclosure: A Literary Form in the New Testament', *NovT* 7 [1964], p. 46) lists four elements of the disclosure: (1) θέλω; (2) noetic verb in the infinitive; (3) person addressed; and (4) information. By incorporating White's broader definition (*Light from Ancient Letters*, pp. 207-208), Mullins's last three requirements are fulfilled in 1 Tim. 3.14-15. The noetic verb is changed to a subjunctive (εἰδῇς) when the finite θέλω is omitted.

3. White, *Light from Ancient Letters*, p. 207.

4. Turner (*Style*, p. 303) states that ἐστιν is to be supplied before ἵνα, but a more likely understanding is that the main finite clause ταῦτά σοι γράφω has been elided (so Lock, *The Pastoral Epistles*, pp. 41-42).

5. The figurative use of ἀναστρέφω to refer to human conduct (but not necessarily ethical conduct) is frequently paired with the preposition ἐν to denote 'behavior *in a particular manner*', as well as the *place* of behavior, as it is here (see 2 Cor. 1.12, which contains both uses in one clause). The verb is commonly used to mean 'to conduct oneself', 'to behave', or 'to live' in a metaphorical extension of the usual meaning 'to turn back' or 'return'; cf., e.g., Eph. 2.3 and the only other infinitival usage in the New Testament in Heb. 13.18.

6. For other similar clausal constructions in the PE, see 1 Tim. 3.7; 2 Tim. 2.6, 24; Tit. 1.11. The exegete wishes Paul would have clarified the subject of the infinitive as 2 Pet. 3.11, a conceptually similar clause, does: ποταμοὺς δεῖ ὑπάρχειν ὑμᾶς ἐν ἁγίαις ἀναστροφαῖς καὶ εὐσεβείαις.

of God' (AV). Assessing the referent of the unexpressed subject of the infinitive has significance for understanding the teleological role which this disclosure formula plays in the macrostructure of 1 Timothy.

There are five reasonable candidates for the subject of ἀναστρέφεσθαι: (1) Timothy, (2) the leaders mentioned in the foregone discourse, (3) all church members (exclusive of leaders) mentioned in the letter, (4) the entire Ephesian church, and (5) Christians in general.[1] The first option assumes Timothy as the primary motivation behind the letter's framing. The last four understand a wider audience as the primary motivation. Although some entertain the view that Timothy may be the subject of the infinitive,[2] most surmise that the subject involves the larger church membership as represented in the letter.[3] That the previous and following injunctions encapsulat-

---

1.   To make matters more obscure, perhaps the subject of ἀναστρέφεσθαι (present middle/passive infinitive) is the 'things' (ταῦτα) Paul has written in his letter, with the verb functioning passively (i.e. '...how it is necessary that these things be conducted in the house of God'). This interpretation, however, does not determine who is the agent of the passive verb.

2.   See Kelly, *The Pastoral Epistles*, p. 87, and Lock, *The Pastoral Epistles*, pp. 42-43, who entertain this view but opt for understanding the church as the subject. Against this, Guthrie (*The Pastoral Epistles*, p. 87) suggests that the subject 'probably refers to Timothy since he is the subject of the main verb'. So also Ellicott, *The Pastoral Epistles*, p. 65; and Holtz, *Die Pastoralbriefe*, pp. 88-89, who translates with the second person singular: 'damit du weißt, wie du dich im Hause Gottes'. Some MSS and Fathers add σε after δεῖ (e.g. D* L[vg] Arm Ambst Origen), but Elliott (*The Greek Text*, p. 57) correctly dismisses these as explanatory additions of scribes and translators. Bernard (*The Pastoral Epistles*, p. 61) is all too pejorative when he warrants, 'The insertion of σε after δεῖ... or the limitation of the words to Timothy (*how* thou *oughtest to behave thyself* &c.), is quite misleading'.

3.   See, e.g., Lock, *The Pastoral Epistles*, p. 43; Kelly, *The Pastoral Epistles*, p. 87; Fee, *1 and 2 Timothy, Titus*, p. 91; Hanson, *The Pastoral Epistles*, p. 82; Simpson, *The Pastoral Epistles*, p. 58; B.S. Easton, *The Pastoral Epistles: Introduction, Translation, Commentary and Word Studies* (New York: Charles Scribner's Sons, 1947), p. 134; Brox, *Die Pastoralbriefe*, pp. 155-56; Donelson, *Ethical Argument*, pp. 154, 171; Prior, *Second Letter to Timothy*, pp. 64-66, 202 n. 80. Dibelius and Conzelmann (*The Pastoral Epistles*, p. 60) fail to address this interpretative question, but their translation takes the subject as indefinite (i.e. 'one'). Verner (*The Household of God*, pp. 1, 13-16) does not investigate this grammatical question, despite the importance of these clauses for his thesis. P.H. Towner in his monograph, *The Goal of our Instruction: The Structure of Theology and Ethics in the*

ing these verses are directed towards church members supports the latter reading. On the other hand, Paul repeatedly instructs Timothy to entrust, command and teach 'these things' (παράγγελλε ταῦτα καὶ δίδασκε; e.g. 4.6, 11; 5.7). This would seem to indicate that the immediate responsibility for administering the codes of 'church conduct' lies upon the shoulders of Timothy. The larger macrostructure, in other words, demonstrates that Paul's words here first and foremost concern the letter's recipient, Timothy. This reading can also be evidenced by the grammar of this microstructure.

Usually, after a verb of perception, the unexpressed subject of an infinitive may be equated with the grammatical subject of the finite verb.[1] 1 Tim. 3.15 does not conform exactly to the instances cited in making this rule, however, since the impersonal verb δεῖ follows the verb of knowing and is the finite clause which governs the infinitive. Nevertheless, a study of uses of δεῖ with the infinitive following verbs of saying/perceiving in the New Testament shows that when a shift in person occurs from the subject of the verb of saying/perceiving to the subject of the infinitive, *the new subject is always explicitly expressed*, and with the accusative case. In Lk. 2.49, for example, a second

---

Pastoral Epistles (JSNTSup, 34; Sheffield; JSOT Press, 1989), esp. pp. 129-36, also gives sparse treatment of the grammar, apparently assuming that 'church' is the subject and focal point of these clauses. In like manner, H. von Lips (*Glaube–Gemeinde–Amt: Zum Verständnis der Ordination in den Pastoralbriefen* [FRLANT, 122; Göttingen: Vandenhoeck & Ruprecht, 1979], p. 95) emphasizes the role of the church, with no treatment of the grammatical ambiguity. Spicq (*Les épîtres pastorales*, II, p. 105) translates thus: '...il faut se comporter dans une maison de Dieu'. Even if the indefinite 'one' is taken as the subject of the infinitive, the essential question remains: is Timothy part of the conduct code and, if so, to what extent?

1. BDF (§392[1]) states, 'The subject of the infinitive is often necessarily (δύνασθαι) or as a rule (θέλειν) identical with that of the governing verb'. Some question arises whether the impersonal verb δεῖ is the governing verb, and, if so, whether there would be an understood subject which carries over to the infinitive. Since εἰδῇς governs the entire δεῖ clause and thus sets the immediate context for determining the subject of the infinitive, the understood subject, 'you' (sing.), should govern the infinitive ἀναστρέφεσθαι. BDF (§§407-408) claims that the unexpressed subject in an impersonal construction (e.g. δεῖ + infinitive) is to be supplied by the immediately surrounding context or that the subject has been omitted for the sake of greater indefiniteness. That the immediate linguistic context concerns Timothy is demonstrated by the dative second person personal pronoun σοι and the second person singular verb εἰδῇς.

person plural verb of knowing is followed by a ὅτι clause with δεῖ + infinitive (οὐκ ᾔδειτε ὅτι ἐν τοῖς τοῦ πατρός δεῖ εἶναί με). The change in subject is specified by the addition of the accusative pronoun με.[1] If the church members of Ephesus are the unexpressed subjects of the infinitive ἀναστρέφεσθαι in v. 15, then one would expect ὑμᾶς ('you') or αὐτούς ('they') to have been used in the text. On the other hand, in cases where the subject of the verb of saying/perceiving and the subject of the infinitive are identical and the surrounding context helps to clarify this similarity, the accusative case subject is occasionally omitted. In 2 Thess. 3.7, for example, a second person plural verb of knowing is followed by δεῖ + infinitive but the accusative case subject is not added even though an accusative direct object is present (αὐτοὶ γὰρ οἴδατε πῶς δεῖ μιμεῖσθαι ἡμᾶς; cf. v. 9).[2] Therefore, although accusative case subjects identical to the subject of the verb of saying/perceiving are sometimes included,[3] a survey of grammatical constructions in the New Testament similar to 1 Tim. 3.15 suggests that Timothy is the most likely candidate for the subject of ἀναστρέφεσθαι. It is unnecessary to look outside of the immediate context to find a subject for the infinitive when one is represented in the second person singular verb εἰδῇς.[4] If the above interpretation is adopted, Timothy, as the subject of the middle/passive infinitive ἀναστρέφεσθαι (functioning as a middle), is the one who must conduct himself in an appropriate manner within the household of God.[5] In further support of this reading of the microstructure, 4.12 contains the nominative case form of ἀναστρέφεσθαι, ἀναστροφή, which Paul employs to describe the type (τύπος) of conduct Timothy

1. Cf. Jn 3.7; 12.34; 20.9; Acts 9.16; 23.11; Rev. 10.11.
2. Cf. Acts 5.29; 27.21; 1 Cor. 8.1. Cf. Lk. 12.12 and Rom. 12.3, where the unexpressed subject of the infinitive is different from that of the finite verb but the context (ὑμᾶς; ἐν ὑμῖν) makes it clear that a change has taken place.
3. See, e.g., Eph. 6.20; Col. 4.4; 1 Thess. 4.1; Rev. 11.5.
4. Cf. Grimes, *Thread of Discourse*, pp. 280-92, who discusses the principle of 'deletion recoverability', a linguistic phenomenon which Paul is apparently employing here.
5. The house of God (ἐν οἴκῳ θεοῦ) is used with reference to the local church at Ephesus, but also has in view the universal church or family of God. The metaphorical extension probably was derived from the house church (cf. 2 Tim. 1.16) and/or the household family structure (cf. 1 Tim. 3.5); cf. Houlden, *The Pastoral Epistles*, pp. 82-83.

should exemplify to believers (τῶν πιστῶν). His conduct, of course, would include his responsibility to carry out Paul's injunctions concerning church members and leaders. Additionally, in 3.15 the relative clause (ἥτις ἐστὶν ἐκκλησία θεοῦ ζῶντος, στῦλος καὶ ἑδραίωμα τῆς ἀληθείας) which follows the purpose clause functions rhetorically as a reminder to Timothy of the importance of his conduct. His behavior should be in accord with the church of the living God which is a pillar and bulwark of the truth.[1] Timothy's failure to see to it that Paul's directives are carried out would be inconsistent with the nature of God's household.

In addition to the disclosure formula, 1 Tim. 3.14-15 contains another formula commonly found in Pauline letters:[2] a *travelogue*, with its rhetorical function as a reminder of 'apostolic presence'.[3]

---

1.   στῦλος and ἑδραίωμα refer to either the church, Timothy, or the 'mystery', which refers to Christ in the following hymn. The majority of commentators understand 'church' as the referent (e.g. Guthrie, *The Pastoral Epistles*, p. 88; Kelly, *The Pastoral Epistles*, pp. 86-88; Fee, *1 and 2 Timothy, Titus*, pp. 91-92; Lock, *The Pastoral Epistles*, pp. 43-44). But if Timothy is given a stronger footing in the text, he remains a possible referent of these terms. Indeed στῦλος is normally applied to persons in the New Testament (e.g. Gal. 2.9; Rev. 3.12). According to this reading, the relative clause ἥτις ἐστὶν ἐκκλησία θεοῦ ζῶντος is a brief parenthesis before returning to the subject of the infinitive, στῦλος καὶ ἑδραίωμα, a synecdoche for 'Timothy'. The use of the nominative case (as opposed to the accusative) either is caused by the disruption of the brief parenthesis or, better yet, merely represents use of a legitimate grammatical construction, since the subject of the infinitive may be put in the nominative case if it is the same as the subject of the governing verb. This general rule even applies to cases with δεῖ intervening between the finite verb and the infinitive (BDF, §405). Such an interpretation is attributed to 'the Fathers and some writers of a later date' (Simpson, *The Pastoral Epistles*, p. 59). Nevertheless, most modern scholars have rejected it.

2.   See, e.g., Phlm. 21-22; 1 Cor. 4.19; 2 Cor. 12.14, 20-21; Gal. 4.20; Phil. 2.24; 1 Thess. 3.11. Whether 1 Timothy is Pauline or not, a pseudepigrapher, borrowing from Paul, would have found Paul's formula compatible with his literary needs.

3.   In his trend-setting essay for New Testament Pauline epistolography, 'The Apostolic Parousia: Form and Significance', in *Christian History and Interpretation: Studies Presented to John Knox* (ed. W.R. Farmer, C.F.D. Moule and R.R. Niebuhr; Cambridge: Cambridge University Press, 1967), p. 249, R.W. Funk notes that the 'apostolic parousia' takes place in sections where Paul indicates 'his reason for or disposition in writing, his intention or hope to dispatch an emissary, and his intention or hope to pay the congregation a personal visit'. Cf.

Although Paul typically lays claim to his apostleship in the opening of his letter (e.g. 1 Tim. 1.1: Παῦλος ἀπόστολος),[1] a stronger appeal to apostolic presence is often found in the travelogue formula. In 1 Tim. 3.14-15 the disclosure formula is accompanied by the travelogue formula, expressed by means of the participial clause ἐλπίζων ἐλθεῖν πρὸς σὲ ἐν τάχει. Since the disclosure formula often worked to stimulate appropriate behavior, the prospect of Paul's physical presence (as indicated by the travelogue) would certainly heighten Timothy's responsiveness to the letter's requests. Rhetorically speaking, Paul uses his 'apostolic authority to persuade recipients into adopting his prescribed course of action'.[2] However, to a certain extent authority contingent upon Paul's apostolic presence is being sanctioned to Timothy who now becomes responsible for the welfare of the church.[3] This understanding is suggested by the protasis of the conditional clause beginning in v. 15 (ἐὰν δὲ βραδύνω). By being delayed, Paul inducts Timothy as his authoritative replacement who must now carry out the instructions of the letter. In addition, Timothy is hounded by the constant reminder that Paul may arrive at any moment at the church's doorstep, ready to inspect his disciple's conduct in the house of God.

Some, however, have played down the forceful rhetoric behind this travelogue, primarily by appealing to the pseudepigraphical nature of

White, *Light from Ancient Letters*, p. 202, who, with regard to Hellenistic letters, remarks, 'The request or demand for the recipient's presence or the sender's own anticipated visit sometimes conveyed a threatening nuance... [and] served to frighten the recipient into responsible and immediate action'. Similarly, H. Koskenniemi states, 'Es wird nämlich als die wichtigste Aufgabe des Briefes angesehen, eine Form eben dieses Zusammenlebens während einer Zeit räumlicher Trennung darzustellen, d.h. die ἀπουσία zur παρουσία machen' (*Studien zur Idee und Phraseologie des griechischen Briefes bis 400 n. Chr.* [Annales Academiae Scientiarum Fennicae; Helsinki: Akateeminen Kirjapaino, 1956], p. 38).

1. See, e.g., Rom. 1.1; 1 Cor. 1.1; 2 Cor. 1.1; Gal. 1.1.
2. White, *Light from Ancient Letters*, p. 219.
3. In this way Paul maintains 'apostolic presence' through an emissary who is already at the church. In fact, the three ways in which Paul is said to have achieved a sense of apostolic authority through 'presence'—the letter, an apostolic courier or emissary, and the intention of a personal visit—find triple fulfillment in 1 Timothy (contra White, 'Saint Paul and the Apostolic Letter Tradition', p. 443). Cf. P. Trummer, *Die Paulustradition der Pastoralbriefe* (Frankfurt am Main: Peter Lang, 1978), pp. 124-125.

the letter. Houlden argues that this clause simply 'establishes the nature of the Pauline tradition: Paul's absence (and death) is no obstacle to the continuance of his authority'.[1] This interpretation distends the semantic range of βραδύνω too far. The only other place the verb is used in the New Testament is in 2 Pet. 3.9 (οὐ βραδύνει κύριος τῆς ἐπαγγελίας). Here the author argues against those who are uncertain about the coming of the Lord. He claims that the Lord is not slow in keeping his promise, as some understand slowness, but God is patient so that others might come to repentance. In v. 10 the author expects and is himself certain of the reality of the coming of the Lord (ἥξει δὲ ἡμέρα κυρίου). Here, although there is the idea of slowness, there is not a sense of doubt about the reality of the event, even though it may be delayed. The UBS lexicon correctly gives βραδύνω the sense of an extension of 'a period of time, with the implication of slowness and/or delay'.[2] If Paul wished to convey the idea that he might not show up at all, something along the lines of ἐὰν μὴ ἔρχωμαι might be expected; but even so, the subjunctive simply projects a possible situation, not necessarily a 'real' one.[3] Therefore, the author is not denying the possibility of Paul's arrival; rather, he expects it, in spite of possible delay.[4]

The travelogue's function is twofold then. Not only does it emphasize the importance of Paul's commands to Timothy (e.g. 4.7), but it forces Timothy to realize that his obedience to these directives, even

1. Houlden, *The Pastoral Epistles*, p. 82; cf. Barrett, *The Pastoral Epistles*, p. 63, and Dibelius and Conzelmann, *The Pastoral Epistles*, p. 60.
2. J.P. Louw and E.A. Nida (eds.), *Greek–English Lexicon of the New Testament Based on Semantic Domains* (2 vols.; New York: United Bible Societies, 1988), II, p. 246. βραδύνω is also used in the papyri to note delays in communication or business transactions (see, e.g., *P.Abinn.* 19.30 [342–51 CE]; *P.Berl. Leihg.* II, 46.9 [136 CE]; *P.Mich.* VIII, 506.8 [II/III CE]; *P.Oxy.* I, 118.37 [III CE]; *P.Oxy.* XIX, 2228.1.20 [283? CE]).
3. On the 'projective' sense of the subjunctive mood, see S.E. Porter, *Verbal Aspect in the Greek of the New Testament, with Reference to Tense and Mood* (Studies in Biblical Greek, 1; New York: Peter Lang, 1989), pp. 170-73.
4. If βραδύνω is given its normal sense, two interpretations of the travelogue are possible for a pseudepigraphical reading of 1 Timothy: (1) the possibility of Paul's coming expressed in the travelogue is merely a creation of the author which imitates the normal Pauline form, and (2) the possibility of Paul's coming is envisioned as occurring in the end times. Cf. Trummer, *Die Paulustradition der Pastoralbriefe*, p. 124.

though Paul may be delayed (ἐὰν δὲ βραδύνω), faces the scrutiny of the apostle's personal presence in the future.[1] Again it becomes conspicuous how this microstructure stands in conformity with the larger macrostructure. Timothy, the letter's intended recipient, is being exhorted to administer Paul's injunctions in the letter.

The above reading of 1 Tim. 3.14-15 has twofold significance. First, it argues for an alternative understanding of an important passage concerning the purpose, or at least one purpose, of 1 Timothy. This purpose directly involves the person of Timothy. Timothy is encouraged to conduct himself properly as a leader of the Ephesian church, no doubt in light of the heresies infiltrating its midst. Secondly, this uncommon reading supports the above macrostructural conclusion that Timothy is the intended recipient of the letter. Or stated conversely, the macrostructure finds particular expression in this microstructure. The disclosure of information is directed first and foremost to Timothy. Additionally, the travelogue directly concerns the interplay between Paul's possible delay and Timothy's substitutionary role, as well as between Paul's impending presence and Timothy's solicited obedience.

4. Conclusion

Dibelius and Conzelmann claim that the focus of 1 Timothy is 'directed to two main points: church order and the refutation of heretics'.[2] This one-sided analysis has a propensity to neglect Timothy's role in the text. By focusing on Timothy as the primary recipient of the letter, as the above macrostructural and microstructural analysis suggests, the problem of the letter's cohesiveness is solved or at least significantly diminished. The eyes of Timothy provide the solution. In other words, since the letter is written to Timothy and the instructions and information disclosed therein are

1. By following the basic thesis that personal sections serve to authenticate the letter as Pauline, Dibelius and Conzelmann (*The Pastoral Epistles*, p. 3) identify this section as an 'artificial statement of purpose' and miss the powerful rhetorical function which this passage would play even in the argument of a pseudepigrapher.

2. Dibelius and Conzelmann, *The Pastoral Epistles*, p. 5. Cf. Lock, *The Pastoral Epistles*, p. xiii, whose threefold characterization of the PE further propagates this one-sided perspective: '1 Ti is entirely pastoral, and perhaps intended to be of universal application; Titus is mainly pastoral...; 2 Ti is mainly personal'.

directed towards him, determining the cohesiveness of the letter depends upon whose eyes it is read through. If an original church member (as portrayed in the text) read the letter (e.g. a slave), much of it would remain irrelevant or, at best, ancillary to his or her own situation. However, as Timothy deciphers the respective pericopes concerning various ecclesiastical issues, their cohesiveness becomes conspicuous: *he* is the unifying factor. He is to carry out the manifold instructions of the letter. They all interrelate to Timothy. They all 'make sense' to him.[1]

Most examination of the PE has centered on Paul's persona as it is represented in these letters. Paul, at least the 'Paul' scholars know from his *Hauptbriefe*, it is said, could not have penned these pale imitations. The organized, or might I say 'over-organized', church structure as represented in the letters, especially in 1 Timothy, has occasioned the main thrust of such an argument. Meanwhile, the persona of Timothy has been put to one side, being replaced with the Ephesian church as the intended recipient of the letter. Discourse analysis of the larger macrostructural evidence in 1 Timothy suggests that, pseudepigraphical or not, Timothy should be dusted off, cleared of the cobwebs, and put back in the spotlight where he belongs. He is more than a Pauline advocate, a role attributed to him by Dibelius and Conzelmann. He is the unifying thread which binds the text into a cohesive unit. He is the intended recipient of the letter.

---

1. Timothy's role as the intended recipient of the letters perhaps explains why the author of the PE does not spell out the exact nature of the false teaching of the heretics, a phenomenon which, according to several scholars (e.g. R.J. Karris, 'The Background and Significance of the Polemic of the Pastorals', *JBL* 92 [1973], pp. 549-64), argues against the Pauline authorship of the PE.

THE THEORY OF CONSTRUCTION GRAMMAR
AND ITS APPLICATION TO NEW TESTAMENT GREEK

Paul Danove

1. *Introduction*

In this paper I present a general overview of the theory of linguistic
analysis and description, Construction Grammar, as proposed in the
writings of Charles J. Fillmore of the University of California at
Berkeley.[1] The discussion begins with a survey of the characteristics
of Construction Grammar and then turns to an examination of its presuppositions concerning the nature and proper domain of linguistic
inquiry. These considerations establish the bases for a brief review of
Construction Grammar's method of analysis, description and representation. The discussion closes with two examples of the application
of this method. The first example is an analysis of the transitive
occurrences of the verb ἀκούω to determine whether there is a
semantic difference evident in the distribution of its second required
complement (either in the genitive or accusative case). The second
example is a brief consideration of the grammatical context of 1 Jn
2.20 to determine whether 1 John's overall distribution of grammatical constructions for the verb οἶδα can contribute to the resolution of
a text-critical problem.

---

1.   The full statement of Construction Grammar's presuppositions and manner of
grammatical representation appears in C.J. Fillmore's forthcoming manuscript, *On
Grammatical Constructions*. Since this manuscript is not yet in print, citations from it
generally receive further reference(s) to published articles which treat the same
topics. Particularly helpful for a general overview of this grammar is Fillmore's 'The
Mechanisms of Construction Grammar', in *Papers from the Fourteenth Annual
Meeting of the Berkeley Linguistics Society* (Berkeley: Berkeley Linguistics Society,
1988), pp. 35-55.

2. *The Presuppositions of Construction Grammar*

Construction Grammar is a descriptive,[1] non-transformational[2] grammar which renders the locutions of a language systematically according to their syntactic and semantic properties. In this framework, syntax is defined as 'the study of the selection and manipulation (of words), the possibilities governing their grouping into larger structural units (phrases and sentences), and the *functions* which these larger structural units serve in linguistic processes'; and semantics treats 'the ways in which linguistic structures serve in representing states of affairs'.[3] Construction Grammar's concern for syntactic functions includes

> such relationships as *modification* (by which one expression adds further details to the concept expressed by another expression), *complementation* (by which certain expressions satisfy requirements contracted by another expression), and *coordination* (by which two linguistic entities of equal status are joined to each other).[4]

As a non-transformational grammar, Construction Grammar's goal is the precise rendering into grammatical constructions of complex (linguistic) objects 'consisting of particular syntactic patterns associated with specific semantic structures'.[5]

Since it is descriptive, Construction Grammatical analysis proceeds in immediate reference to received locutions. The analysis first isolates predicators (usually 'verbs') and then determines the syntactic and semantic requirements which these predicators impose upon their

---

1. Fillmore, *Constructions*, pp. 5-6; cf. C.J. Fillmore, 'Grammatical Construction Theory and the Familiar Dichotomies', in R. Dietrich and C.F. Graumann (eds.), *Language Processing in Social Context* (North Holland: Elsevier, 1989), pp. 20 and following.

2. Fillmore, *Constructions*, p. 3; cf. Fillmore, 'Dichotomies', p. 20. For a discussion of the general nature of transformational grammars, see E. Bach, *An Introduction to Transformational Grammars* (New York: Holt, Rinehart & Winston, 1964), pp. 63-64.

3. Fillmore, *Constructions*, p. 2; cf. Fillmore, 'Dichotomies', p. 19; and C.J. Fillmore, P. Kay and M. Catherine O'Connor, 'Regularity and Idiomacity in Grammatical Constructions: The Case of *Let Alone*', *Language* 64 (1988), p. 501.

4. Fillmore, *Constructions*, p. 2; cf. Fillmore *et al.*, '*Let Alone*', pp. 512-18.

5. Fillmore, *Constructions*, p. 12; cf. Fillmore, 'Dichotomies', pp. 21-22, 34.

complements.[1] For example, in the sentence 'They called Chris' the predicator ('called') requires two complements (here, 'they' and 'Chris'). The predicator also requires (1) that the first complement ('they') have the syntactic function 'subject', the semantic function 'agent' (i.e., the 'doer' of an action) and lexical instantiation as a maximal noun phrase (i.e., a noun with any appropriate modifiers or a pronoun), and (2) that the second complement ('Chris') have the syntactic function 'object', the semantic function 'patient' (i.e., the one to whom something is done) and lexical instantiation as a maximal noun phrase. In this manner, Construction Grammar is competent to analyze the complementation structure of any predicator.

3. *The Theoretical Basis for Integrating Syntax and Semantics: Semantic Frames*

Construction Grammar's ability to provide a simultaneous analysis and description of syntax and semantics finds its rationale in Fillmore's proposal for discussing semantic relationships in terms of deep semantic cases.[2] The proposed deep cases are covert in that they lack obvious morphemic realizations (i.e., they do not have particular distinctive markings at the surface level of language). Rather, they are empirically discoverable relationships which form a finite set of semantic possibilities having validity in many languages.[3] Semantic cases describe certain interpretative distinctions which are necessary for human communication:

> [They] comprise a set of universal, presumably innate, concepts which identify certain types of judgments human beings are capable of making about events that are going on around them, judgments about such matters as who did it, who did it happen to, and what got changed.[4]

Granted this, Fillmore concludes that, just as the choice of a given verb in the communication process imposes deep case requirements on its complement noun phrases, so too verbs are selected according to

1. Fillmore, 'Dichotomies', pp. 13, 34; Fillmore *et al.*, *'Let Alone'*, p. 501.
2. C.J. Fillmore, 'The Case for Case', in E. Bach and R.T. Harms (eds.), *Universals in Linguistic Theory* (New York: Holt, Rinehart & Winston, 1968), p. 3.
3. Fillmore, 'Case', pp. 5, 19-20.
4. Fillmore, 'Case', p. 24.

the case environment (i.e., 'case frames') which the sentence will provide.[1]

Fillmore locates the notion of deep cases in internal, as opposed to external, semantics: that is, 'deep cases are among the types of semantic relations that elements of sentence structures have with each other in context, rather than with the system of contrasts and oppositions that differentiate constituents paradigmatically'.[2] The union of semantic and syntactic cases gives rise to the construct, 'case frame', which provides a bridge between descriptions of situations and their underlying representations by assigning semantico-syntactic roles to the particular participants in the situation (or 'scene') represented by the sentence.[3] According to this proposal, the study of semantics becomes the study of the cognitive scenes activated by utterances.[4]

Recourse to cognitive scenes to explain the process whereby meaningful communication occurs brings a concomitant requirement to expand the notion of linguistic competence. Traditionally, linguists have assumed that speakers draw upon two kinds of knowledge: that is, grammatical knowledge, which 'contains the general or systematic facts about language and has the form of a set of integrated generative and/or interpretive rules', and lexical knowledge, which 'contains the idiosyncratic information, information that must be learned item by item for each morpheme, word or idiom in language'.[5] An interpreter's need to construct cognitive scenes in the process of interpretation requires that the interpreter have 'access to an enormous number of cognitive schemata and...know which words and morphemes...are within these schemata'.[6]

Fillmore terms the linguistic construct which addresses the interpreter's need a 'semantic' frame and defines this construct as 'a collection of linguistic forms or processes (including the information

1.   Fillmore, 'Case', pp. 26-29.

2.   C.J. Fillmore, 'The Case for Case Reopened', in P. Cole and J.M. Sadoch (eds.), *Syntax and Semantics*. VIII. *Grammatical Relations* (San Francisco: Academic Press, 1977), p. 60.

3.   Fillmore, 'Reopened', p. 61. The case frame is the basis of combining syntactic and semantic functions into a single Valence Description.

4.   Fillmore, 'Reopened', pp. 73-74.

5.   C.J. Fillmore, 'The Need for a Frame Semantics within Linguistics', *Statistical Methods in Linguistics* (1976), p. 6.

6.   Fillmore, 'Need', p. 13.

contained in appropriate case frames) related in precise ways to specific cognitive schemata...which might impose certain perspectives (including expectations) on these'.[1] Thus, Fillmore concludes that

> In characterizing a language system we must add to the description of grammar and lexicon a description of cognitive and interactional 'frames' in terms of which the language-user interprets his environment, formulates his own messages, understands the messages of others, and accumulates or creates an internal model of his world.[2]

Since Construction Grammar presupposes this understanding of linguistic frames,[3] it is able to address several issues which previous linguistic theories have left unexamined and/or unnoticed. Two such examples will help to clarify this situation.

First, imagine the following scenario: on two successive days someone receives a postcard from a friend who is travelling, and each postcard contains only one sentence, the first being 'I spent two hours on land this afternoon', and the second being 'I spent two hours on the ground this afternoon'. There is nothing in the description of grammar or lexicon which can account for the reader's understanding that the first sentence was written while 'at sea' and the second while 'in the air'.[4] Here, it is neither the meaning of the individual words nor their grammatical organization which gives these sentences their particular meanings but the conceptual contexts and relationships which they evoke in the reader.

The second example of a cognitive schema and its associated linguistic frame is the commercial transaction. The advantage of this schema is that it helps to highlight the perspectives which certain schemata may impose. The linguistic frame associated with this schema is built upon the verbs 'buy', 'sell', 'pay', 'spend', 'cost' and 'charge', the nouns 'money', 'payment', 'merchant' and 'customer', and other related terms. Each of these lexical forms imposes a

1. Fillmore, 'Need', p. 13.

2. C.J. Fillmore, 'Frame Semantics and the Nature of Language', *Annals of the New York Academy of Sciences: Conference on the Origin and Development of Language and Speech* 280 (1976), p. 23.

3. C.J. Fillmore, 'Topics in Lexical Semantics', in R.W. Cole (ed.), *Current Issues in Linguistic Theory* (Bloomington: Indiana University Press, 1977), p. 90.

4. Fillmore, 'Frame', pp. 26-27.

perspective upon (or highlights certain segments of) the schema.[1] This implies that the sender's choice of perspective in communication entails concomitant and simultaneous determination of deep (semantic) cases and surface (syntactic) cases. The situation is similar on the interpreter's side of the communication, in that the recognition of given verbs and noun phrase complements with particular deep and surface case structures activates a given schema and determines the particular perspective for viewing the scene. Here, syntactic and semantic methods are seen to provide descriptions of two distinct aspects of the same communicative process and, especially from the interpreter's side, two distinct but necessarily complementary ways of describing the experience inviting interpretation. Thus, the recognition of cognitive schemata and of linguistic frames provides the basis for unifying syntactic and semantic methods in linguistic analysis.

4. *Construction Grammar's Method of Analysis and Representation*

Construction Grammar represents the grammatical constructions of a language through a graphic diagram called a Valence Description. The Valence Description of a predicator is a characterization of the linguistic complements required (or permitted) by a certain predicator. In this graphic representation, the first line gives the syntactic function(s) of the predicator's complement(s), the second the semantic

---

1.   Fillmore, 'Need', p. 20. Note the manner in which each of the following sentences highlights different segments of the commercial transaction:

He sold her the parrot for $300.	merchant, customer, merchandise, price
She bought the parrot for $300.	customer, merchandise, price
She spent $300 on the parrot.	customer, price, merchandise
She paid him $300 for the parrot.	customer, merchant, price, merchandise
The parrot cost her $300.	merchandise, customer, price
He charged her $300 for the parrot.	merchant, customer, price, merchandise

In this example, the selection of particular verbs in the linguistic frame imposes certain perspectives on the schema of the commercial transaction by raising certain noun phrases to positions of prominence in the structure of the sentence (as subjects), by relegating others to secondary positions (as objects), and by omitting still others. Since each verb imposes a particular perspective, it is clear that semantic considerations as well as their concomitant syntactic constraints are intimately united in communication.

function(s), and the third the lexical realization(s). The sentence, 'They called Chris', serves as the basis of the Valence Description of the predicator, *call*:

Sentence: They called Chris.

Valence Description		*Function (Description)*
V		(the lexical item described is a verb)
call		(the base form of the verb)
1	2	syntactic function (1 = subject, 2 = direct object)
Agt	Pat	semantic function (Agt = agent, Pat = patient)[1]
N	N	lexical realization (N = maximal noun phrase)

The column headed with 1 indicates that the subject of the verb (the first complement) is the doer of the action (Agt) and is a maximal noun phrase (N). The column headed with 2 indicates that the direct object (the second complement) is acted upon by the subject (Pat) and is a maximal noun phrase (N). The number of columns relates the fact that this verb requires two complements (subject and object) arranged in a hierarchy wherein the subject (1) has pre-eminence of grammatical importance over the direct object (2).[2] The fact that semantic functions are realized through an agent and a patient indicates that the verb is transitive; and the combination of syntactic and semantic functions indicates that the verb is active voice (because the subject is also the agent). The bottom line indicates that the complements are maximal noun phrases.[3] In order to round out this presentation, I offer a further example of a Valence Description as a means of clarifying certain points which are significant in my subsequent analysis:

1.   These and all other semantic function designations correspond to the appropriate semantic case designations discussed above.

2.   This pre-eminence in English (and in Greek) is evinced in the fact that the verb 'agrees with' the subject (but not with the object).

3.   Fillmore, *Constructions*, ch. 3. My future analysis of Greek verbs (predicators) inserts a line of descriptive representation between the semantic function (line 2) and the lexical realization (line 3). This line (the new third line) concerns itself with the syntactic case in which a noun, adjective, pronoun, or participle appears or which a preposition 'governs'. This is necessary in Greek wherein (1) a subject may be nominative, genitive (genitive absolute), dative (infinitival clauses after certain verbs), or accusative (accusative absolute, accusative and infinitive construction) and (2) a given preposition may 'govern' more than one case (e.g., ἐπί).

Sentence: I contributed five dollars to the United Way.

$$
\begin{array}{ccc}
 & \text{V} & \\
 & \text{contribute} & \\
1 & 2 & \text{P} \\
\text{Agt} & \text{Pat} & \text{Goal} \\
\text{N} & \text{N} & \text{prep.}
\end{array}
$$

This Valence Description represents the fact that the verb, *contribute*, requires three complements characterized by Agent, Patient and Goal semantic functions. This requirement indicates that the linguistic frame associated with this verb imposes a perspective which highlights three parties of the action involved: a Giver, a Gift and a Receiver. The fact that the frame evoked by *contribute* places certain constraints upon the manner in which the verb's complements can be realized explains why a clause containing this verb may be well formed and grammatical even when the second complement (the Patient-Gift) is missing. For example, if I enter a conversation at the point when someone says, 'I contributed to the United Way', this statement would make perfect sense (i.e., it would be meaningful to me) even though the conversation has provided no indication of the nature or size of the gift. This is so because the frame evoked by *contribute* permits an identification of the missing element as the Patient-Gift and constrains the denotation of the missing complement as something which would be considered a gift. Thus, the second complement of *contribute* has the characteristic that it may be null (i.e., omitted) and that, when omitted, its denotation remains indefinite (i.e., not precisely defined). Such a complement receives the designation 'indefinite null complement' or 'INC'.

The situation is different for the third complement. Although this complement also may be omitted, such omission can occur only in a very precisely defined circumstance. For example, if I again enter a conversation at the point when someone says, 'I contributed five dollars', this sentence, as it stands, is ungrammatical for me. Here, the frame evoked by *contribute* permits me to identify the missing complement as a Goal-Receiver but the absence of this complement prevents meaningful communication. If the other parties of the conversation seem to experience no difficulty with this statement, I realize that the Goal-Receiver must have been stated before I entered the conversation; and, if interested, I would ask the speaker, 'To whom?' or 'For what?' Thus, the third complement of *contribute* has the characteristic that it may be null (i.e., omitted). However, in the case when it is omitted, its denotation must be definite (i.e., precisely defined in its immediate context). This manner of complementation receives the designation 'definite null complement' or 'DNC'.[1]

The constraints governing the omission of indefinite null complements and definite null complements, therefore, are pragmatic:

> With definite null complements the missing element must be retrieved from something *given* in the context; with indefinite null complements the referent's identity is unknown or a matter of indifference. One test for the INC/DNC distinction has to do with determining whether it would sound odd for a speaker to admit ignorance of the identity of the referent of the missing phrase. It's not odd to say things like 'He was eating; I wonder what he was eating'; but it is odd to say things like 'They found out; I wonder what they found out'. The missing object of the surface intransitive verb, *find out*, is definite. The point is that one does not wonder about what one already knows.[2]

The generalized Valence Description of the verb, *contribute* (i.e., the Valence Description which specifies the possible ways this verb may appear in specific locutions), receives the following representation:

	V		
	contribute		
1	(2)	[P]	(INC), [DNC]
Agt	Pat	Goal	
N	N	prep.	

---

1. Fillmore, *Constructions*, ch. 6; cf. C.J. Fillmore, 'Pragmatically Controlled Zero Anaphora', in *Papers from the Twelfth Annual Meeting of the Berkeley Linguistics Society* (Berkeley: Berkeley Linguistics Society, 1986), pp. 95-107; *idem*, '"U"-Semantics, Second Round', *Quaderni di Semantica* 7 (1986), p. 57; and *idem*, 'Topics in Lexical Semantics', in Cole (ed.), *Current Issues in Linguistic Theory*, pp. 96-97.

2. Fillmore, 'Zero Anaphora', p. 96. For other methods of describing those complement slots capable of being unfilled under DNC interpretations, see the discussion of 'definite noun phrase deletion' in A. Mittwoch, 'Idioms and Unspecified NP Deletion', *Linguistic Inquiry* 2 (1971), pp. 255-59; 'latent objects' in P. Matthews, *Syntax* (Cambridge: Cambridge University Press, 1981); 'contextual deletion' or 'contextual suppression' in D. J. Allerton, *Valence and the English Verb* (New York: Academic Press, 1982); and 'pragmatically controlled model-interpretive null anaphora' in I. Sag and J. Hankamer, 'Toward a Theory of Anaphoric Processing', *Linguistics and Philosophy* 7 (1984), pp. 325-45.

5. *Two Examples of Construction Grammatical Analysis*

a. *Transitive Uses of the Verb* ἀκούω

The first example of the application of Construction Grammatical methods is an examination of the transitive uses of the verb ἀκούω. This verb is found to have two distinct grammatical constructions when transitive. Both constructions have the first complement, the Subject-Experiencer, in the nominative case; but one construction has the second complement, the Object-Patient, in the genitive case, and the other has the second complement, also the Object-Patient, in the accusative case:

ἀκούω		ἀκούω	
1	2	1	2
Agt	Pat	Agt	Pat
nom.	gen.	nom.	acc.
N	N	N	N

In terms of Construction Grammatical description, both constructions have associated linguistic frames which highlight the same two parties of the linguistic frame (Experiencer and Patient) but are distinct in that their constituent case frames require different syntactic roles for the Patient.

In discussing these complementation structures, grammarians of the New Testament usually cite classical rules governing the distribution of the two transitive structures and then present a rule to describe the differences in their distribution in the New Testament. This essay first examines the distributional rules offered for the New Testament uses of ἀκούω and then proposes a new avenue of inquiry which leads to the formulation of a modified set of rules meant to assist grammarians and translators.

Distributional rules for the two transitive complementation structures of ἀκούω generally begin by drawing a sharp distinction between the verb's transitive use with an accusative second complement and the content accusative construction. This latter construction also has its second complement in the accusative case; but, here, the second complement designates not the object of hearing but the content of that which is heard.[1] The classical rule governing the

---

1.   The Valence Description for the content accusative construction is

distribution of the two transitive complementation structures and the content accusative construction of ἀκούω generally is rendered in three parts:[1]

1. The person speaking appears in the genitive.
2. The sound which one hears is in the genitive, unless it is a speech, λόγος, which may be in either the genitive or the accusative.
3. That of or about which one hears is in the accusative.

Though widely applicable in classical Greek, this rule no longer holds in all its parts for the Greek of the New Testament. The following discussion examines the limits of applicability of this rule.

The third part, governing the 20 occurrences of the content accusative construction (Appendix: List A), is consistently valid in the New Testament.[2] An investigation of the contents of List A reveals that the only example of a non-accusative complement, Acts 23.16, results from the attraction of the object, a relative pronoun, to the case of its antecedent.[3] Since the attraction of the relative to the case of its antecedent is a well-attested phenomenon in New Testament

ἀκούω

1	C
Exp.	Cont
nom.	acc.
N	N

1. M. Zerwick, *Biblical Greek Illustrated by Examples* (trans. J. Smith; Rome: Pontifical Biblical Institute, 1963), p. 24; cf. N. Turner, *A Grammar of New Testament Greek*. III. *Syntax* (Edinburgh: T. & T. Clark, 1963), p. 233; F. Blass and A. Debrunner, *A Greek Grammar of the New Testament and Other Early Christian Literature* (trans. R.W. Funk; Chicago: University of Chicago Press, 1961), p. 95; and H.W. Smyth, *Greek Grammar* (Cambridge, MA: Harvard University Press, 1966), pp. 324-25.

2. The 20 occurrences of the content accusative construction (Mt. 11.2; 14.1; 24.6; Mk 13.7; Lk. 9.7; 21.9; Acts 5.11; 17.32; 23.16; 28.15; Gal. 1.13; Eph. 1.15; 3.2; 4.21; Phil. 1.27; Col. 1.4; 2 Thess. 3.11; Phlm. 5; Jas 5.11; and 3 Jn 4) receive the translations, 'hear of', 'hear about', or 'hear that' in the RSV.

3. Since this example indicates that attraction to the case of the antecedent takes precedence over semantically regulated considerations, my subsequent discussion, including the formulation of rule-governed distributional rules, assumes the operation of such a general grammatical principle.

Greek, the presence of the genitive in Acts 23.16 presents no difficulty for maintaining the third part of the rule as stated.[1]

Examination of the 195 transitive occurrences of ἀκούω (Appendix: List B) reveals that 66 of the 67 second complements referring to speakers (i.e., human beings, angels, beasts and objects attributed with speech) occur in the genitive (Appendix: List C). Here, the only example of a speaker in the accusative case occurs in the phrase, καὶ πᾶν κτίσμα...ἤκουσα λέγοντας (Rev. 5.13). This sentence presents significant grammatical difficulty in that there is either (1) a lack of gender concordance between noun and participle or (2) a lack of an explicit antecedent for the participle. The former and more probable option, the lack of gender concordance, would indicate that the noun κτίσμα originally need not refer explicitly to speaking creatures but is granted this reference through the choice of the gender (masculine/animate) of the participle.[2] Here, the participle would refer to speakers, but the original grammatical constraints (permitting the accusative case) would continue to hold. The second option, the lack of an explicit antecedent for the participle, would indicate that the referent of the participle is a group of speakers but that the simple use of the genitive without an explicit antecedent would generate more confusion than the simple use of the accusative which would establish at least a tenuous relationship with the instantiated noun κτίσμα. Since either option constitutes an exceptional situation, the occurrence of the accusative in Rev. 5.13 cannot be the basis of a general rule. Thus, the first part of the rule also continues to hold for New Testament Greek.

The second part of the classical rule, governing the case of the sound which is heard, however, no longer holds in the New Testament. The lack of rigor in accounting for the distribution of these second complements has led New Testament grammarians to various approaches to the problem. Nigel Turner, for example, accepts a semantic distinction between the genitive and accusative complementation structures in John (the genitive with the meaning 'obey' [Jn 5.25, 28; 10.3, 6; etc.], and the accusative with the meaning

---

1. BDF, pp. 153-54.
2. This option receives the support of the RSV and of M. Zerwick, *Analysis Philologica Novi Testamenti Graeci* (Rome: Pontifical Biblical Institute, 1966), p. 575.

'hear', elsewhere) and a possible distinction in the similar occurrences in Acts 9.7 and 22.9.[1] Beyond this, however, Turner finds no semantic basis for a general distinction in case usage. A second possibility, put forth by Theodore H. Mueller, is that there is no real difference in meaning between the two complementation structures and that 'the different usages could be due to dialectal influences or represent the speaking habits of different socio-economic groups'.[2] This resolution also offers no semantic basis for distinguishing case usage and fails to address the fact that both structures can appear in the same author.

Zerwick takes a more traditional approach, suggesting a rule patterned on the classical rules which highlight semantic considerations associated with the second complement.[3]

1. The accusative designates 'what is directly grasped by the hearing (sound, news, what is said)', that is, the accusative indicates the physical perception of sound (e.g., Jn 3.8; 5.37; Rev. 19.1).

2. The genitive designates 'the source of what is heard, whether the person speaking or a voice conceived not as a sound but as speaking', that is, the genitive is used if the 'voice' (a) is explicitly represented as speaking (e.g., Acts 11.7; 22.7; Rev. 11.12) or (b) is represented as teaching, ordering or something similar (e.g., Jn 5.25; 10.3; 18.37).

Though widely applicable, these rules fail to account for apparent examples (1) of the genitive relating that which is said (Lk. 6.18; Jn 7.40; 12.47) or (2) of the accusative referring to a speaking voice (Acts 9.4; 26.14).

The various proposals indicate the difficulty in establishing a distribution for second complements governed by the semantic considerations associated with this complement. The following discussion investigates the 128 non-speaker transitive occurrences of ἀκούω (195 in List B minus 67 in List C) to determine whether there is a semantic consideration which will permit the statement of a further rule-governed distribution of second complements. This investigation

---

1. Turner, *Syntax*, pp. 233-34.
2. T.H. Mueller, *New Testament Greek: A Case Grammar Approach* (Fort Wayne, IN: Concordia Theological Seminary Press, 1978), p. 46.
3. Zerwick, *Biblical Greek*, p. 24; cf. BDF, p. 95.

moves beyond semantic considerations associated with the second complement, which have proved inadequate, to considerations associated with the subject complement. However, since the first complements admit to no fruitful distinction in their immediate contexts (clauses or verb phrases), it will be necessary to examine linguistic contexts larger than the clause or verb phrase.[1] Thus, the following analyses assume that the choice of one or the other complementation structure (1) is motivated by the case environment which it will provide (see above) and (2) relates particular semantic expectations operative over an extended context (see above).

The 128 non-speaker transitive occurrences of ἀκούω divide unequally into 29 genitive second complements and 99 accusative second complements. Examination of the 29 genitive occurrences reveals that, in 27 of the 29 examples, the first complement of ἀκούω appears as the subject of an immediately following verb phrase or clause.[2] In each example, this clause presents a response to the 'hearing' (whether real, potential or simply desired) which occurs in the ἀκούω verb phrase or clause.[3] That is, the genitive in 27 of 29 occurrences indicates that the 'hearing' produces an impact upon the hearer; and this impact receives explicit reference. Though the first of the two remaining occurrences, Col. 1.23, has no explicitly noted response, it represents an occasion of the attraction of the relative (οὗ) to the case of its antecedent (εὐαγγελίου). As such, it does not violate the proposed observation concerning a response. The second occurrence, Rev. 16.1, does present a difficulty in that there is no explicit response by the subject. However, the nature of the narration does present an implicit response insofar as the subject, the book's

---

1. The appeal to semantic considerations in contexts of extension greater than a clause or verb phrase is similar to that required for the analysis of anaphora and employs the concept of semantic frames.

2. Mk 14.64; Lk. 6.47; 15.25-26; Jn 5.25; 5.28-29; 6.60; 7.40; 10.3-4; 10.16; 10.27; 12.47; 18.37-38; 19.13; Acts 7.34; 9.7; 11.7; 22.1-2; 22.7; 2 Tim. 1.13-14; Heb. 3.7-8; 3.15; 4.7; 12.19; Rev. 3.20; 11.12; 14.13; 21.3. Though in 2 Tim. 1.13 the relative pronoun, ὧν, is attracted to the case of the antecedent, λόγων, this occurrence has an explicitly stated response in 1.14.

3. For example, in Rev. 11.12, καὶ ἤκουσαν φωνῆς μεγάλης ἐκ τοῦ οὐρανοῦ λεγούσης αὐτοῖς ἀνάβατε ὧδε. καὶ ἀνέβησαν... the referent of the subject of ἀκούω appears as the subject of the verb, ἀναβαίνω, whose clause connotes a response to that which was heard.

narrator, first hears a command to the seven angels (16.1) and then immediately reports the execution of the command by the angels (16.2). Though this report does not begin with an explicit statement such as 'And I saw', the seeing is implied; and its omission may be justified by narrative considerations precluding the interjection of a narratorial notice about seeing in the midst of the rapidly unfolding story.

These observations indicate that, except for the one occasion of attraction of the relative to the case of its antecedent (Col. 1.23), the remaining 28 occurrences of ἀκούω with genitive second complements (Appendix: List D) appear in the context of a response, usually explicit and once implicit. Recognition of this permits the formulation of a distributional rule which restricts the occurrence of the genitive complement on semantic considerations. For convenience in stating this rule, I propose to treat the expectation of a contextual response on the part of the subject as a semantic feature governing verb usage and term this semantic feature '+ impact'. This convention permits the statement of a general distributional rule:

> For the verb, ἀκούω, non-speaker second complements in the genitive case indicate that the verb is characterized by the semantic feature, '+ impact', that is, they indicate that the subject complement responds to that which is heard.

An immediate consequence of this rule is the recognition that all examples of the uses of ἀκούω which do not produce a response by the subject, that is, all occurrences characterized by the feature, '– impact', must have their second complement in the accusative case. However, this does not demand that the remaining 99 transitive occurrences be characterized by the feature '– impact'. Rather, an examination of the 99 remaining occurrences reveals that only 53 have the feature, '– impact' (Appendix: List E). Of these, 52 have the second complement in the accusative case as expected; and the one example of a complement in the genitive case (Col. 1.23) represents another occasion of attraction of the relative to the case of the antecedent. The remaining 47 occurrences are found to have the feature, '+ impact' (Appendix: List F). Of these, 46 have the second complement in the accusative case; and the one example of a complement in the dative case (Lk. 2.20) represents a further occurrence of attraction to the case of the antecedent.

The presence of uses of ἀκούω characterized by the feature '+ impact', with second complements in both the genitive and the accusative cases, indicates that a one-to-one correspondence between feature and second complement case is impossible. This is seen in the comparison of minimal and near-minimal pairs of verb phrases in List G, which reveals that both structures accommodate the semantic feature '+ impact'. However, this lack of one-to-one correspondence between feature and case does not compromise the results of this analysis; for the analysis (1) permits the statement of distributional rules which account for the case of the second complement of every occurrence of ἀκούω in the New Testament, (2) establishes parameters for discussing various exegetical problems, and (3) offers a basis for general guidelines in translation. The remainder of this discussion addresses each of these topics in succession.

First, the analysis permits a reformulation of parts 1 and 2 of the classical rule governing the distribution of second complement cases for transitive occurrences of ἀκούω in the New Testament usage. This rule assumes an appeal to two semantic features, one of which concerns the subject (+ or – impact) and the other of which concerns the object (+ or – speaker).

Rule: Except for occasions of attraction of a relative second complement to the case of its antecedent, the second complement of a transitive occurrence of ἀκούω

1.   appears in the genitive case if it is characterized by the feature, '+ speaker';
2.   appears in the accusative case if it is characterized by the features, '– speaker' and '– impact';
3.   appears in the genitive or accusative case if it is characterized by the features, '– speaker' and '+ impact'.

Secondly, the analysis establishes parameters for discussing various exegetical problems. One example is the previously noted discussion concerning the implications of the differences in case between the similar statements in Acts 9.7 and 22.9:

Acts 9.7:   ἀκούοντες μὲν τῆς φωνῆς μηδένα δὲ θεωροῦντες
Acts 22.9:   τὸ μὲν φῶς ἐθεάσαντο, τὴν δὲ φωνὴν οὐκ ἤκουσαν τοῦ λαλοῦντός μοι

Here, Turner follows the third edition of Zerwick's *Graecitas Biblica* in drawing a distinction between the genitive in 9.7 which indicates the hearing of a sound and the accusative in 22.9 which indicates the understanding of a voice.[1] In his English language grammar, Zerwick however follows his double reformulation of the second part of the classical rule (given above) to propose that in 9.7 the source of the sound appears in the genitive and that in 22.9 the source of the sound, which should appear in the genitive, now appears in the accusative due to the addition of the source of the voice in the genitive.[2] In the first case Turner's suggestion, as Zerwick indicates, seems to be an 'ad hoc' distinction insofar as the proposed semantic difference is not generally applicable. However, Zerwick's suggestion, which relies upon a singular occurrence of case change from the genitive to the accusative in 22.9, seems equally arbitrary.

The results of my analysis, however, indicate a more straightforward resolution to this apparent difficulty. Here, the occurrence of ἀκούω in 9.7 is characterized by the semantic feature '+ impact', which permits the second complement to be in either the genitive or the accusative case. Thus, the occurrence of the genitive is in keeping with reformulated Rule 3. The occurrence of the accusative in 22.9, however, is demanded by reformulated Rule 2, for this occurrence is characterized by the features, '– speaker' and '– impact'. Similar reasoning may be used to explain a second example of an apparent minimal pair of verb phrases, Jn 8.47 and 12.47, which, in fact, are distinguished by differences in the feature 'impact'.

Jn 8.47:   ὁ ὢν ἐκ τοῦ θεοῦ τὰ ῥήματα τοῦ θεοῦ ἀκούει   [– impact]
Jn 12.47:   καὶ ἐὰν τίς μου ἀκούσῃ τῶν ῥημάτων   [+ impact]

Thirdly, the analysis offers a basis for general guidelines in translation. As noted earlier, Turner suggests that translations of occurrences of ἀκούω with a genitive second complement in John have the meaning 'obey' while other grammarians expand their observations to include such translations as 'heed' and 'listen to'.[3] These translations fit well with the first reformulated rule that the use of the genitive with a non-speaker occurs only in the context of a noted response to what is heard. However, since second complements of uses of ἀκούω

1. Turner, *Syntax*, p. 233; cf. M. Zerwick, *Graecitas Biblica* (Rome: Biblical Institute Press, 1946), sec. 50.

2. Zerwick, *Biblical Greek*, p. 25.

3. Turner, *Syntax*, p. 234; cf. BDF, p. 95 and Smyth, *Greek Grammar*, p. 323.

characterized by the feature, '+ impact', may appear in either the genitive or the accusative case, translations employing 'obey', 'heed' or 'listen to' may be appropriate for any such occurrence. Here, the choice of one or another English translation has as much to do with the nature of the constraints imposed by English grammar as it does with the original constraints imposed by the Greek verb phrase.

These observations permit the formulation of a graphic representation of the distributional rules as proposed in this article. The representation includes the proposed translational options and situates the various lists generated during the analysis:

translation: 'obey, heed, listen to'

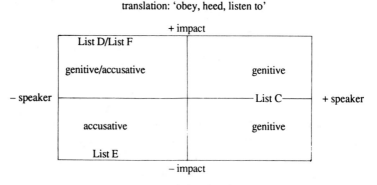

translation: 'hear'

b. *A Possible Example of a Definite Null Complement*
The second example of the application of Construction Grammatical analysis appears in a brief consideration of the grammatical context of 1 Jn 2.20. This verse presents considerable textual-critical difficulties in that the manuscript tradition is rather evenly divided between two alternative readings:[1]

---

1.   According to K. Aland *et al.* (eds.), *The Greek New Testament* (Stuttgart: Biblia-Druck, 3rd edn, 1983), p. 816, πάντες receives the support of א, B, P, Y and of several uncials and minuscules; and πάντα receives the support of A, C, K and of several uncials and minuscules. B.M. Metzger (*A Textual Commentary on the Greek New Testament* [Stuttgart: Biblia-Druck, 1975], p. 709) notes that the committee adopted πάντες with the rating {D} and rejected πάντα, which 'was regarded as a correction introduced by copyists who felt the need of an object after οἴδαμεν'.

καὶ ὑμεῖς χρῖσμα ἔχετε ἀπὸ τοῦ ἁγίου, καὶ οἴδατε **πάντες**.
καὶ ὑμεῖς χρῖσμα ἔχετε ἀπὸ τοῦ ἁγίου, καὶ οἴδατε **πάντα**.

The following discussion does not seek to draw any firm conclusions but only to provide collateral information concerning the *UBSGNT*[3] preference for the reading with πάντες. The grammatical constructions associated with the uses of the verb οἶδα consistently require at least two complements for both verbs (Appendix: List H). An analysis of the surface intransitive occurrences of οἶδα reveals that, in each case, the permissibly omitted second complement is a DNC (Appendix: List I).[1] That is, in each occurrence of a surface intransitive usage, the content of the omitted second complement receives explicit instantiation in the context immediately preceding its occurrence. In the case of 1 Jn 2.20, the adoption of the reading with πάντες would require that the second complement be a DNC and the context would require that the DNC be the clause, ὅτι οὐκ εἰσὶν πάντες ἐξ ἡμῶν (1 Jn 2.19). A review of List H1 reveals that the use of οἶδα with a ὅτι clause as the second complement occurs more frequently in 1 John than in any other New Testament book.[2] This is in contrast to the subject/object complementation structure (required by the choice of πάντα) which is much less frequent in 1 John (List H2), both absolutely and in relation to the other New Testament books.[3] These considerations are not of such a nature as to place any constraints upon the creativity of the author of 1 John, who was free to use either construction. However, they do reveal that the Committee's choice of πάντες brings the text into harmony with the distinctive style of 1 John.

---

1. Here, 'surface intransitive' indicates that there is no explicit second complement in the text.
2. This construction occurs 11 times in 1 John (of a total of 118 times in the New Testament). This is a relatively greater frequency than that of any other New Testament book and more than 7 times the frequency of the New Testament overall.
3. This construction occurs twice in 1 John (of a total of 94 times in the New Testament). This is relatively half the frequency of the Gospel of John (29 times) and only 1.3 times the relative frequency of the New Testament overall.

APPENDIX[1]

List A. *Content Accusative Construction with the Verb* ἀκούω *(20 Occurrences)*

Matthew	11.2	τὰ ἔργα
	14.1	τὴν ἀκοήν
	24.6	πολέμους
Mark	13.7	πολέμους
Luke	9.7	τὰ γινόμενα
	21.9	πολέμους
Acts	5.11	ταῦτα
	17.32	ἀνάστασιν νεκρῶν
	23.16	τὴν ἐνέδραν
	28.15	τά
Galatians	1.13	τὴν ἐμὴν ἀναστροφήν
Ephesians	1.15	τὴν πίστιν
	3.2	τὴν οἰκονομίαν
	4.21	αὐτόν
Philippians	1.27	τά
Colossians	1.4	τὴν πίστιν
2 Thessalonians	3.11	τινας περιπατοῦντας
Philemon	5	τὴν ἀγάπην, τὴν πίστιν
James	5.11	τὴν ὑπομονήν
3 John	4	τὰ ἐμὰ τέκνα περιπατοῦντα

List B. *Surface Transitive Construction with the Verb* ἀκούω *(195 Occurrences)*

	Genitive Case		Accusative Case	
Matthew	2.9	τοῦ βασιλέως	7.24	τοὺς λόγους τούτους
	17.5	αὐτοῦ	7.26	τοὺς λόγους τούτους
	18.15	σου	10.14	τοὺς λόγους
			10.27	ὅ
			11.4	ἅ
			12.19	τὴν φωνήν

1.   *   = attraction to case of antecedent
    " " = scriptural quotation

	Genitive Case		Accusative Case	
			12.42	τὴν σοφίαν
			13.17	ἅ
			13.18	τὴν παραβολήν
			13.19	τὸν λόγον
			13.20	τὸν λόγον
			13.22	τὸν λόγον
			13.23	τὸν λόγον
			15.12	τὸν λόγον
			19.22	τὸν λόγον
			21.33	ἄλλην παραβολήν
			21.45	τὰς παραβολάς
			26.65	τὴν βλασφημίαν
Mark	6.11	ὑμῶν	4.16	τὸν λόγον
	6.20	αὐτοῦ	4.18	τὸν λόγον
	6.20	αὐτοῦ	4.20	τὸν λόγον
	7.14	μου	4.24	τί
	9.7	αὐτοῦ		
	12.28	αὐτῶν		
	12.37	αὐτοῦ		
	14.58	αὐτοῦ		
	14.64	τῆς βλασφημίας		
Luke	2.46	αὐτῶν	1.41	τὸν ἀσπασμόν
	2.47	αὐτοῦ	*2.20	οἷς
	6.18	αὐτοῦ	4.23	ὅσα
	6.47	τῶν λόγων	4.28	ταῦτα
	9.35	αὐτοῦ	5.1	τὸν λόγον
	10.16	ὑμῶν	7.9	ταῦτα
	10.16	ἐμοῦ	7.22	ἅ
	15.1	αὐτοῦ	8.15	τὸν λόγον
	15.25	συμφωνίας, χόρων	8.21	τὸν λόγον
	16.29	αὐτῶν	9.9	τοιαῦτα
	16.31	Μωϋσέως, προφητῶν	10.24	ἅ
	18.36	ὄχλου	10.39	τὸν λόγον
	19.48	αὐτοῦ	11.28	τὸν λόγον
	21.38	αὐτοῦ	11.31	τὴν σοφίαν
			14.15	ταῦτα
			16.14	ταῦτα πάντα
			18.23	ταῦτα
			19.11	ταῦτα
John	1.37	αὐτοῦ λαλοῦντος	3.8	τὴν φωνὴν αὐτοῦ
	3.29	αὐτοῦ	3.32	ὅν

Genitive Case		Accusative Case	
5.25	τῆς φωνῆς	5.24	τὸν λόγον
5.28	τῆς φωνῆς αὐτοῦ	5.37	φωνὴν αὐτοῦ
6.60	αὐτοῦ	8.43	τὸν λόγον
7.32	ὄχλου γογγύζοντος	8.47	τὰ ῥήματα
7.40	τῶν λόγων τούτων	9.40	ταῦτα
9.31	ἁμαρτωλῶν	14.24	ὅν (τὸν λόγον)
9.31	τούτου	19.8	τοῦτον τὸν λόγον
10.3	τῆς φωνῆς αὐτοῦ		
10.8	αὐτῶν		
10.16	τῆς φωνῆς μοῦ		
10.20	αὐτοῦ		
10.27	τῆς φωνῆς μοῦ		
11.41	μου		
11.42	μου		
12.47	τῶν ῥημάτων		
18.37	μου τῆς φωνῆς		
19.13	τῶν λόγων τούτων		

	Genitive Case		Accusative Case	
Acts	2.6	λαλούντων αὐτῶν	2.22	τοὺς λόγους τούτους
	2.11	λαλούντων αὐτῶν	4.4	τὸν λόγον
	"3.22"	αὐτοῦ	5.5	τοὺς λόγους τούτους
	"3.23"	τοῦ προφήτου	5.24	τοὺς λόγους τούτους
		ἐκείνου	7.54	ταῦτα
	4.19	ὑμῶν	9.4	φωνὴν λέγουσαν
	6.11	αὐτοῦ λαλοῦντος	10.33	πάντα τὰ προστεταγ-
	6.14	αὐτοῦ λέγοντος		μένα
	"7.34"	τοῦ στεναγμοῦ	10.44	τὸν λόγον
	8.30	αὐτοῦ ἀναγινώσ-	13.7	τὸν λόγον
		κοντος	13.44	τὸν λόγον
	9.7	τῆς φωνῆς	15.7	τὸν λόγον
	10.46	αὐτῶν λαλούντων	17.8	ταῦτα
	11.7	φωνῆς λεγούσης	17.21	τι καινότερον
	14.9	τοῦ Παύλου	19.10	τὸν λόγον
		λαλοῦντος	21.12	ταῦτα
	15.12	Βαρναβᾶ, Παύλου	22.9	τὴν φωνήν
	15.13	μου	22.14	φωνήν
	17.32	σου	26.14	φωνὴν λέγουσαν
	18.26	αὐτοῦ		
	22.1	τῆς ἀπολογίας		
	22.7	τῆς φωνῆς μοι		
	22.22	αὐτοῦ		
	24.4	ὑμῶν		

	Genitive Case		Accusative Case	
	24.24	αὐτοῦ		
	25.22	τοῦ ἀνθρώπου		
	25.22	αὐτοῦ		
	26.3	μου		
	26.29	μου		
Romans	10.14	οὗ		
1 Corinthians			"2.9"	ἅ
2 Corinthians			12.4	ἄρρητα ῥήματα
Galatians			4.21	τὸν νόμον
Ephesians			1.13	τὸν λόγον
Philippians			4.9	ἅ
Colossians	1.23	οὗ		
1 Timothy	4.16	σου		
2 Timothy	1.13	ὧν (λόγων)		
Hebrews	"3.7"	τῆς φωνῆς αὐτοῦ		
	"3.15"	τῆς φωνῆς αὐτοῦ		
	"4.7"	τῆς φωνῆς αὐτοῦ		
	12.19	ἧς (φωνῆς)		
2 Peter			1.18	ταύτην τὴν φωνήν
1 John	4.5	αὐτῶν	1.1	ὅ
	4.6	ἡμῶν	1.3	ὅ
	4.6	ἡμῶν	1.5	ἥν (ἀγγελίαν)
	5.14	ἡμῶν	2.7	ὅν
	5.15	ἡμῶν	2.24	ὅ
			2.24	ὅ
			3.11	ἥν (ἀγγελίαν)
Revelation	3.20	τῆς φωνῆς	1.3	τοὺς λόγους
	6.1	ἑνὸς ἐκ τῶν . . .	1.10	φωνὴν μεγάλην
		ζῴων	4.1	ἥν (φωνήν)
	6.3	τοῦ δευτέρου ζῴου	5.11	φωνὴν ἀγγέλων
	6.5	τοῦ τρίτου ζῴου	5.13	τὰ κτίσμα
	8.13	ἑνὸς ἀετοῦ	6.6	φωνήν
	11.12	φωνῆς μεγάλης	6.7	φωνήν
	14.13	φωνῆς	7.4	τὸν ἀριθμόν
	16.1	μεγάλης φωνῆς		

Genitive Case		Accusative Case	
16.5	τοῦ ἀγγέλου	9.13	φωνὴν μίαν
16.7	τοῦ θυσιαστηρίου	9.16	τὸν ἀριθμόν
21.3	φωνῆς μεγάλης	10.4	φωνήν
		10.8	ἥν (φωνήν)
		12.10	φωνὴν μεγάλην
		14.2	φωνήν
		14.2	φωνήν
		18.4	ἄλλην φωνήν
		19.1	φωνὴν μεγάλην
		19.6	φωνήν
		22.8	ταῦτα
		22.18	τοὺς λόγους

List C. *Second Complement Speaking Creatures (67 Occurrences: 66 Genitive and 1 Accusative)*

		Genitive Case	Accusative Case
Matthew	2.9	τοῦ βασιλέως	
	17.5	αὐτοῦ	
	18.15	σου	
Mark	6.11	ὑμῶν	
	6.20, 20; 9.7;	αὐτοῦ	
	12.37; 14.58		
	7.14	μου	
	12.28	αὐτῶν	
Luke	2.46; 16.29	αὐτῶν	
	2.47; 6.18; 9.35;	αὐτοῦ	
	15.1; 19.48; 21.38		
	10.16	ὑμῶν	
	10.16	ἐμοῦ	
	16.31	Μωϋσέως, προφητῶν	
	18.36	ὄχλου	
John	1.37	αὐτοῦ λαλοῦντος	
	3.29; 10.20	αὐτοῦ	
	7.32	ὄχλου γογγύζοντος	
	9.31	ἁμαρτωλῶν	
	9.31	τούτου	
	10.8	αὐτῶν	
	11.41, 42	μου	
Acts	2.6, 11; 10.46	λαλούντων αὐτῶν	

	Genitive Case	Accusative Case
"3.22"; 18.26; 22.22; 24.24; 25.22	αὐτοῦ	
"3.23"	τοῦ προφήτου ἐκείνου	
4.19	ὑμῶν	
6.11	αὐτοῦ λαλοῦντος	
6.14	αὐτοῦ λέγοντος	
8.30	αὐτοῦ ἀναγινώσκοντος	
14.9	τοῦ Παύλου λαλοῦντος	
15.12	Βαρναβᾶ, Παύλου	
15.13; 26.3, 29	μου	
17.32	σου	
24.4	ὑμῶν	
25.22	τοῦ ἀνθρώπου	

Romans	10.14	οὗ	

1 Timothy	4.16	σου	

1 John	4.5	αὐτῶν	
	4.6; 4.6; 5.14, 15	ἡμῶν	

Revelation	6.1	ἑνὸς ἐκ τῶν. . . ζῴων	
	6.3	τοῦ δευτέρου ζῴου	
	6.5	τοῦ τρίτου ζῴου	
	8.13	ἑνὸς ἀετοῦ	
	16.5	τοῦ ἀγγέλου	
	16.7	τοῦ θυσιαστηρίου	
	5.13		τὰ κτίσμα

List D. *Non-Speaker Genitive Second Complement with + Impact for the Verb (28 Occurrences)*

	Genitive Occurrence	Response	
Mark	14.64	14.64	οἱ δὲ πάντες κατέκριναν αὐτὸν ἔνεχον θανάτου εἶναι
Luke	6.47	6.47	ποιῶν αὐτούς
	15.25	15.26	προσκαλεσάμενος ἕνα
John	5.25	5.25	οἱ ἀκούσαντες ζήσουσιν
	5.28	5.29	ἐκπορεύσονται
	6.60	6.60	εἶπαν
	7.40	7.40	ἔλεγον
	10.3	10.4	τὰ πρόβατα αὐτῷ ἀκολουθεῖ

144   *Biblical Greek Language and Linguistics*

	Genitive Occurrence	Response	
	10.16	10.16	γενήσονται μία ποίμνη
	10.27	10.27	ἀκολούθουσίν μοι
	12.47	12.47	μὴ φυλάξῃ
	18.37	18.38	λέγει αὐτῷ
	19.13	19.13	ἤγαγον ἔξω τὸν Ἰησοῦν
Acts	"7.34"	7.34	κατέβην
	9.7	9.7	μηδένα δὲ θεωροῦντες
	11.7	11.7	ἀναστάς, Πέτρε, θῦσον καὶ φάγε. (11.8) εἶπον δέ
	22.1	22.2	ἀκούσαντες/παρέσχον
	22.7	22.8	ὦγὼ δὲ ἀπεκρίθην
2 Timothy	1.13		ὧν (λόγων)
Hebrews	"3.7"	3.8	μὴ σκληρύνητε τὰς καρδίας ὑμῶν
	"3.15"	3.15	μὴ σκληρύνητε τὰς καρδίας ὑμῶν
	"4.7"	4.7	μὴ σκληρύνητε τὰς καρδίας ὑμῶν
	12.19	12.19	παρῃτήσαντο
Revelation	3.20	3.20	ἀνοίξῃ τὴν θύραν
	11.12	11.12	ἀνάβατε ὧδε· καὶ ἀνέβησαν
	14.13	14.13	γράψον
	16.1	16.1	
	21.3	21.3	ἰδού

List E. – *Impact for the Verb (53 Occurrences: 52 Accusative and 1 Genitive)*

Matthew	10.14; 13.19, 22	λόγους / λόγον
	11.4; 13.17	ἅ
	12.19	τὴν φωνήν
	12.42	τὴν σοφίαν
	13.18; 21.33	παραβολήν
Mark	4.18	τὸν λόγον
	4.24	τί
Luke	1.41	τὸν ἀσπασμόν
	4.23	ὅσα
	5.1; 10.39	τὸν λόγον
	7.22; 10.24	ἅ
	11.31	τὴν σοφίαν
	19.11	ταῦτα

John	5.37	φωνὴν αὐτοῦ
	8.43	τὸν λόγον
	8.47	τὰ ῥήματα
	14.24	ὅν (τὸν λόγον)
Acts	2.22; 10.44; 13.7,44; 19.10	λόγους / λόγον
	10.33	τὰ προστεταγμένα
	17.21	τι καινότερον
	22.9	τὴν φωνήν
1 Corinthians	"2.9"	ἅ
2 Corinthians	12.4	ἄρρητα ῥήματα
Galatians	4.21	τὸν νόμον
Colossians	*1.23	οὗ (τοῦ εὐαγγελίου)
2 Peter	1.18	ταύτην τὴν φωνήν
1 John	1.1; 2.24, 24	ὅ
	2.7	ὅν
	3.11	ἥν (ἀγγελίαν)
Revelation	5.11	φωνὴν ἀγγέλων
	6.6; 12.10; 14.2, 2; 18.4; 19.1; 19.6	φωνήν
	7.4; 9.16	τὸν ἀριθμόν
	9.13	φωνὴν μίαν
	22.18	τοὺς λόγους

List F. *Accusative Patient with + Impact on the Experiencer (47 Occurrences)*

Matthew	7.24, 26	τοὺς λόγους τούτους
	10.27	ὅ
	13.20, 23; 15.12; 19.22	τὸν λόγον
	21.45	τὰς παραβολάς
	26.65	τὴν βλασφημίαν
Mark	4.16, 20	τὸν λόγον
Luke	*2.20	οἷς
	4.28; 7.9; 14.15; 16.14; 18.23	ταῦτα
	8.15, 21; 11.28	τὸν λόγον
	9.9	τοιαῦτα
John	3.8	τὴν φωνὴν αὐτοῦ
	3.32	ὅ
	5.24; 19.8	τὸν λόγον

	9.40	ταῦτα
Acts	4.4; 15.7	τὸν λόγον
	5.5, 24	τοὺς λόγους τούτους
	7.54; 17.8; 21.12	ταῦτα
	9.4; 26.14	φωνὴν λέγουσαν
	22.14	φωνήν
Ephesians	1.13	τὸν λόγον
Philippians	4.9	ἅ
1 John	1.3	ὅ
	1.5	ἥν (ἀγγελίαν)
Revelation	1.3	τοὺς λόγους
	1.10; 6.7; 10.4	φωνήν
	4.1; 10.8	ἥν (φωνήν)
	22.8	ταῦτα

List G. *Minimal Pairs (Same Impact)*

Lk. 6.47   πᾶς ὁ... ἀκούων μοῦ τῶν λόγων καὶ ποιῶν αὐτούς...

Mt. 7.24   πᾶς οὖν ὅστις ἀκούει μοῦ τοὺς λόγους τούτους καὶ ποιεῖ αὐτούς...

Mt. 26.65-66   τί ἔτι χρείαν ἔχομεν μαρτύρων; ἴδε νῦν ἠκούσατε τὴν βλασφημίαν

Mk 14.63-64   τί ἔτι χρείαν ἔχομεν μαρτύρων; ἠκούσατε τῆς βλασφημίας

Acts 9.4   καὶ πεσὼν ἐπὶ τὴν γῆν ἤκουσεν φωνὴν λέγουσαν αὐτῷ

Acts 11.7   ἤκουσα δὲ καὶ φωνῆς λεγούσης μοι

Acts 26.14   πάντων τε καταπεσόντων ἡμῶν εἰς τὴν γῆν ἤκουσα φωνῆς λεγούσης μοι

Acts 22.7   ἔπεσά τε εἰς τὸ ἔδαφος καὶ ἤκουσα φωνῆς λεγούσης μοι

Rev. 12.10   καὶ ἤκουσα φωνὴν μεγάλην ἐν τῷ οὐρανῷ λέγουσαν

Rev. 21.3   καὶ ἤκουσα φωνῆς μεγάλης ἐκ τοῦ θρόνου λεγούσης

Rev. 10.4   καὶ ἤκουσα φωνὴν ἐκ τοῦ οὐρανοῦ λέγουσαν

Rev. 14.13   καὶ ἤκουσα φωνῆς ἐκ τοῦ οὐρανοῦ λεγούσης

List H: *Uses of* οἶδα

List H1: ὅτι *Clause Complement*

	οἶδα	
	1	2
	Exp.	Cont
	nom.	V +
	N	ὅτι

Matthew	6.32; 9.6; 15.12; 20.25; 22.16; 25.26; 26.2; 27.18; 28.5
Mark	2.10; 10.42; 12.4
Luke	2.49; 5.24; 8.53; 12.30; 19.22; 20.21
John	3.2; 4.25, 42; 6.61; 8.37; 9.10, 24, 25, 29, 31; 11.22, 24, 42; 12.50; 13.1, 3; 16.30; 19.10, 28, 35; 20.24; 21.4, 12, 15, 16, 24
Acts	2.30; 3.17; 12.9, 11; 16.3; 20.25, 29; 23.5; 26.27
Romans	2.2; 3.19; 5.3; 6.9, 16; 7.14, 18; 8.22, 28; 14.14; 15.29
1 Corinthians	3.16; 5.6; 6.2, 3, 9, 15, 16, 19; 8.1, 1, 4; 9.13, 24; 11.3; 12.2; 15.58
2 Corinthians	1.7; 4.14; 5.1, 6; 11.31
Galatians	2.16; 4.13
Ephesians	6.8, 9
Philippians	1.16, 19, 25; 4.15
Colossians	3.24; 4.1
1 Thessalonians	5.2
1 Timothy	1.18
2 Timothy	2.23
Titus	3.11
Philemon	21
Hebrews	12.12
James	3.1; 4.4
1 Peter	1.18
2 Peter	1.14
1 John	2.29; 3.2, 5, 14, 15; 5.13, 15, 15, 18, 19, 20
3 John	12

List H2. *Transitive*

	οἶδα	
	1	2
	Exp.	Pat
	nom.	acc.
	N	N

Matthew	9.4; 12.25; 22.29; 25.12, 13; 26.72, 74
Mark	1.43; 4.13; 5.33; 6.20; 10.19; 11.17; 12.15, 24; 14.71
Luke	6.8; 18.20; 22.34, 57
John	1.26, 31, 33; 4.10, 22, 22, 32; 6.42; 7.15, 28, 29; 8.19, 19, 55, 55, 55; 10.4, 5; 11.49; 13.7, 11, 17; 14.4; 15.21; 16.30; 18.2, 4; 20.9; 21.17
Acts	3.16; 5.7; 7.17; 10.37; 20.22; 24.22; 26.4
Romans	7.7; 13.11; 14.14
1 Corinthians	2.2, 11, 12; 13.2; 14.11
2 Corinthians	5.11, 16; 9.2; 12.2, 3
Galatians	4.8
Ephesians	5.5; 6.21
1 Thessalonians	1.4; 2.1; 3.3; 4.4; 5.12
2 Thessalonians	"1.8"; 2.6
2 Timothy	3.15
Titus	1.16
Hebrews	"8.11"; 10.30
1 John	2.21, 21
Jude	5; 10
Revelation	2.2, 9, 17, 19; 3.1, 8, 15; 19.12

List H3: *Relative Clause Complement*

$$οἶδα$$

1	C
Exp.	Cont
nom.	V +
N	Rel.

Matthew	6.8 ὧν
Luke	9.33 ὅ; 22.60 ὅ
John	3.11 ὅ; 13.7 ὅ; 18.21 ἅ
1 Thessalonians	1.5 οἷοι

List H4. *Interrogative Clause Complement*

$$οἶδα$$

1	C
Exp.	Cont
nom.	V +
N	Int.

Matthew	20.22 τί; 24.42 ποία; 24.43 ποία; 26.70 τί
Mark	1.24 τίς; 9.6 τί; 10.38 τί; 14.40 τί; 14.68 τί
Luke	4.34 τίς; 23.34 τί; 12.39 ποία
John	5.13 τίς; 6.6 τί; 7.28 τί; 7.28 τί; 9.21 τίς; 13.18 τίνας; 15.5 τί; 16.18 τί
Acts	"7.40" τί; 19.32 τίνος
Romans	8.26 τὸ τί; 8.27 τί ὅτι; 11.2 τί
1 Corinthians	14.16 τί
Ephesians	1.18 τίς
Colossians	2.1 ἡλίκος
1 Thessalonians	4.2 τίνος
2 Timothy	3.14 παρὰ τίνος

List H5. *[Patient] and Relative Clause Complements*

	1 Exp. nom. N	οἶδα [2] Pat	C Cont Rel. Adv.
Matthew	27.65 ὡς		
Mark	4.27 ὡς		
Luke	20.7 πόθεν		
John	7.15 πῶς		

List H6. *[Patient] and Interrogative Clause Complements*

	1 Exp. nom. N	οἶδα [2] Pat	C Cont V + Int. Adv.
Mark	13.33 πότε; 13.35 πότε		
Luke	6.27 ὑμᾶς πόθεν; 13.25 ὑμᾶς πόθεν; 13.27 ὑμᾶς πόθεν; 13.27 πόθεν		
John	2.9 πόθεν; 3.8 πόθεν καὶ ποῦ; 7.27 τοῦτον πόθεν; 8.14 πόθεν καὶ ποῦ; 8.14 πόθεν ἢ ποῦ; 9.21 πῶς; 9.12 ποῦ; 9.25 εἰ; 9.30 πόθεν; 12.35 ποῦ; 14.4 ὅπου; 14.5 πῶς; 14.5 ποῦ		
1 Corinthians	1.16 εἰ; 7.16 εἰ; 7.16 εἰ		
2 Corinthians	12.2 εἴτε; 12.2 εἴτε; 12.3 εἴτε. . . εἴτε		
Colossians	4.6 πῶς		
2 Thessalonians	3.7 πῶς		
1 Timothy	3.15 πῶς		

1 John	2.11 ποῦ
Revelation	2.13 ποῦ; 12.35 ποῦ; 20.2 ποῦ; 20.13 ποῦ

List H7: *Topic and Content Complements*

	οἶδα		
	1	2	C
	Exp.	Topic	Cont
	nom.	acc.	V +
	N	N	ὅτι
John	9.25 εἰ		
Acts	16.3 πατέρα		
1 Corinthians	16.15 οἰκίαν		
1 Timothy	1.9 τοῦτο		
2 Timothy	1.15 τοῦτο		

List H8. *Infinitive Verb Phrase Complement*

	οἶδα	
	1	2
	Exp.	Cont
	nom.	V + i
	N	inf.
Matthew	7.11	
Luke	11.13; 12.56	
Philippians	4.12 (2×)	
1 Thessalonians	4.4	
1 Timothy	3.5	
James	4.17	
1 Peter	5.9	
2 Peter	2.9	

List I: *Surface Intransitive Uses of* οἶδα

	οἶδα	
	1	[DNC]
	Exp.	
	nom.	
	N	
Matthew	21.27; 27.65	
Mark	11.33	
Luke	11.44	
Acts	2.22	
2 Corinthians	12.2, 3	

1 Thessalonians   2.2, 5; 3.4
James   1.19
2 Peter   1.12
1 John   2.20
Revelation   7.14

List J. *Definite Null Complements*

Mt. 21.27	[21.25]	τὸ βάπτισμα τὸ Ἰωάννου πόθεν ἦ; ἐξ οὐρανοῦ ἦν ἦ ἐξ ἀνθρώπου;
Mt. 27.65	[27.65b]	ἀσφαλίσασθε
Mk 11.33	[11.30]	τὸ βάπτισμα τὸ Ἰωάννου ἐξ οὐρανοῦ ἦ ἐξ ἀνθρώπου;
Lk. 11.44	[11.44a]	ὅτι ἐστὲ ὡς τὰ μνημεῖα τὰ ἄδηλα
Acts 2.22	[2.22a]	Ἰησοῦν τὸν Ναζαραῖον. . .ἐν μέσῳ ὑμῶν
2 Cor. 12.2	[12.2a]	εἴτε ἐν σώματι. . .εἴτε ἐκτὸς τοῦ σώματος
2 Cor. 12.3	[12.3a]	εἴτε ἐν σώματι. . .εἴτε χωρὶς τοῦ σώματος
1 Thess. 2.2	[2.2a]	προπαθόντες καὶ ὑβρισθέντες
1 Thess. 2.5	[2.5a]	οὔτε ποτε ἐν λόγῳ κολακείας ἐγενήθημεν
1 Thess. 3.4	[3.4a]	ὅτι μέλλομεν θλίβεσθαι
Jas 1.19	[1.18]	ἀπεκύησεν ἡμᾶς λόγῳ ἀληθείας, εἰς τὸ εἶναι ἡμᾶς. . .κτισμάτων
2 Pet. 1.12	[1.12a]	περὶ τούτων
1 Jn 2.20	[2.19b]	ὅτι οὐκ εἰσὶν πάντες ἐξ ἡμῶν
Rev. 7.14	[7.13b]	οὗτοι οἱ περιβεβλημένοι τὰς στολὰς τὰς λευκὰς τίνες εἰσὶν καὶ πόθεν ἦλθον;

HOW DO WE KNOW A PHRASE IS A PHRASE?
A PLEA FOR PROCEDURAL CLARITY IN THE APPLICATION OF LINGUISTICS TO BIBLICAL GREEK

Micheal W. Palmer

Introduction: The Need for Discussion of Procedure

As interest in the application of linguistics to the biblical languages increases, it will become more and more important to present clearly the assumptions guiding research in this area. If our results are to be accepted as viable, the methods we use must be made explicit, since the correctness of the results of linguistic and grammatical analysis depends on the validity of the modes of argumentation and the analytical procedures by means of which they are reached. In an environment where various linguistic theories are being applied to the same body of data, this need for methodological explicitness is particularly significant.

In 1984 E.V.N. Goetchius pointed out that Chomsky's methods could not be applied to Hellenistic Greek 'without making certain procedural modifications'.[1] Goetchius asserted that these modifications were necessary because a select corpus of utterances recorded from native speakers is all that students of Hellenistic Greek have at their disposal. All native speakers of Hellenistic Greek are dead.

This paper is, in one sense, a response to the limitation Goetchius has suggested. It suggests some possibilities for procedures compatible with the data at hand. The paper does not provide a representative overview of recent discussions of linguistic methodology, nor does it debate recent developments in linguistic theory.[2] Instead, it treats in

---

1. E.V.N. Goetchius, review of *Hellenistic Greek Grammar and Noam Chomsky: Nominalizing Transformations*, by D.D. Schmidt, *JBL* 103 (1984), p. 282.

2. For a competent, concise introduction to the basic concepts and issues

broad terms three major areas of concern for a discussion of linguistic procedure and then focuses on one: procedures for testing syntactic hypotheses. I present examples and arguments for some widely used syntactic tests while recognizing that no set of procedures, no matter how stringently applied, can insure the accuracy or correctness of any linguistic argument. Nonetheless, discussions of procedure may lead to productive critical reflection on the limitations and possibilities for linguistic analysis of biblical texts.

In what follows I assume a distinction between the substantive aspect and the methodological aspect of a scientific investigation. Rudolf P. Botha has stated this distinction in the following way:

> The scientific knowledge established in a field of inquiry and the unsolved problems with which it is concerned constitute its SUBSTANTIVE ASPECT. The techniques, methods and procedures used in the discovery and validation of this knowledge and the forms of statement in terms of which the knowledge is represented collectively form its METHODOLOGICAL ASPECT.[1]

I am concerned with what Botha called the methodological aspect of linguistic investigation.

Further, one may distinguish between the theoretical assumptions a linguist makes about the nature of language and the specific procedures used in the analysis of a particular language. The two are, of course, interrelated in that a theory of language dictates to a certain extent the questions which a researcher will be able to formulate, and thus limits investigation from the outset.[2]

While several attempts to apply modern linguistics to New Testament Greek have been accompanied by expositions of the

involved in current linguistic theory as they impact biblical studies, see S.E. Porter, 'Studying Ancient Languages from a Modern Linguistic Perspective', *FN* 2 (1989), pp. 147-72.

1.   R.P. Botha, *Methodological Aspects of Transformational Generative Phonology* (The Hague: Mouton, 1971), p. 14.

2.   The formation of linguistic hypotheses and their testing are both affected by the notion of a paradigm as presented in T. Kuhn's book, *The Structure of Scientific Revolutions* (Chicago: University of Chicago Press, 1962). While Kuhn assigns a variety of interpretations to the term 'paradigm', the notion of a paradigm as a construct which supplies instrumentation, a framework, analogy or organizing principle governing scientific inquiry is of particular relevance here since such a paradigm sets the parameters for the way the data will be treated.

theoretical assumptions involved, little attention has been given to the issue of procedures. In general, methods from modern linguistics have not been widely used in the analysis of New Testament Greek.[1] Most of the few works applying insights from modern linguistics have focused on the value of new linguistic models and not on the relevant discussions of procedure.[2]

1.   Apart from several articles, a few books of interest are J.Barr, *The Semantics of Biblical Language* (Oxford: Oxford University Press, 1961); J.P. Louw, *Semantics of New Testament Greek* (Chico, CA: Scholars Press, 1982); M. Silva, *Biblical Words and their Meaning: An Introduction to Lexical Semantics* (Grand Rapids: Zondervan, 1983); D.A. Black, *Linguistics for the Student of New Testament Greek* (Grand Rapids: Baker, 1988); and P. Cotterell and M. Turner, *Linguistics and Biblical Interpretation* (Downers Grove, IL: IVP, 1989). A few structuralist grammars have appeared. See, for example, E.V.N. Goetchius, *The Language of the New Testament* (New York: Charles Scribner's Sons, 1965); D.N. Larson, *A Structuralist Approach to Greek, with Special Emphasis on Learning the Koine Dialect* (Lincoln, IL: Lincoln Christian College Press, 1971); and R.W. Funk, *A Beginning–Intermediate Grammar of Hellenistic Greek* (3 vols.; Missoula, MN: Society of Biblical Literature, 1973). One work representing an early version of Case Grammar has appeared: T. Mueller, *New Testament Greek: A Case Grammar Approach* (Fort Wayne, IN: Concordia Seminary Press, 1978). A version of transformational-generative grammar popular in the 1970s was employed by D.D. Schmidt in his 1979 dissertation, *Hellenistic Greek Grammar and Noam Chomsky: Nominalizing Transformations* (Chico, CA: Scholars Press, 1981). R. Wonneberger has also employed a form of generative grammar in his *Syntax und Exegese: Eine generative Theorie der griechischen Syntax und ihr Beitrag zur Auslegung des Neuen Testamentes, dargestellt an 2. Korinther 5, 2f und Römer 3, 21-26* (Frankfurt: Peter Lang, 1979). For a significant application of semantic theory to the New Testament texts, see the new UBS lexicon, J.P. Louw and E.A. Nida (eds.), *Greek–English Lexicon of the New Testament Based on Semantic Domains* (New York: United Bible Societies, 1988). More recently, S.E. Porter has applied systemic linguistics to the problem of verbal aspect in *Verbal Aspect in the Greek of the New Testament, with Reference to Tense and Mood* (Studies in Biblical Greek, 1; New York: Peter Lang, 1989). Another recent approach to verbal aspect is available in B. Fanning, *Verbal Aspect in New Testament Greek* (Oxford: Clarendon Press, 1990).

2.   Schmidt (*Hellenistic Greek Grammar*) dedicated the first chapter of his monograph to the theoretical revolutions in linguistics in the past two hundred years and their impact on the study of Hellenistic Greek, but he did not deal directly with issues of procedure. Black (*Linguistics*) gives the subtitle 'How Do Linguists Go About Their Work?' to a section of his first chapter, but proceeds to discuss the general aims of descriptive, historical and comparative linguistics without discussing procedure in any detail.

In some cases the limitations of working with ancient texts are recognized, but solutions are not proposed. E. Wendland and E.A. Nida, for example, offer the following statement in their article, 'Lexicography and Bible Translating':

> The limited corpus of the New Testament and of other Koine Greek texts makes it impossible to undertake the fine-grid distinctions which would be possible if there were more data available and particularly if informants of New Testament Greek were available.[1]

They offer no discussion, however, of how their semantic theory may be adapted to this limitation. In fact, some of their statements might lead the skeptic to conclude that the limitation has been ignored. They state, for example, 'in Greek itself *gunai* has an associative meaning which is far more favorable than the English term *woman*'.[2] While this may be a completely valid conclusion, how did they reach it? How can associative meaning be measured given the limited corpus available?

Wendland and Nida give the approach of Osgood, Suci and Tannenbaum as an example of one way to quantify associative meaning (as distinguished from designative meanings), but this approach is dependent on native speaker informants.[3] How can it be applied to the New Testament? I believe, in fact, that the approach of Wendland and Nida can be (and has been) applied quite effectively to the New Testament texts, but we would all benefit from a clear exposition of the methods actually employed and the role of the modern, scholarly informant in this process.

The lack of attention to method evident in much of the recent literature is somewhat understandable given the radical departure of modern linguistic theories from more traditional views of language and their recent introduction into biblical studies. The new systems are often highly technical and difficult to master.[4] Several of the

---

1. E. Wendland and E.A. Nida, 'Lexicography and Bible Translating', in J.P. Louw (ed.), *Lexicography and Translation* (Cape Town: Bible Society of South Africa, 1985), p. 31.

2. Wendland and Nida, 'Lexicography', p. 18.

3. Wendland and Nida, 'Lexicography', pp. 17-19. The work they cite is C.E. Osgood, G.J. Suci and P.H. Tannenbaum, *The Measurement of Meaning* (Urbana, IL: University of Illinois Press, 1957).

4. For discussion of this and other issues which have hindered application of

major theories presently in use, however, can make significant contributions to an accurate description of the language.

If the application of linguistics to biblical Greek is to gain wide support among biblical scholars we cannot overlook the problem of procedure. Most of our colleagues are not trained in linguistics and many, perhaps because of their lack of exposure to the relevant literature, are quite skeptical about the methodological validity of our enterprise. For that reason, I now turn to a broad formulation of the process involved in much of recent syntactic analysis.

Outline of a Method for Syntactic Analysis[1]

A method of analysis common in recent linguistic study utilizes syntactic tests to distinguish discrete units (constituents) within sentences and larger units of discourse and to compare these units in order to describe their similarities and differences.[2] The researcher proposes

linguistics to New Testament Greek, see D.D. Schmidt, 'The Study of Hellenistic Greek Grammar in the Light of Contemporary Linguistics', in C.H. Talbert (ed.), *Perspectives on the New Testament: Essays in Honor of Frank Stagg* (Macon, GA: Mercer University Press, 1985), pp. 27-38.

1. This section is an adaptation of material from my PhD dissertation, forthcoming from Peter Lang Publishers. For the expanded version, see M.W. Palmer, *Levels of Constituent Structure in New Testament Greek* (Studies in Biblical Greek; New York: Peter Lang, forthcoming).

2. For an example of the application of this method to the study of English from the perspective of recent currents in generative grammar, see A. Radford, *Transformational Grammar: A First Course* (Cambridge: Cambridge University Press, 1988). Since his book is directed toward beginners with no previous exposure to linguistics, Radford makes extensive use of syntactic tests and explains his procedure at crucial points throughout the study. While Radford provides a significant example of this analytical method, it is not limited to the theoretical perspective he represents (government-binding theory). Theories as diverse as generalized phrase structure grammar (represented by G. Gazdar, E. Klein, G. Pullum and I. Sag, *Generalized Phrase Structure Grammar* [Cambridge, MA: Harvard University Press, 1985]) and lexical-functional grammar (represented by R. Kaplan and J. Bresnan, 'Lexical-Functional Grammar: A Formal System for Grammatical Representation', in J. Bresnan [ed.], *The Mental Representation of Grammatical Relations* [Cambridge, MA: The MIT Press, 1982]) utilize the same basic analytical procedure, though employing different conceptual models. Even tagmemic analysis (as represented by K.L. Pike and E. Pike, *Grammatical Analysis* [Arlington, TX: Summer Institute of Linguistics, rev. edn, 1982]) utilizes the same procedure while assuming a strikingly

generalizations to explain the behavior of these discrete units, then tests them in light of further data. I will divide the discussion of procedure, on this basis, into three broad areas:[1]

1. Collection of data.
2. Formulation of hypotheses.
3. Testing of hypotheses.

The analysis of an ancient language poses unique problems for the application of this method.[2] Points 1 and 3 are complicated by the finite nature of the available body of data. Because the data are limited to a finite corpus, crucial gaps will always remain so that some questions cannot be answered.[3]

At point 2 the analyst faces the same restrictions as the analyst of a modern language who is not a native speaker of the language under analysis, except that the analyst of an ancient language has the added restriction of the unavailability of native speaker informants. Nonetheless, this general model is an old one and has been successfully applied in the study of ancient languages.[4]

As applied by contemporary linguists, however, this method differs from prestructuralist approaches in the assumptions it makes about language description as well as in the specific procedures used to test

different paradigm for its understanding of language.

1.   It should be recognized that, while these three aspects of procedure may be discussed separately (to some extent), they are almost never applied in strict chronological sequence. The three tasks are often carried out more or less simultaneously, or with the researcher repeatedly switching among the three. Several hypotheses may be formulated and tested during the gathering of data for the analysis of one phenomenon.

2.   Several works addressing these problems are available. See especially D.W. Lightfoot, *Principles of Diachronic Syntax* (Cambridge: Cambridge University Press, 1979), pp. 1-80.

3.   Lightfoot noted that 'it is probably impossible to write a full grammar of a dead language, albeit as richly attested as Classical Greek or Early Modern English. There will always be crucial gaps in a finite corpus and questions which must be left unresolved' (*Diachronic Syntax*, p. 6).

4.   The general outline does not vary significantly from that of comparative philology, the linguistic method used in most of the major reference grammars now available for New Testament Greek. For a discussion of these grammars and their assumptions about method and constituent structure, see Palmer, *Levels of Constituent Structure*.

hypotheses. It is assumed that syntactic categories, for example, are to be defined in terms of the behavior of syntactic units, not in terms of vague, subjective semantic notions such as 'a noun is the name of a person, place, or thing'.[1] The tests used to confirm or disprove a proposed hypothesis generally attempt to reflect this empirical orientation.

It is also assumed that linguistic analyses should be undertaken from a synchronic perspective. Synchronic analysis is the analysis of the state of a language at any one given point in time. Diachronic analysis, on the other hand, is the examination of language change from one time to another. David Crystal, following the logic of Ferdinand de Saussure, has claimed,

> it is impossible to consider the way a language has changed from one state to another without first knowing what the two states to be compared are: a synchronic description is prerequisite for a proper diachronic study.[2]

This perspective is shared by the vast majority of linguists today.

Most recent linguistic analysis of the language of the New Testament has been concerned with synchronic description. Perhaps for this reason, little attention has been given to recent work in historical linguistics and most of us have, understandably, avoided the misuse of diachronic data. Knowledge of diachronic data may at some points suggest alternative ways of looking at the synchronic data, but may not be used as supporting argument for a particular analysis of the way an author used a given word or construction.

Notwithstanding this orientation, since those who study language from a diachronic perspective must work with texts, and often with ancient texts, previous work in the area of diachronic linguistics can provide valuable insight into appropriate procedures. David Lightfoot, for example, has provided important cautions about the

---

1. A definition of the Greek noun, for example, might be stated along the following lines: a noun is a lexical item which has context-free gender (in contrast to adjectives, whose gender varies with the grammatical context in which they occur).

2. D. Crystal, *Linguistics, Language and Religion* (New York: Hawthorn Books, 1965), p. 58. One example illustrates the depth of the conviction that a synchronic description is prerequisite for diachronic study. Lightfoot, a linguist working with diachronic syntax, wrote, 'A fundamental prerequisite for work in diachronic syntax is that one should be able to compare the grammars of at least two stages of a language' (*Diachronic Syntax*, p. 5).

limitations of work on the syntax of ancient texts.[1] Some of those
cautions are noted below.

Gathering Data 1: The Limited Corpus[2]
Modern linguists analyzing their own languages may rely at least in
part on personal knowledge of the language under analysis. The
analyst of an ancient language, however, must select a text or body of
texts (known as a 'corpus') for analysis.

Lightfoot has pointed out that, in working with an early stage of a
language, the analysis of syntax faces an obstacle much greater than
that faced by work on the phonetic and phonological segments of the
grammar.[3] The functional phonological units utilized by a particular
language community are finite; they may be listed exhaustively. The
number of phrases, sentences and suprasentential units produced by
that same community, on the other hand, is potentially infinite. No
matter how large the corpus, it can never be complete. Even a language extremely well attested (such as first-century Greek) is only
partially attested.

A linguist analyzing an ancient language confronts a problem similar to that faced by a child learning the language. The child hears, and
the grammarian sees written, a finite (yet potentially infinite) set of
syntactic structures. Yet the child does not know whether certain other
hypothetical structures are not heard because they would be ungrammatical and thus are not spoken, or simply because they have not yet
occurred within the child's hearing.[4] The modern grammarian
investigating an ancient language is bound to a set of texts which,
similarly, will from time to time lack the crucial example which
might justify one hypothesis in favor of another. Since the linguist
cannot know why such examples are missing, some issues must be left
unresolved.

Lightfoot has also noted that the grammarian must be sensitive to
the possibility that the available texts represent different forms of the

1. See, for example, Lightfoot, *Diachronic Syntax*, pp. 5-7.
2. This section is adapted from Palmer, *Levels of Constituent Structure*.
3. Lightfoot, *Diachronic Syntax*, p. 5.
4. The term 'ungrammatical' will be taken to mean 'stated in a way which no
native speaker would accept' and should not be interpreted to mean 'bad' or
'possible, but undesirable'.

language.[1] Exactly which texts are chosen for analysis, then, will depend to a large degree on what the analyst wishes to describe: the language at a given point in time, the development of the language through time, the language of a particular group of writers (all of the same speech community, or representatives of various speech communities), the language of one individual writer, or language universals.[2]

These issues must be considered in the selection of the appropriate body of documents to be accepted as sources of evidence for the phenomena under investigation. Once a corpus has been chosen, data may be collected regarding specific phenomena occurring in those documents and hypotheses tested on the basis of those data. Several computer tools are now available to assist with the collection of data relevant to the phenomena being studied.

Gathering Data 2: Computers in the Syntactic Analysis of New Testament Texts

The advent of the computer continues greatly to expand the possibilities for text analysis through increased speed and quicker access to a wider variety of texts than available only a few years ago. The computer cannot, however, replace the linguist's competence in the language under analysis and provides reliable data only under the following conditions:

1.   Any databases used are accurate.
2.   All programs used are designed with a program logic appropriate to the task.
3.   The operator is competent in the use of these computer tools.

Here I assess the value of three computer tools for the analysis of constituent structure: the Ibycus System, GRAMCORD, and LBase.[3]

---

1.   Lightfoot, *Diachronic Syntax*, p. 5.

2.   For a larger discussion of this issue, see Palmer, *Levels of Constituent Structure*, ch. 3, 'Methodology'. There I give an argument for the corpus assumed below in this paper.

3.   Ibycus is a computer system designed by D.W. Packard for use in classical studies and is used by the Packard Humanities Institute, 300 Second St., #201, Los Altos, CA 94022, in the development of databases for the humanities. GRAMCORD is a database and program produced by the GRAMCORD Institute, 2218 NE Brookview Dr., Vancouver, WA 98686, for performing grammatical searches of

The Ibycus Scholarly Computer searches specialized databases (the Thesaurus Lingua Graecae, and the Packard Humanities Institute databases) for user-defined strings of text or specific citations in any of the documents in the database being used. The primary value of the Ibycus system for the analysis of constituent structure is its ability to search easily and quickly through massive databases containing thousands of texts.

The databases contain only text, however, no grammatical information. Performing a search for the stem ἀποστελλ- is a simple matter, but finding every instance of the verb ἀποστέλλειν is more complex since the databases do not indicate that the aorist forms of that verb belong to the same verb as its present forms (which are built on a slightly different stem). Similarly, Ibycus cannot search for a particular grammatical category such as 'genitive case nouns'. The user may take advantage of the logical OR function to give a list of genitive case endings for which the system should search, but Ibycus will find anything with those endings, not just the nouns. For similar reasons, it is impractical to use Ibycus to search for attributive adjectives, genitive absolutes or any other construction requiring specific reference to syntactic criteria.

This does not mean, however, that Ibycus is of no value in the analysis of grammatical function or constituent structure. Ibycus may be used to locate specific words whose grammatical functions may then be examined manually to see if they match the functions postulated for the same words in other contexts. This procedure may serve as an informal check against which to weigh the viability of proposed hypotheses.

GRAMCORD avoids the primary limitation of the Ibycus system for work on syntax (lack of grammatical information) but works with a much more limited corpus (one including only biblical texts). The inclusion of grammatical tags on the words in the database, while providing a distinct advantage, raises a different problem. What about those instances in which the researcher disagrees with the analysis given a particular word? GRAMCORD provides no means for

biblical texts. LBase is a program developed by Silver Mountain Software and distributed by Gamma Productions Inc., 710 Wilshire Blvd, Suite 609, Santa Monica, CA 90401, for editing and analysis of text databases.

altering its database. Consequently, the user is simply at the mercy of those who compiled it.

GRAMCORD may be used with confidence for syntactic analysis only in those instances in which the analyst is in agreement with the judgments of those who compiled the database. The user must study the program in detail to understand what grammatical tags are given to which forms and under what circumstances in order to decide for what purposes the program may be used.

Several limitations related to these aspects of the program design are discussed in the *GRAMCORD User's Guide*.[1] GRAMCORD searches primarily for morphological tags (tags placed in the database on the basis of morphology such as case endings and tense endings). Tags given on the basis of syntactic function are limited mostly to forms which display little or no inflectional variation (such as adverbs and conjunctions).[2] This criterion for tagging words makes it impractical to search for an item such as an objective genitive, since the syntactic function of any given genitive case noun in relation to the noun it modifies is not specified in the database and such information cannot be added by the user.

GRAMCORD may be used to search for constructions in terms of traditional categories (upon which the database is built); these constructions may then be reinterpreted. In some instances (such as the status of nouns in larger syntactic categories) the grammatical tags in the GRAMCORD database will probably provide little interference since nouns may be identified by strict morphological criteria. GRAMCORD may be used more freely in such cases to search for constructions which a particular analysis indicates should occur in the corpus.

LBase provides the user with a tool for modifying its grammatically tagged database files. Several of the grammatically tagged databases currently available (such as those distributed by the Center for Computer Analysis of Texts, University of Pennsylvania) may be easily converted to LBase format and edited to suit the needs of the analyst.

A major limitation of LBase is its inability to handle discontinuous

1. P.A. Miller, *GRAMCORD User's Guide* (Deerfield, IL: GRAMCORD Institute, 1984), pp. 68-70.
2. Miller, *User's Guide*, p. 69.

constituents.[1] In Lk. 1.2, for example, LBase is unable to recognize τοῦ λόγου as forming part of a larger noun phrase including αὐτόπται καὶ ὑπηρέται, since the two units are separated by γενόμενοι.

This limitation is acute when analyzing phrase-level constituents, since such discontinuous constituents are quite common, but LBase is well suited for research into constituent structure at the level of individual words and phrases which do not have discontinuous elements. Its usefulness at the level of individual words is significant because of the freedom it allows in modifying the databases on which it operates.

Whether by computer or by manually searching through the available texts, a large amount of data must be gathered to test hypotheses and inspire new ones about the function and structure of syntactic units within the corpus. The following section examines the nature of these hypotheses.

Formulating Hypotheses[2]

In any scientific enterprise, both inductive and deductive reasoning are essential.[3] Albert Einstein argued that the simplest conception of a natural science is 'that according to the inductive method', but,

> great steps forward in scientific knowledge originated only to a small degree in this manner. For if the researcher went about his work without any preconceived opinion, how should he be able at all to select out those facts from the immense abundance of the most complex experience, and just those which are simple enough to permit lawful connections to become evident?[4]

1.   A discontinuous constituent is a unit, usually at the level of the phrase, which, while forming a single functional unit, is interrupted by some other element in the sentence which does not belong to that unit.

2.   This section is adapted from ch. 3, 'Methodology', of Palmer, *Levels of Constituent Structure.*

3.   Inductive reasoning, often associated with F. Bacon, William of Ockham and J.S. Mill, starts from observed data and proceeds to a generalization (a rule or law). Deductive reasoning, on the other hand, starts from a law or general principle. Deductions made on the basis of this law are then judged by their correspondence with observed data.

4.   A. Einstein, 'Induktion und Deduktion in der Physik', *Berliner Tageblatt*, 25 December 1919, as quoted in D. Lightfoot, *The Language Lottery: Toward a Biology of Grammars* (Cambridge, MA: The MIT Press, 1982), p. 87.

The linguist, also, must begin with some expectation of what she or he will find, though this expectation may be modified in the course of the analysis. The research must have a goal, and this goal will shape the questions asked of the data. Through observation of the available data, hypotheses are formed which attempt to explain the structure and behavior of that data in terms of structural descriptions and grammatical rules or principles. Deductions may then be made on the basis of these rules and tested against further data.

The formation of a hypothesis regarding the structure of some linguistic unit or the form of a particular rule is an inductive process. While we cannot say much about that process, we can say something about how such hypotheses must be formulated in serious research. Rudolph P. Botha has argued,

> More and more present-day linguists and grammarians concede the inescapability of the general methodological maxim that the correctness of the results of linguistic and grammatical analyses depends on the validity of the modes and patterns of argumentation by means of which they are reached.[1]

Arguments typical of linguistic research are of a type called *non-demonstrative* arguments, or arguments from probability. In order for such arguments to be accepted as valid, the assumptions which undergird them must be clearly stated. As far as possible, all relevant assumptions about language in general and the language under analysis in particular must be made explicit when treating data affected by those assumptions.

Two significant assumptions about the formulation of hypotheses underlie all of what follows. The first is that all valid empirical hypotheses are testable—a hypothesis which is not testable cannot be falsified.[2] The requirement that empirical hypotheses be testable does not mean that every theoretical construct proposed by a linguistic

---

1.　R.P. Botha, *The Methodological Status of Grammatical Argumentation* (The Hague: Mouton, 1970), p. 9.

2.　This assumption is evident in F.R. Eckman's statement that 'all nondefinitional statements must have empirical consequences which make them subject to falsification' ('Empirical and Nonempirical Generalizations in Linguistics', in J.R. Wirth [ed.], *Assessing Linguistic Arguments* [New York: Hemisphere, 1976], p. 36).

theory be observable, but that it must have empirical consequences making it subject to falsification.[1]

This requirement does not mean that linguistic hypotheses which are not testable are untrue. Victoria Fromkin has asserted,

> It is the case that there are many linguistic hypotheses... which may not be observationally verified by any experimental tests but which are nonetheless true, true in the sense that they reveal generalizations, relationships, regularities which would be obscured without them.[2]

It does mean, however, that such hypotheses, while valuable, are not *empirical* hypotheses in the standard sense.[3]

While it is reasonable in principle that all empirical hypotheses must be testable, there are times in the development of any science when advances preclude such verification. Einstein noted that there are times when we have at our disposal data which cannot be accounted for by any theory in existence and that it may equally well happen that the existing theories lead to conclusions which fall outside our present experience and 'may need many years of empirical research to ascertain whether the theoretical principles correspond with reality'.[4] The application of syntactic tests in such situations may not lead to immediately obvious solutions; a paradigm shift may be needed which will

1. Eckman, 'Empirical', p. 36. J.D. Ringen, in a highly critical assessment of transformational grammar, argues that linguistic facts are 'no more (and no less) empirical facts than are certain logical, mathematical, and philosophical facts' ('Linguistic Facts: A Study of the Empirical Scientific Status of Transformational Generative Grammars', in D. Cohen and J.R. Wirth [eds.], *Testing Linguistic Hypotheses* [Washington, DC: Hemisphere, 1975], p. 2). Even so, they must have empirical consequences.

2. 'When Does a Test Test a Hypothesis, or, What Counts as Evidence?', in Cohen and Wirth (eds.), *Testing Linguistic Hypotheses*, p. 45.

3. One example of such an untestable statement common in the linguistic literature is the assertion of word order restrictions on syntactic deep-structure within the Chomskian tradition of transformational generative grammar. Since transformational grammar asserts that transformations may alter word order between deep and surface structure, there is no way to validate by experimentation any claim about word order in deep structure. Supporting arguments are entirely theory-internal and are similar to forms of argumentation in the nonempirical sciences such as formal logic or pure mathematics. For a helpful treatment of the distinction between empirical and nonempirical facts, see Ringen, 'Linguistic Facts', pp. 1-41.

4. A. Einstein, *Essays in Science* (New York: Philosophical Library, 1934), p. 9.

permit the researcher to view the same data in a new way, independently of any empirical tests.

A second assumption, logically related to the requirement that empirical hypotheses be testable, governs the nature of such testing: the truth of an empirical hypothesis is determined by checking it against independent evidence.[1] An empirical hypothesis is *confirmed* if it is supported by such evidence, *disconfirmed* if it is contradicted by such evidence, and *unconfirmed* if it is impossible to obtain any supporting or conflicting evidence.

These assumptions undergird a second methodological principle: any empirical linguistic hypothesis must be stated in such a way as to allow its truth value to be tested against independent evidence.

Testing Hypotheses[2]

A number of empirical tests may be used in the evaluation of data from New Testament Greek. These tests are currently used to confirm or disconfirm hypotheses both in synchronic analyses of modern languages and in diachronic syntax. They generally rely on the following types of phenomena: distribution, movement, coordination, modifier placement, agreement and concord, replacement, and deletion.[3]

If two constituents share the same distribution,[4] for example, they may be said to be constituents of the same type (unless, of course, they fail to behave in similar ways with respect to another test). If a given group of words does not share the same distribution as any other group, cannot be moved to another point in a sentence, coordinated with a similar word group, modified in ways similar to other like word groups, replaced by a pro-form,[5] nor deleted under certain discourse conditions, then it cannot be posited as a constituent of the sentence in which it occurs.

1. 'Independent evidence' will be taken to mean evidence other than that upon which the hypothesis was formulated, but drawn from a body of texts which has been accepted as viable evidence.
2. This section is adapted from ch. 3, 'Methodology', of Palmer, *Levels of Constituent Structure*.
3. Tests relying on several of these types of phenomena are illustrated below. Definitions of the phenomena are given with the illustrations.
4. That is, the contexts in which they may occur are equivalent.
5. The term 'pro-form' is used to designate a variety of forms including pronouns which substitute for other elements in a sentence.

Many of these tests have been taken over from earlier work in structural linguistics and have continued to be used in a number of more recent approaches to language. Leonard Bloomfield supported his syntactic analyses in the 1930s on the basis of distribution, pronominalization and ellipsis.[1] Zellig Harris admitted only distributional criteria.[2] Rulon Wells used, in addition to distribution, criteria relating to pronominalization, structural ambiguity, and phonology.[3] Early generative grammar made use of similar tests. Chomsky, in his 1955 *Logical Structures*, used coordination, adverb placement, phonological criteria and structural ambiguity.[4] Kenneth and Evelyn Pike take as the 'most fundamental means of identifying class' (i.e. constituent type) the use of distributional data,[5] while Radford uses all of these criteria.[6]

1. L. Bloomfield, *Language* (London: George Allen & Unwin, 1935), pp. 146-47, 160-61, 184-206, 247-63, 264-80.
2. Z. Harris used the term 'co-occurrence' to designate distributional criteria in his presidential address to the Linguistic Society of America in 1955 ('Co-Occurrence and Transformation in Linguistic Structure', in *Papers in Structural and Transformational Linguistics* [Formal Linguistics Series; New York: Humanities Press, 1970], pp. 390-457). In 1946 he used the term 'substitution' to refer to similar criteria ('From Morpheme to Utterance', *Language* 22 [1946], pp. 161-83). 'Distribution', however, is the more common term and was used by Harris in his *Methods in Structural Linguistics* (Chicago: University of Chicago Press, 1951), pp. 5-6.
3. R. Wells, 'Immediate Constituents', *Language* 23 (1947), pp. 81-117.
4. N. Chomsky, *The Logical Structure of Linguistic Theory* (New York: Plenum Press, 1975), esp. pp. 224, 228-30 and 238.
5. Pike and Pike, *Grammatical Analysis*, p. 67. Pike and Pike, like most tagmemic analysts, use a slot-filler technique to discover such distributional data. In the analysis of modern languages this process consists of the use of elicitation questions such as 'What do you call "x"?' when a bilingual helper is available. Where no bilingual helper is available, the analyst may simply ask for words designating objects by simply pointing to the appropriate object. Once a basic list of words which function more or less like nouns is established, more complex phrases which function in ways similar to nouns (noun phrases in the terminology used below) may be elicited and analyzed, determining which elements perform a central role (fill the primary slot) and which play a marginal role (fill modifier slots). In the analysis of ancient texts no helpers of any kind are available and this procedure must be significantly modified.
6. Radford, *Grammar*. Tests using all these criteria are used throughout the book, but see especially ch. 2, 'Structure', for explanations.

A potential problem arises in the case of corpus-based research: it is possible that some sentences may be included in the corpus which the authors themselves would reject as ill-formed if they were to reread them.[1] The grammarian must also be ready to characterize such sentences as ill-formed. This standard poses a problem for research on an ancient language. How may such judgments be made without the assistance of native speakers? Any such judgment made by a modern grammarian is, of course, open to significant challenge. In some cases, however, the text tradition has left clues indicating problematic constructions.[2] In any event, the characterization of a construction as ungrammatical must be accompanied by strong supporting arguments.

Some issues simply cannot be decided on the basis of the empirical data. Victoria Fromkin has observed,

> it is not always possible to find or conduct a 'crucial experiment' to decide between two hypotheses or two theories. Linguistics is no different in this sense from other sciences where there may exist alternative hypotheses which cannot be decided on by reference to empirical data, even if such data are provided by experimental methods.[3]

When this is the case, we are forced to decide between alternative hypotheses by choosing the one which is simplest in the common sense of the term. Similarly, lack of evidence is not sufficient to negate a hypothesis; for that purpose counterevidence is needed. Lack of evidence means only that a hypothesis is unconfirmed.

In many cases, however, it is possible to find sound evidence for the testing of linguistic hypotheses. The syntactic tests proposed below may be used in the development of that kind of evidence. They have limited application and cannot resolve every syntactic problem, but

---

1. It is, of course, possible that some such sentences are intentionally ill-formed for the sake of impact or a desired effect. Intentionality, however, does not make such a sentence well-formed in the technical sense of complying with the general principles of the writer's grammar. That grammar would still characterize these sentences as ill-formed.

That some New Testament sentences were perceived as ill-formed by later scribes is quite clear from their alterations to the texts. Note Rev. 1.4 where attempts have been made to alleviate the case contradiction after ἀπό.

2. See, for example, the problem in Rev. 1.4 cited in the previous note.

3. Fromkin, 'When Does a Test Test a Hypothesis', p. 56.

are in wide use to provide support or counterevidence for a wide variety of hypotheses within various linguistic paradigms.

Evidence for the Viability of Syntactic Tests: Phrase-Level Syntactic Categories

Some syntactic tests may be developed on the basis of what we already know about constituent categories. This section looks specifically at phrasal categories. The corpus assumed consists of Luke–Acts, Romans, 1 and 2 Corinthians, Galatians and 1 Thessalonians.[1]

While Greek sentences are undoubtedly structured out of words belonging to various categories, they are also structured out of phrases belonging to a set of phrasal categories. The evidence for phrase-level categories is of various types, with the most diverse coming from syntactic processes. Evidence from morphology and semantics is also available, however.[2] I begin with a brief look at one form of semantic evidence.

Semantic Evidence[3]

Semantic evidence for phrasal categories may be adduced from a phenomenon known as *structural ambiguity*. Structural ambiguity occurs when a given unit may be assigned more than one phrase structure. The clause ὁ γὰρ νόμος τοῦ πνεύματος τῆς ζωῆς ἐν Χριστῷ Ἰησοῦ

---

1. The existence of phrase-level syntactic categories is widely accepted. This section merely uses what is typically taken as evidence for such categories to show how syntactic tests may be used. In *Levels of Constituent Structure*, I argue for other levels of syntactic categories.

2. Morphological evidence is available from such processes as case agreement within noun phrases. All items capable of being marked for case within an immediate phrase adjust to the case of the phrase head.

The term *case* is used in more than one way in current linguistic discussion. I am using it here to refer to morphological case (i.e., case endings on such items as the article, adjectives, nouns, and participles). In much of recent linguistic literature the term has been employed to designate certain aspects of the relationship of participants to events or states in discourse. For an example of this latter use of the term in a context relevant to New Testament Greek, see Louw and Nida, *Greek–English Lexicon*, I, pp. 796-97.

3. This section is adapted from Palmer, *Levels of Constituent Structure*, ch. 4, 'Syntactic Structure'.

ἠλευθέρωσέν σε (Rom. 8.2), for example, is ambiguous between the following two interpretations:

1. [the law of the spirit of life in Christ Jesus] has set you free
2. the law of the spirit of life [has set you free in Christ Jesus]

On the first interpretation, the phrase ἐν Χριστῷ Ἰησοῦ is taken adjectivally as a modifier of some element in the noun phrase ὁ...νόμος τοῦ πνεύματος τῆς ζωῆς and the clause may be roughly diagrammed as follows:

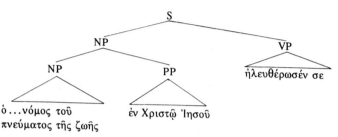

In this structure the PP ἐν Χριστῷ Ἰησοῦ is taken as a part of the larger NP and, hence, to function adjectivally as a modifier of some element in that NP. According to the second interpretation above, the clause may be represented by the simplified tree below:

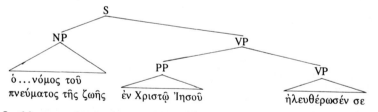

In this case, the PP ἐν Χριστῷ Ἰησοῦ is interpreted as a part of the larger VP and thus functions adverbially.

The ambiguity, then, is created by a difficulty in interpreting the phrase-level structure of the clause in question. It represents an inability of the reader to decide to which phrase-level constituent the phrase ἐν Χριστῷ Ἰησοῦ belongs, and is resolved when a decision is made about the phrase-level constituent structure of the clause. The existence of such ambiguity, then, lends support to the claim that New Testament Greek sentences are structured out of phrase-level constituents.

That this type of ambiguity is structural in nature is demonstrable by the fact that Greek has a device which, without altering the phrase order or adding any new meaning, but depending on the phenomenon of phrase-level case marking, disambiguates such constructions. The insertion immediately before the preposition of an article whose case, gender, and number match those of the preceding NP eliminates the ambiguity which concerns us here by tying the PP to the NP rather than the VP. Note the following example (Acts 8.1):

Ἐγένετο... διωγμὸς μέγας
There arose. . . a great persecution

[PPἐπὶ [NPτὴν ἐκκλησίαν [PPτὴν ἐν ἹεροσολύμοιςPP]NP]PP]
[against the church in Jerusalem]

Here the repetition of the article τήν marks the PP ἐν Ἱεροσολύμοις as a part of the larger NP so that it cannot be taken as a modifier of ἐγένετο. The first of the following two interpretations, then, is ruled out while the second is not:

There arose in Jerusalem a great persecution against the church [in general]

There arose a great persecution against the church [which was] in Jerusalem

The insertion of the second article in such constructions eliminates one of the two otherwise possible interpretations by forcing a particular decision about the phrase-level constituent structure of the clause—a phenomenon which depends on the assumption that sentences have phrase-level constituent structure.

On the basis of such evidence, one might propose that phrase-level constituent categories are necessary postulates of Greek grammar, but what procedures are needed to confirm or disprove this hypothesis or, if the hypothesis is valid, to define these categories? The following section on syntactic evidence presents further evidence for phrase-level categories and proposes certain syntactic tests which may be used to define them.

Syntactic Evidence[1]

The bulk of evidence for phrase-level categories comes from syntax. Facts about *distribution* provide one form of syntactic evidence for

1. This section is adapted from Palmer, *Levels of Constituent Structure*, ch. 4, 'Syntactic Structure'.

172   *Biblical Greek Language and Linguistics*

phrase-level constituents.[1] Some elements in the sentence, for example, may be moved forward for emphasis or stylistic variation.[2] In Lk. 8.16 the NP τὸ φῶς ('the light') occurs immediately after the verb βλέπωσιν:

ἵνα οἱ εἰσπορευόμενοι βλέπωσιν τὸ φῶς
so that those who enter may see the light

In Lk. 11.33 the exact same clause occurs with the NP τὸ φῶς preposed:

ἵνα οἱ εἰσπορευόμενοι τὸ φῶς βλέπωσιν

Similarly, a phrasal subject of a main verb may occur as a unit either after the main verb or at the beginning of a sentence:

ὁ ἀγαθὸς ἄνθρωπος...προφέρει τὸ ἀγαθόν (Lk. 6.45)
the good man... produces good

ὄψεται πᾶσα σάρξ (Lk. 3.6)
all flesh will see

Likewise, a prepositional phrase may be placed after the main verb or at the beginning of a sentence.

τὸ γὰρ ἅγιον πνεῦμα διδάξει ὑμᾶς ἐν αὐτῇ τῇ ὥρᾳ ἃ δεῖ εἰπεῖν (Lk. 12.12).
For the Holy Spirit will teach you in that very hour what you must say

Ἐν αὐτῇ τῇ ὥρᾳ προσῆλθάν τινες Φαρισαῖοι (Lk. 13.31).
At that very hour some Pharisees came

Notably, however, there are constraints on what types of units exhibit this freedom of placement. Not just any random sequence of words may be moved from one point to another in a sentence. Sequences such as the following, where the article is placed before the main verb, thereby being separated from the rest of its phrase, do not occur in the corpus:

*ἵνα οἱ εἰσπορευόμενοι τὸ βλέπωσιν φῶς[3]

1. Distribution has to do with which types of words or word sequences may occur in which positions in which types of sentences.
2. See F. Blass and A. Debrunner, *A Grammar of the New Testament and Other Early Christian Literature* (trans. and rev. R.W. Funk; Chicago: University of Chicago Press, 1961), p. 248 §472(2).
3. The asterisk (*) at the beginning of this string of Greek text indicates that the string is not found in the corpus and is considered ungrammatical.

While not just any word or sequence of words may exhibit this freedom of placement, it is significant that any sequence which forms a
phrase-level constituent may. This generalization requires the
assumption that phrase-level constituents are a necessary postulate of
Greek syntax.

Order cannot provide an absolute test of constituent structure since
phrases which are identifiable on the basis of morphology (case
endings, for example) may be split by movement processes (i.e., parts
of phrases are sometimes moved rather than whole phrases). Since all
phrase-level constituents may undergo movement, however, the
occurrence of a particular word group in more than one sentence
position should at least suggest the possibility of phrasal constituent
status. Conversely, any sequence of word types which is thought to
form a phrasal category should be checked for the possibility of
occurrence in multiple sentence positions.[1] Movement, then, may
serve only as a *preliminary* test dependent on confirmation from other
data.

Further distributional evidence is available from the occurrence of
sentence fragments. What kinds of word sequences may serve as sentence fragments in an appropriate discourse context? In Lk. 7.43 the
following sentence fragment occurs: ᾧ τὸ πλεῖον ἐχαρίσατο ('the
one to whom he forgave more'). On the basis of the preceding sentence (Lk. 7.42) one may propose that the full sentence would be
πλεῖον ἀγαπήσει αὐτὸν ᾧ τὸ πλεῖον ἐχαρίσατο ('the one to whom
he forgave more will love him more') and may be roughly diagrammed as follows:[2]

My argument here should not be taken to imply that NPs are never split in the
corpus. They clearly are, as πνεῦμα ἦν ἅγιον ἐπ᾽ αὐτόν at Lk. 2.25 demonstrates (see also Acts 1.5).

1. The failure of such a sequence to occur in multiple sentence positions does
not constitute valid evidence against its constituent status since such failure may
result from the limitation of the corpus.

2. The label S' in the tree below denotes an embedded sentence (traditionally
called a subordinate clause). Syntactic units traditionally called subordinate clauses
are treated as embedded sentences in much of current linguistic theory. The rationale
for such treatment comes from the fact that these clauses have all of the basic elements of a full sentence, differing from main clauses only in the use of such devices
as relative pronouns and complementizers (such as ὅτι). That one sentence may be
embedded inside another is certainly not, however, an innovation of modern linguis-

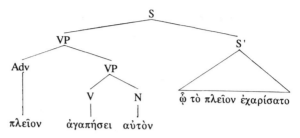

The sentence fragment which occurs in Lk. 7.43 is a phrase-level constituent (S', a subordinate clause) of this reconstructed complete sentence.

It is significant, however, that not just any random sequence of words may serve as a sentence fragment, even if they make sense in the given context. Given the reconstructed full sentence above, the respondent in Lk. 7.43 could not have answered with the bracketed sequence below:[1]

πλεῖον ἀγαπήσει [αὐτὸν ᾧ τὸ πλεῖον ἐχαρίσατο]
More will he love [him the one to whom he forgave more]

Notice that the bracketed sequence does not form a constituent of any kind in the tree diagram above, while the actual sentence fragment found in Lk. 7.43 does.

Note also the sentence fragment which occurs in Lk. 16.6: ἑκατὸν βάτους ἐλαίου ('one hundred baths of oil'). On the basis of the question in the preceding verse, one may reconstruct the full sentence as ὀφείλω ἑκατὸν βάτους ἐλαίου τῷ κυρίῳ σου ('I owe your master one hundred baths of oil'). Leaving aside the phrase τῷ κυρίῳ σου (whose case marks it as a distinct phrase from ἑκατὸν βάτους

---

tic theory. G.B. Winer, in his 1839 grammar treated coordination and subordination of clauses in this way. (See the 1850 English translation, *A Grammar of the Idioms of the Greek Language of the New Testament* [trans. J.H. Agnew and O.G. Ebbeke; New York: Robert Carter & Brothers, 1850], pp. 341-59.)

1.   No sentence fragment consisting of an accusative case form followed by a relative clause occurs in the corpus. While this does not in itself rule out the possibility that one could occur, the absence of such sentence fragments is to be expected if the following analysis is correct.

ἐλαίου), the remainder of this sentence may be represented as follows:[1]

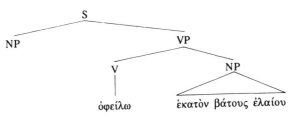

Again, the fragment which occurs in Lk. 16.6 is a phrase-level constituent of the full sentence.

The sequence *αὐτὸν ᾧ τὸ πλεῖον ἐχαρίσατο cited above does not occur as a sentence fragment precisely because it does not form a phrase-level constituent (or a constituent of any kind) of any possible sentence. On the basis of such evidence one may propose the following generalization regarding the formation of sentence fragments: only constituents (and perhaps only phrase-level constituents) may serve as sentence fragments.

Given the assumption that phrase-level constituents form a functional part of the syntax of New Testament Greek, then, we are able to formulate a principled account of what may and what may not serve as a sentence fragment, an account rendered impossible without that assumption.[2]

The occurrence of a given sequence of word types as a sentence fragment, therefore, may serve as a viable test of constituent status. While the lack of occurrence of a sequence as a sentence fragment does not negate its status as a constituent (since such lack of occurrence may result from the size of the corpus or mere chance), the occurrence of a unit as a sentence fragment does demonstrate constituent status.

One further form of distributional evidence involves the placement of adverbs. The presence of case marking on nouns, adjectives, and

---

1. The empty node NP to the left in the tree below indicates simply that the sentence does not contain an explicitly stated subject apart from the verb ending.

2. A common form of ellipsis, while distinct from the phenomenon of sentence fragments, may be explained along similar lines as the omission of the constituent VP. Arguments for that analysis are not given here, however.

participles allows for a freedom of word order not present in a language lacking these inflections, such as English, since the syntactic relationships between these words and other words in the sentence may be determined to some extent on the basis of morphology rather than word order alone.[1] Word order in Greek is not completely free, however, as can be seen from the placement patterns of some adverbs.

On this basis at least two different types of adverbs are distinguishable. Some adverbs have a placement pattern like that of εὐθέως while others follow a pattern like that of πάντοτε. Observe the following sentence:

% ἡ λέπρα % + ἀπῆλθεν + ἀπ᾽ αὐτοῦ +

Assuming a sentence containing an explicitly expressed subject to the left of the main verb (as ἡ λέπρα here), the adverb εὐθέως may occur in either of the positions marked by a % above.[2] In similar sentences πάντοτε occurs only in the positions marked by a + above, and never to the left of the subject.[3] Why this difference?

The crucial factor in explaining these two patterns for a number of adverbs is to explain why those like εὐθέως, and not those like πάντοτε, may occur in the position marked by the first % and why those like εὐθέως never occur in the position marked by the second + (though some do occur in the position marked by the third).

A plausible explanation of these facts may be stated in the following terms: certain adverbs (like εὐθέως) are S-adverbs, being attached only to an S-node, while others (like πάντοτε) are VP-adverbs, being attached only to a VP-node.

Assuming that the structure of the example sentence is roughly as follows, this explanation correctly predicts the placement possibilities for both sets of adverbs:

1. English does have a system of case marking for personal pronouns (she, her, he, him, his), but is lacking such inflection for the forms mentioned here.
2. See, for instance, Lk. 5.13 and Acts 17.10. This description holds for the entire New Testament, not just for the corpus assumed for this paper.
3. See, for example, Lk. 15.31; Rom. 1.9-10; and 1 Cor. 15.58.

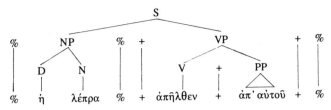

S-adverbs are excluded from the position marked by the second + since that position disallows the possibility of connection to the S-node. VP-adverbs, on the other hand, are excluded from the position marked by the first % since that position disallows the possibility of connection to the VP node.

The distributional difference between these two types of adverbs, then, indicates that phrase-level structures are crucial for any adequate explanation of word order considerations in New Testament Greek, and that the placement of adverbs may serve as a viable test of such structure.

Apart from such distributional evidence that sentences are structured out of phrasal constituents, further syntactic evidence comes from the phenomenon known as *pronominalization*. Robertson claimed that pronouns 'either "point out" or they "refer to" a substantive'.[1] This view of pronouns as words which substitute for nouns is pervasive in smaller works on Greek syntax. Brooks and Winbery state, 'A pronoun...is a word which stands for or in the place of or instead of a noun'.[2] This view of pronouns, however, is clearly inadequate and is based on a view of language which does not incorporate phrase-level constituents.

---

1. A.T. Robertson, *A Grammar of the Greek New Testament in the Light of Historical Research* (Nashville: Broadman, 4th edn, 1934), p. 676.

2. J.A. Brooks and C.L. Winbery, *Syntax of New Testament Greek* (Washington, DC: University Press of America, 1979), p. 74. C.F.D. Moule, in *An Idiom Book of New Testament Greek* (Cambridge: Cambridge University Press, 2nd edn, 1959), p. 93, also accepted the premise that a pronoun 'stands "for a noun" to the extent that it is not enclosed within the article-noun unit'. This view of pronouns as substitutes for nouns (or as having only nouns as antecedents) is very old. In general, this is the assumption of Winer in *Idioms*, pp. 122-43. To Winer's credit, however, he did recognize that the pronoun αὐτός may sometimes refer 'To some words [plural] plainly pointed out by the verb, or by a preceding word' (*Idioms*, p. 126).

178   *Biblical Greek Language and Linguistics*

In Lk. 13.18 the following sentence is found: τίνι ὁμοία ἐστὶν ἡ βασιλεία τοῦ θεοῦ...; ('What is the kingdom of God like?'). The basic syntactic structure of this sentence may be represented as follows:[1]

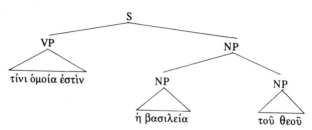

If this sentence were coordinated with a second sentence, such as τίνι ὁμοιώσω τὴν βασιλείαν τοῦ θεοῦ; ('To what shall I compare the kingdom of God?'), the repeated NP (ἡ βασιλεία τοῦ θεοῦ) would usually be replaced by a pronoun, as is the case in Lk. 13.18: [Sτίνι ὁμοία ἐστὶν ἡ βασιλεία τοῦ θεοῦS] καὶ [Sτίνι ὁμοιώσω **αὐτήν**;S]. Note, however, that the pronoun does not replace simply the noun βασιλεία, in which case the coordinated sentence would read: *[Sτίνα ὁμοία ἐστὶν ἡ βασιλεία τοῦ θεοῦS] καὶ [Sτίνι ὁμοιώσω (τὴν) αὐτὴν **τοῦ θεοῦ**;S].

This analysis may at first seem to rely on a subjective proposal about the wording of the full version of the second sentence. There is solid evidence, however, that the full sentence must be as I have proposed (τίνι ὁμοιώσω τὴν βασιλείαν τοῦ θεοῦ;).

If the function of the pronoun αὐτή were as Robertson and others have proposed, then we should be able to replace the pronoun with the noun βασιλεία to recover the full version. This clearly leads to an awkward sentence inappropriate to the context: τίνι ὁμοία ἐστὶν ἡ βασιλεία τοῦ θεοῦ καὶ τίνι ὁμοιώσω βασιλείαν; ('What is the

---

1. The internal structure of the top NP in the following diagram is over-simplified here. This phrase marker fails to distinguish between the relationship of a genitive phrase to the unit it modifies and the relationship of phrases whose case marking matches that of the phrase they modify. For now, however, it is only important to notice that ἡ βασιλεία and τοῦ θεοῦ are two separate structures related within one overarching NP unit. In *Levels of Constituent Structure*, ch. 5, 'Evidence from Noun Phrases', I provide a more adequate representation of the internal structure of such phrases.

kingdom of God like and to what shall I compare [a] kingdom?').

If we assume, however, that the pronoun replaces not a single noun but the phrase-level constituent NP, we may replace the pronoun with that NP and produce a perfectly sensible (if somewhat redundant) sentence: τίνι ὁμοία ἐστὶν ἡ βασιλεία τοῦ θεοῦ καὶ τίνι ὁμοιώσω τὴν βασιλείαν τοῦ θεου; ('What is the kingdom of God like and to what shall I compare the kingdom of God?'). The function of the pronoun, of course, is precisely to remove the redundancy evident in this full version.

The replacement of a given sequence by a pronoun, then, may provide significant evidence for its status as a constituent. Pronominalization, therefore, provides a significant constituent structure test.

Further syntactic evidence comes from *coordination*. Simple coordination occurs when two linguistic units are joined using a coordinating conjunction such as καί, δέ[1] or ἤ. Complex coordination occurs when the two coordinated units share a common element, such as a word or phrase. In *Levels of Constituent Structure*[2] I give detailed evidence for the claim that only constituents of the same type may be coordinated in either of these two ways (i.e. NP with NP, N with N, VP with VP, etc.). Coordination, then, like the placement of adverbs and pronominalization, may serve as a test of constituent structure. If any unit can be shown to be a constituent (such as N, NP, V, VP, etc.), then any other unit coordinated with it must be a constituent of the same type.[3]

The use of constituent structure tests may be complicated by the fact that words may sometimes have the same distribution as phrases. The following section presents evidence for this claim and addresses the relevant use of structure tests.

---

1. This includes the compound negative form, οὐδέ.
2. See Palmer, *Levels of Constituent Structure*, ch. 4, 'Syntactic Structure'.
3. As I point out in *Levels of Constituent Structure*, caution must be exercised when employing coordination as a test since in cases of complex coordination a single unit is shared by the two coordinated units and may thus fool the analyst.

Words Functioning as Phrase-Level Constituents[1]

Up to this point I have assumed a simple distinction between word-level syntactic categories and phrase-level categories. This simple distinction is, however, a misleading oversimplification.

Consider the following sentence:

ἄνθρωπός τις ἐφύτευσεν ἀμπελῶνα (Lk. 20.9)
A certain man planted a vineyard

Given common assumptions about word types (and abundant morphological and syntactic evidence for word-level constituent categories), it is reasonable to propose that ἄνθρωπος is a N, that φυτεύω is a V, and that ἀμπελών is a N. One might also, with little objection, propose that τις functions here as some type of determiner (D; τις does not function as a pronoun here, but as a specifier of ἄνθρωπος). One might then take the sequence ἄνθρωπός τις to be some type of NP. Still further, one might assume that the sequence ἐφύτευσεν ἀμπελῶνα is a VP and, finally, that ἄνθρωπός τις ἐφύτευσεν ἀμπελῶνα is a S (clause, sentence).

Given these assumptions one might argue that the sentence has the following structure:

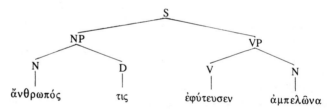

Many linguists, however, would reject this analysis, arguing that ἀμπελῶνα must be considered not only a N but also a NP, so that the nodes immediately above ἀμπελῶνα in the diagram should read:

---

1. This section is adapted from Palmer, *Levels of Constituent Structure*, ch. 4, 'Syntactic Structure'.

Given the usual meaning of the word *phrase* this analysis may seem absurd. *Phrase* is not used here in its usual meaning, however, but as a technical term meaning 'a set of elements which form a constituent'. Such a set may be empty, contain only one element, or contain numerous elements. The term *verb phrase*, then, may be taken to mean roughly, 'a set of elements containing a head verb', or *noun phrase* may be taken to mean 'a set of elements containing a head noun', and neither necessarily implies that the phrase must contain any other elements.[1]

But what empirical evidence is there that such a definition of *phrase* is necessary? Some of the most compelling evidence comes from distribution—that is, the application of distributional tests to answer the question, what kinds of elements may occur in the same syntactic configurations in which ἀμπελών occurs in sentences like the one above?

Observe the following sentences:

καὶ τὸν κονιορτὸν τὸν κολληθέντα ἡμῖν...εἰς τοὺς
  πόδας ἀπομασσόμεθα ὑμῖν (Lk. 10.11)
We wipe off even *the dust that clings. . . to our feet* against you

ἔθυσεν ὁ πατήρ σου τὸν μόσκον τὸν σιτευτόν (Lk. 15.27)
Your father has killed *the fatted calf*

Βαρναβᾶς δὲ ἐβούλετο συμπαραλαβεῖν καὶ τὸν Ἰωάννην τὸν
  καλούμενον Μᾶρκον (Acts 15.37)
Barnabas wanted to take along with them *John called Mark*

Μαριάμ...τὴν ἀγαθὴν μερίδα ἐξελέξατο (Lk. 10.42)
Mary has chosen *the good portion*

ἔδωκεν **δύο δηνάρια** τῷ πανδοχεῖ (Lk. 10.35)
He gave *two denarii* to the innkeeper

Notice that in each sentence the emphasized portion (NP) functions as the simple noun ἀμπελῶνα does in Lk. 20.9 (as the object of a verb). Other syntactic possibilities for NPs are also available to simple nouns. Compare the following:

ἐν τῷ ὀφθαλμῷ σου (Lk. 6.42)
in *your eye*

---

1.   In fact, it may be helpful to speak of a phrase which might normally appear in a sentence as being left 'empty' under certain circumstances.

ἐν ἀγορᾷ (Lk. 7.32)
in *the market*

ὁ κύριος Ἰησοῦς...ἔλαβεν ἄρτον (1 Cor. 11.23)
the Lord Jesus... took bread

πνεῦμα λαμβάνει αὐτόν (Lk. 9.39)
a spirit seizes him

A single noun, then, may have the same distribution as a NP. When this is the case, the noun must be assigned the status of NP.[1]

The same may be said of the relationship of other word-level categories to their corresponding phrase-level categories.

Ἰωάννης ἐδίδαξεν τοὺς μαθητὰς αὐτοῦ (Lk. 11.1)
John *taught his disciples*

εἰσῆλθον... εἰς τὸ ἱερὸν καὶ ἐδίδασκον (Acts 5.21)
they went... into the temple and *taught*

In fact, there are no syntactic configurations in the corpus where a full VP may occur, but an individual verb may not. A verb, then, may have (but does not always have) the same distribution as a VP.

Further evidence for this analysis may be taken from pronominalization facts (i.e., using pronominalization as a test). I argued above that pronouns replace the phrase-level unit NP. If individual nouns may serve as NPs, one would expect to find some cases where a single noun is replaced by a pronoun (though Ns which do not function as NPs are not). In 2 Cor. 3.13 the pronoun αὐτός replaces the (proper) noun Μωϋσῆς (οὐ καθάπερ Μωϋσῆς ἐτίθει κάλυμμα ἐπὶ τὸ πρόσωπον αὐτοῦ), exactly as expected. It is reasonable to assume, then, since any NP may be replaced by a pronoun, yet not just any individual noun may be,[2] that the noun Μωϋσῆς functions here as a NP.

The same implication is evident from the earlier discussion of sentence fragments (i.e., using the occurrence of sentence fragments as a test). I argued above that phrasal constituents could serve as

---

1.   It is not always the case that the distribution of individual nouns is the same as that of a NP, and when it is not, they cannot be assigned the status of NP. There are places where an individual N may occur but a full NP may not, but no places where a full NP may occur, while a simple N may not. Any NP may be filled by a simple N, then, but not all occurrences of N may be assigned the status of NP.

2.   See the argument above.

sentence fragments. Some individual words, however, occur as sentence fragments in the corpus under consideration. In response to the question τίνος ἔχει εἰκόνα καὶ ἐπιγραφήν ('Whose likeness and inscription does it have?', Lk. 20.24), it was not necessary to answer with a full sentence such as ἔχει εἰκόνα καὶ ἐπιγραφὴν Καίσαρος ('It has the likeness and inscription of Caesar'). It would have been sufficient to answer simply εἰκόνα καὶ ἐπιγραφὴν Καίσαρος, leaving out the main verb, or simply, Καίσαρος, as in Lk. 20.24, allowing a single noun to stand as a sentence fragment.

As seen above, there are restrictions on what kind of unit may serve as a sentence fragment. For example, the question could not be answered by καὶ ἐπιγραφὴν Καίσαρος ('and inscription of Caesar').[1] Whereas Καίσαρος serves as a constituent of the sentence ἔχει εἰκόνα καὶ ἐπιγραφὴν Καίσαρος, the group of words, καὶ ἐπιγραφὴν Καίσαρος, does not.

Such evidence suggests that only constituents may serve as sentence fragments, but, unlike the examples presented earlier, the fragment here is a single word. If individual nouns under appropriate discourse conditions may serve as NPs, however, one would expect to find some cases of individual nouns as sentence fragments. This is exactly what we find at Lk. 20.24.

Under this proposal the structure of the full sentence would be as follows:

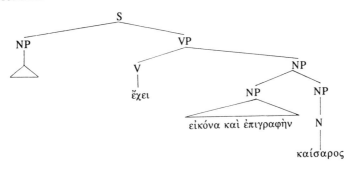

---

1. No sentence fragment beginning with a coordinating conjunction followed by a noun appears in the corpus. While the absence of such fragments does not rule out the possibility that they might have occurred, but just by chance did not, it does conform to what is to be expected if the assumptions of this paper are correct.

The single noun Καίσαρος fills the phrasal constituent NP. While the term *phrasal* (or *phrase-level*) *constituent category* does not demand that the unit it designates contain more than one word, it does demand that if a unit so designated contains only one word, that word must function in a way known to be characteristic of phrases bearing the same phrasal category label (i.e., that it must conform to the same tests of constituent structure). Assuming the earlier treatment of sentence fragments, the role played here by Καίσαρος is, in fact, one known to be characteristic of the phrasal category NP.

Given this understanding of the term *phrasal constituent category*, where it refers to a particular class of syntactic unit which may be filled by an individual word or a group of words, and knowing that phrasal constituents may serve as sentence fragments, one may simplify the generalization made earlier regarding sentence fragments in the following way: only phrasal constituents may serve as sentence fragments.

This view of the term *phrasal constituent category* also has implications for the treatment of coordination proposed earlier. Given the premise that only constituents of the same type may be coordinated (as I suggest above and argue in *Levels of Constituent Structure*), one would expect to find individual nouns coordinated only with other individual nouns. If single nouns may function as NPs, however, the premise would not be disturbed by the appearance of individual nouns coordinated with NPs. In fact, such structures are to be expected. In Lk. 8.51 the following sequence is found:...Πέτρον καὶ Ἰωάννην καὶ Ἰάκωβον καὶ [NPτὸν πατέρα τῆς παιδὸςNP] καὶ [NPτὴν μητέραNP] ('. . . Peter and John and James and the father of the child and her mother'). The names Πέτρος, Ἰωάννης and Ἰάκωβος, all individual (proper) nouns, are coordinated with two NPs. Given the evidence that only identical categories may be coordinated in this way, and since it is clear that the phrases τὸν πατέρα τῆς παιδός and τὴν μητέρα are each NPs, it is reasonable to posit that these individual nouns also function as NPs.[1] That is, assuming that the earlier premise

---

1. In English proper names are always NPs except in a very few, highly specialized discourse settings. This is not the case, however, in Greek. The frequent occurrence of proper names with the article makes their role in Greek somewhat different from the role of proper names in English.

is correct, a coordination test corroborates other evidence that Ns may function as NPs.

The application of syntactic tests, then, indicates that whenever a single word occurs in a syntactic configuration where a parallel phrase-level category may also occur, the word should be assigned the status of a phrase-level category since its distribution is the same as that of a related phrase-level unit and the same grammatical processes which apply to phrase-level units apply also to such words.

Summary

Phrase-level categories are a relatively recent introduction into linguistic theory. The assumption that phrase-level constituents are a necessary postulate of Greek syntax, however, is justified on the basis of a considerable body of evidence taken from morphological (case marking), semantic (structural ambiguity) and syntactic processes (the distribution of noun phrases, sentence fragments, adverb placement, pronominalization, coordination).

The existence of such phrasal constituents suggests the possibility of certain constituent structure tests which may then be applied in the examination of further data and wider problems. The tests themselves, however, are open to question and must be consistently re-evaluated as new data are found. The application of constituent structure tests is complicated by the fact that individual words often function in the same way as phrases. The tests suggested above, however, may be applied to these words to clarify their function as phrasal constituents.

Such syntactic tests can be applied only to hypotheses stated in such a way as to have empirical consequences. Any hypothesis which does not have empirical consequences cannot be tested empirically. The application of any procedure for syntactic analysis is limited by the finite nature of the available body of data. Some hypotheses which do have empirical consequences remain untestable because of this limitation, requiring that some issues be left unresolved. Recent developments in computer technology have provided more rapid access to some types of data within the finite corpus available, but none can provide direct access to data on syntactic units larger than the individual word.[1] In order to be reliable providers of data at any

---

1. Though it should be noted that GRAMCORD does allow rather complex

level, these tools require the user to have a significant understanding of their programming logic and search techniques.

While the constituent structure tests suggested here may allow us to test some linguistic hypotheses, there may sometimes be multiple hypotheses which account equally well for the available data. In such cases one must decide between them on other than empirical grounds.

searches which may significantly speed up the collection of data relevant to the analysis of larger units.

THE FINITE VERB WITH COGNATE PARTICIPLE IN THE NEW TESTAMENT

Mark S. Krause

Introduction

'No one who knows Hebrew or another Semitic language can fail to be impressed by the Semitic tone and flavor of the New Testament...'[1] Similar statements can be found in other treatments of the grammar of the Greek New Testament. Yet Stanley. E. Porter, in a rather exhaustive survey of possible New Testament Semitisms, concludes that for the Greek verb there is 'no clear instance of Semitic intervention'.[2] Some of this apparent disagreement may simply be on the level of definition. Porter defines a true Semitism as 'intervention, when a form that cannot reasonably be formed or paralleled in Greek must be attributed to the influence of a Semitic construction'.[3] He acknowledges Semitic influence on the level of enhancement, however.

The question for the student of Greek is this: are there places in the Greek New Testament which are so heavily Semitic that they cannot

---

1. D.A. Black, 'New Testament Semitisms', *BT* 39 (1988), p. 216. Black, following many others, lists four main causes for New Testament Semitisms:

   a. Koine Greek had borrowed many Semitic elements by New Testament times.
   b. It is probable that all the New Testament authors but Luke were Jews, for whom a Semitic language would have been their first language.
   c. The LXX had an influence on the New Testament writers.
   d. Aramaic or Hebrew sources were used by the New Testament authors.

2. S.E. Porter, *Verbal Aspect in the Greek of the New Testament, with Reference to Tense and Mood* (New York: Peter Lang, 1989), p. 141.
3. Porter, *Verbal Aspect*, p. 118. Porter cites Lk. 13.16, ἦν ἔδησεν ὁ σατανᾶς ἰδοὺ δέκα καὶ ὀκτὼ ἔτη, as an instance where the ἰδού must be seen as functioning temporally, as the Aramaic אָה or the Hebrew הִנֵּ is sometimes used.

be understood within the normal rules of Greek grammar? Presumably such passages would need to be understood using the grammatical rules of Hebrew or Aramaic. Or, is Porter correct in asserting that there is no place where the language of the New Testament authors can be understood only by resorting to Semitic grammar (i.e., true examples of 'Semitic intervention')?[1]

In his invaluable *An Idiom Book of New Testament Greek*, C.F.D. Moule devotes chapter 25 to the question of Semitisms in the New Testament.[2] One of the more intriguing examples offered is the possible adaptation of the Hebrew[3] idiom of a finite verb with a cognate infinitive absolute to show emphasis or perhaps frequency. This would be rendered in Greek by the finite verb + cognate participle (the closest Greek equivalent to the infinitive absolute), or by the finite verb + cognate dative noun.

The New Testament usage of the finite verb with cognate participle will be the object of investigation for this paper. Where does this construction appear? Which instances may be understood as reflections of the Hebrew verb with cognate infinitive absolute? Should this construction be seen as an example of Semitic intervention (to use Porter's distinction)? And finally, how should this construction be treated in translation?

Notational Matters

The Greek and Hebrew constructions here being studied have been dubbed with various appellations by grammarians. The Greek finite verb with cognate participle has been called the 'Hebraistic Intensifying Participle',[4] the 'redundant participle',[5] or the 'pleonastic

1. It should be remembered that Porter's claim really deals only with the verbal system, as will this study.
2. (Cambridge: Cambridge University Press, 2nd edn, 1959), pp. 171-91. Moule points out that *Semiticism* would be a more accurate term (p. 171).
3. As Moule points out (*Idiom Book*, p. 177) this construction is exceedingly rare in Aramaic. This may be due to Aramaic's lack of distinction between the infinitive absolute and the infinitive construct. See A.F. Johns, *A Short Grammar of Biblical Aramaic* (Berrien Springs, MI: Andrews University Press, 1972), p. 24.
4. A.T. Robertson and W.H. Davis, *A New Short Grammar of the Greek Testament* (New York: Harper & Brothers, 10th edn, 1933; repr. Grand Rapids: Baker, 1977), p. 382.
5. Also by A.T. Robertson in *A Grammar of the Greek New Testament in the*

participle',[1] among others. For notational purposes this construction will be referred to as Greek verb + cognate participle. The Hebrew finite verb with cognate infinitive absolute has been called the 'infinitive absolute with verbal adjunct',[2] the 'intensifying infinitive',[3] the 'internal object', and the like.[4] This construction will be referred to as the Hebrew verb + cognate infinitive absolute.

Hebrew: Finite Verb with Infinitive Absolute

The Hebrew verb form known as the infinitive absolute can be used in various ways, but 'By far the most frequent use of the infinitive absolute in Hebrew is its substantival employment as the object of a verb derived from the same stem or of a verb of kindred meaning'.[5] C.L. Seow explains that the infinitive absolute may come after the verb, although usually it comes before, and stands '...to emphasize the certainty, force, or decisiveness of the verbal idea'.[6] The infinitive

---

Light of Historical Research (Nashville: Broadman, 4th edn, 1934), p. 1110. Such pejorative terms are not as acceptable as they once might have been. To call a grammatical feature of one language 'redundant' because it would be so in another language reflects the bias of the grammarian. For example, from the Greek perspective the many subjective pronouns in English might be seen as redundant, since the Greek verb is capable of defining a pronominal subject independently, but such pronouns are hardly redundant in English.

1.   P.S. Karleen, 'The Syntax of the Participle in the Greek New Testament' (PhD dissertation, University of Pennsylvania, 1980), p. 165. Karleen includes other types of constructions under this designation (such as Jn 3.27, ἀπεκρίθη Ἰωάννης καὶ εἶπεν) which are not reflections of the Hebrew infinitive absolute, and will not be considered here.

2.   Porter, *Verbal Aspect*, p. 139.

3.   B. Waltke and M. O'Connor, *An Introduction to Biblical Hebrew Syntax* (Winona Lake, IN: Eisenbrauns, 1990), p. 584.

4.   E. Hammershamb, 'On the So-Called *Infinitivus Absolutus* in Hebrew', in D.W. Thomas and W.D. McHardy (eds.), *Hebrew and Semitic Studies Presented to Godfrey Rolles Driver* (Oxford: Clarendon Press, 1963), p. 87.

5.   Hammershamb, 'So-Called *Infinitivus Absolutus*', p. 87. For agreement that this is the most common use of the infinitive absolute, see T.O. Lambdin, *Introduction to Biblical Hebrew* (New York: Charles Scribner's Sons, 1971), p. 58; C.L. Seow, *A Grammar for Biblical Hebrew* (Nashville: Abingdon Press, 1987), p. 182.

6.   Seow, *Grammar*, p. 182. Gesenius explains the purpose of the cognate infinitive absolute as '...to define more accurately or to strengthen the idea

absolute is able to perform this function with most other verb forms, even the participle:

Perfect		
1 Sam. 2.30	אמור אמרתי	('I surely said' = 'promised')
Imperfect		
Gen. 18.10	שוב אשוב	('I shall surely return')
Imperative		
Job 13.17	שמעו שמוע	(RSV: 'Listen carefully')
Participle		
Judg. 20.39	נגוף נגף	(NRSV: 'surely defeated')

The intensive nature of the Hebrew verb + cognate infinitive absolute construction is meant to emphasize the assertion made by the main verb, not the root idea.[1] Thus, in Gen. 18.10, God is not speaking of the nature of his 'return' so much as its certainty. The Hebrew verb + cognate infinitive absolute construction is essentially adverbial, then, adding special emphasis or intensity to the verb.[2]

Rendering Hebrew Verb + Cognate Infinitive Absolute in the LXX

Nigel Turner calls the New Testament Greek verb + cognate participle construction 'thoroughly Septuagintal'.[3] This type of observation makes it prudent to investigate the way the LXX renders the Hebrew verb + cognate infinitive absolute. By Turner's count,[4] the

---

of the verb' (W. Gesenius, *Gesenius' Hebrew Grammar* [ed. E. Kautzsch; trans. A.E. Cowley; Oxford: Clarendon Press, 2nd edn, 1910], p. 342).

1.   Waltke and O'Connor, *Introduction*, p. 584. They also make the point that in this construction the verb and infinitive absolute will share not only the same root, but usually the same stem. For a striking example, see Isa. 22.17 where מטלטלך מלטלה is probably a participle and infinitive absolute in the *pilpel* stem.

2.   Hammershamb, 'So-Called *Infinitivus Absolutus*', p. 87: 'In this way the Semitic languages circumvent their paucity of adverbs compared with the Indo-European languages, where however, constructions with internal object, also called *paronomasia* or *figura etymologica* are not infrequently met with'.

3.   N. Turner, *A Grammar of New Testament Greek*. III. *Syntax* (Edinburgh: T. & T. Clark, 1963), p. 156.

4.   *Syntax*, p. 156. While Turner's figures may be open to question, they undoubtably show a general pattern in the LXX.

Hebrew verb + cognate infinitive absolute is translated in the LXX in the following ways:

171×   by our target construction, Greek verb + cognate participle
123×   by a finite verb + a cognate dative noun[1]
23×   by a finite verb + a cognate accusative noun[2]
5×   by an appropriate adverb[3]

In addition to these numbers, Henry St. John Thackeray finds about 50 times where the Hebrew verb + cognate infinitive absolute is not rendered at all in the LXX (that is, it is rendered simply with the Greek finite verb).[4] There is also one instance where the Hebrew verb + cognate infinitive absolute is literally rendered in the LXX with a Greek infinitive.[5] Thackeray notes that the first two of these constructions (Greek verb + cognate participle and with cognate dative) do not occur in the LXX books originally written in Greek.[6]

A look at actual instances may shed some light on the LXX's tendencies in rendering the Hebrew verb + cognate infinitive absolute. Consider the following:

---

1.   This construction also occurs in the New Testament (e.g. Lk. 22.15: ἐπιθυμίᾳ ἐπεθύμησα [RSV: 'I have earnestly desired']). While some may detect an awkward Semitic flavor in this, it is not unintelligible Greek and will not be considered here.

2.   A fairly common Greek construction. See BDF, §153; cf. §156.

3.   Examples:

Exod. 15.1   כי־גאה גאה = ἐνδόξως γὰρ δεδόξασται
('for he has magnified himself gloriously')
Num. 22.17   כי־כבד אכבדך = ἐντίμως γὰρ τιμήσω σε
('for I shall honorably honor you')

4.   H.St J. Thackeray, 'Renderings of the Infinitive Absolute in the LXX', *JTS* 9 (1908), p. 600. Thackeray observed that almost all of these renderings were in the Pentateuch (primarily in Deuteronomy) and in Jer. 1–28.

5.   Josh. 17.13: והורש לא הורישו = ἐξολεθρεῦσαι δὲ αὐτοὺς οὐκ ἐξωλέθρευσαν (difficult to render from Greek, 'but they did not destroy to destroy them').

6.   H.St J. Thackeray, *A Grammar of the Old Testament in Greek according to the Septuagint*. I. *Introduction, Orthography, and Accidence* (Cambridge: Cambridge University Press, 1909), p. 49. Elsewhere ('Renderings', p. 600) Thackeray includes an example from Sir. 28.1: διατηρῶν διατηρήσει ('he will surely establish'), but offers no examples from LXX books that have no tradition of a Hebrew original.

Job 13.17   שמעו שמוע   LXX: ἀκούσατε ἀκούσατε

Here the emphatic nature of the Hebrew verb + cognate infinitive absolute is rendered by duplication of the aorist imperative: 'Hear! Hear!'

1 Sam. 20.3   ידע ידע אביך   LXX: γινώσκων οἶδεν ὁ πατήρ σου

The Hebrew verb + cognate infinitive absolute is translated by a finite verb (οἶδεν) and a participle. The participle is of similar meaning, but not a true cognate.[1] The construction should be translated as intensive, however: 'your father surely knows'.

Judg. 11.25   הרוב רב עם־ישראל   LXX(B): μὴ μαχόμενος ἐμαχέσατο
                                          μετὰ Ισραηλ . . . ;

The μή is added with the question mark (;) to render the Hebrew interrogative (ה). The Hebrew verb + cognate infinitive absolute is translated with the cognate present participle and the aorist verb with intensive force, 'did he not fight intensely...?'[2]

Amos 5.5   כי הגלגל גלה יגלה   LXX: ὅτι Γαλγαλα αἰχμαλωτευομένη
                                        αἰχμαλωτευθήσεται

The LXX is unable to retain the striking alliteration of the Hebrew in its play on Gilgal, but faithfully translates the Hebrew verb + cognate infinitive absolute with a monumental Greek verb + cognate participle construction which has intensive force: 'for Gilgal will surely be taken captive'.

Zech. 11.17   זרעו יבוש תיבש   LXX: ὁ δεξιὸς αὐτοῦ ἐκτυφλούμενος
                                        ἐκτυφλωθήσεται

The LXX adds the minor detail of 'right' hand (δεξιός), and renders the Hebrew jussive with the Greek future passive. The Hebrew verb + cognate infinitive absolute is translated with the Greek verb + cognate participle, even if the verbal ideas do not quite match up (יבש, 'dry up,

---

1.   Thackeray ('Renderings', p. 599) notes that the Hebrew verb + cognate infinitive absolute was sometimes translated with a Greek verb + non-cognate participle, e.g., ἐπαναστρέφων ἥξω for שוב אשוב (Gen. 18.10). Another variation consists of reducing the participle from a compound to a simple verb form, e.g., ζητῶν ἐξεζήτησεν for דרש דרש (Lev. 10.16).

2.   The alternate text, LXX(A), has μὴ μάχῃ ἐμαχέσατο, aorist verb with cognate dative noun.

wither'; ἐκτυφλόω, 'make blind'). If it can be assumed that the Greek
verb has taken on a metaphorical sense, the translation of the verb
would be intensive, 'his arm will be totally blinded' → 'his power will
be totally nullified'.

There are two other types of examples which are, perhaps, even
more instructive of the LXX tendencies in translating the Hebrew verb
+ cognate infinitive absolute.

הישוב אליה עוד הלוא חנוף תחנף הארץ ההיא (Jer. 3.1)
('Will he return to her again? Will not that earth be utterly defiled?')
μὴ ἀνακάμπτουσα ἀνακάμψει πρὸς αὐτὸν ἔτι; οὐ μιαινομένη
μιανθήσεται ἡ γυνὴ ἐκείνη;
('Will she truly return to him again? Will not that woman be utterly
defiled?')

There are several differences in the content (Hebrew 'earth' versus
LXX 'woman'; the LXX's reversal of the subject and indirect object in
the first clause as compared to the Hebrew), but for my purposes the
verbal construction should be noted. The Hebrew text has merely a
finite verb in the first clause, but the Hebrew verb + cognate infinitive
absolute construction in the second. The LXX has the Greek verb +
cognate participle in both clauses. This LXX rendering in the first
clause is unjustified by the Hebrew text and by the context. Where
does it come from? Is it possible that the LXX translator has adopted
the Greek verb + cognate participle construction as a way of rendering those verbs he wishes to emphasize? This is unlikely, for there is
nothing in the Hebrew text of Jer. 3.1 to suggest an intensive sense for
ישוב. A more likely suggestion is made by Thackeray, who explains
such readings as indicative that the LXX translators were working with
a different Hebrew text than the one we now have.[1]

Thackeray offers an even more engaging example from Prov. 24.22:
δεχόμενος δὲ ἐδέξατο αὐτόν ('but he surely received him'). This is
a text for which no Hebrew equivalent is extant, but presumably the
LXX is rendering an emphatic Hebrew verb + cognate infinitive

---

1. Thackeray, 'Renderings', p. 600. Thackeray lists the following (along with
Jer. 3.1) as examples where the LXX has the Greek verb + cognate participle with no
Hebrew verb + cognate infinitive absolute extant: Gen. 19.17; Exod. 11.9;
Lev. 14.48; Num. 5.6; 1 Kgdms 1.5; 2 Kgdms 17.11; 3 Kgdms 11.34; 22.6; Jer.
12.11; 22.24; 41.2. It is interesting to note that one third of these occur in Jeremiah,
where the LXX text is very different from the MT.

absolute construction with the Greek verb + cognate participle.[1]

In summary, in numerous examples the LXX translators attempt to retain the intensive force of the Hebrew verb + cognate infinitive absolute construction. This is done in several ways, but often with the Greek verb + cognate participle. Further, although there are a few examples of the Greek verb + cognate participle in the LXX without an underlying Hebrew verb + cognate infinitive absolute, these are probably explained on the level of textual variation, not as a way the LXX uses to emphasize certain verbs.

Greek Verb + Cognate Participle in Non-Biblical Greek

Does the Greek verb + cognate participle with intensive force occur in Greek outside of the New Testament? A wide range of responses can be found to this question.[2] A cautious approach is expressed by BDF, which says '...in pure Greek only remotely related examples are to be found'.[3] Conybeare and Stock answer an emphatic 'No', by saying, 'The cognate accusative is quite Greek and the cognate dative is to be found in pure Greek, but we should search in vain among classical authors for the intensive use of the participle'.[4]

William Edward Jelf is sometimes mentioned as a grammarian who thought that the Greek verb + cognate participle with an intensive sense was a regular construction in classical Greek. Indeed, Jelf calls the construction a 'peculiar Greek idiom', and gives several examples.[5] Yet a careful reading of Jelf's treatment in §705.3 and an examination of his examples reveal a lack of any suggestion that such a construction is used in classical Greek as a method of intensifying the verb (as the Hebrew verb + cognate infinitive absolute construction does).

The examples from classical literature given below demonstrate that the construction, Greek verb + cognate participle, may be found. The question for my purposes is whether or not this construction ever occurs with a sense similar to the LXX usage. That is, does the

1. Thackeray, 'Renderings', p. 600.
2. See discussion in Porter, *Verbal Aspect*, pp. 139-40.
3. BDF, §422.
4. F.C. Conybeare and St G. Stock, *A Grammar of Septuagint Greek* (Grand Rapids: Zondervan, 1980 [1905]), §81.
5. W.E. Jelf, *A Grammar of the Greek Language, Chiefly from the German of Raphael Kuehner* (Oxford: John Henry Parker, 1842), p. 330.

construction intend a single verbal idea with intensive force? Or, should the finite verb and the participle be seen as separate verbal ideas, with the cognate relationship being a matter of coincidence or literary technique determined by the author's subjective choice? More pointedly, is the classical author pulling this construction from the stock of methods for expressing a single verbal idea with emphatic or intensive force?[1]

μὲν βλέποντες ἔβλεπον μάτην (Aeschylus, *Prometheus Bound* 447)
LCL: 'though they had eyes to see, they saw to no avail'
MSK: 'while seeing they saw in vain'[2]

ὡς ὁρῶμεν οὐχ ὁρώμενοι (Euripides, *The Bacchanals* 1050)
LCL: 'that so we might behold all unbeheld'
MSK: 'as we might see while not seeing'

ἀλλ' ὑπακούων σχολῇ ὑπήκουσα; (Xenophon, *Cyropaedia* 8.4.9)
LCL: 'Or, obeying, did I ever obey reluctantly?'

γινώσκουσα γινώσκω ἐγώ, ὅτι κύριος ὁ θεὸς παραδίδωσιν ὑμιν τὴν γῆν ταύτην (*1 Clement* 12.5)
LCL: 'I know assuredly that the Lord God is delivering to you this land'

The passages from Aeschylus, Euripides and Xenophon are indeed finite verbs with cognate participles, but clearly have no sense of the intensive meaning signified by the Hebrew verb + cognate infinitive absolute.[3]

The citation from *1 Clement* is the most difficult to explain. In ch. 12 Clement is relating the story of Rahab, at points following the text of Joshua quite closely. At this point he seems to be quoting Josh. 2.9, but neither the LXX nor the MT has an intensive verb construction.[4] Why would Clement resort to the Greek verb + cognate participle construction here, when he apparently uses it nowhere

---

1.   Citations are from the LCL, as are the translations. MSK indicates the author's translation.

2.   LSJ, s.v. μάτην suggesting the meaning 'in vain' for this citation.

3.   An additional often-cited example is *P.Tebt.* 421.12: ἐρχόμενος δὲ ἔρχου (ε)ἰς Θεογονίδα. This, however, is admittedly a third-century AD or later source, and of seemingly dubious value. Turner (*Syntax*, p. 157) doubts it is a true example, translating it 'when you come, come to Th'.

4.   Hebrew: ידעני כי־נתן יהוה לכם את־הארץ
     LXX: ἐπίσταμαι ὅτι δέδωκεν ὑμῖν κύριος τὴν γῆν

else?[1] Several things should be considered.

1. In ch. 12 Clement is using Rahab as an example of faith and hospitality (πίστιν καὶ φιλοξενίαν, 12.1). For Rahab to be able to say (in 12.5) that she *certainly knows* that the Lord is giving the land to the Israelites would be in keeping with Clement's picture of her as a woman of faith.

2. Clement's grammatical intention with the Greek verb + cognate participle must be understood as an intensive use of the verb; nothing else makes sense. His apparent lack of use of this construction elsewhere for intensive purposes makes its use here suspicious. Could it be that Clement was following a Greek text of Joshua which had this reading?[2]

In summary, a claim that Greek verb + cognate participle exists in non-biblical Greek rests upon scanty evidence, especially if the claim is pressed to understand this as a method in non-biblical Greek to intensify the verb.

Greek Verb + Cognate Participle in the New Testament

A computer search of the Greek New Testament using the GRAMCORD system for a verbal form with a cognate participle occurring within five words before or after yielded 154 possible instances in the New Testament. Nine of these seem potentially to reflect the Semitic construction, Hebrew verb + cognate infinitive

---

1. My search of the entire text of *1 Clement* uncovered only one other Greek verb + cognate participle construction at 56.3, παιδεύων ἐπαίδευσέν με ὁ κύριος. This occurs in a quotation from Ps. 118.18 (LXX 117.18), which has an underlying Hebrew verb + cognate infinitive absolute, יסר יסרני יה. The LCL translation 'with chastisement did the Lord chastise me', shows the misunderstanding of this construction by the translator. It should be rendered intensively, 'The Lord surely disciplined me'.

Cognate constructions of any type are not frequent in *1 Clement* (e.g., 16.11: δικαιῶσαι δίκαιον ['to justify a righteous man']; 32.1: τῶν ὑπ᾽ αὐτοῦ δεδομένων δωρεῶν ['of the gifts given by him']).

2. Many of *1 Clement*'s 'quotations' of Scripture are in a loose manner, adding, subtracting or expanding details in accordance with his purpose. For example, cf. the many differences in detail between the Cain and Abel story in *1 Clem.* 4 and in Gen. 4. This may be frustrating to the modern student hoping to use *1 Clement* for textual studies, but should not be seen as unusual for his day and age.

absolute,[1] and each will be considered. One additional passage (Eph. 5.5) is often mentioned in treatments of the New Testament Greek verb + cognate participle and will also be considered.

Quotations of Isaiah 6.9

Because quotations of Isa. 6.9 account for nearly half of the possible New Testament occurrences of the Greek verb + cognate participle which will be considered, they will be examined in some depth.

Isa. 6.9	MT	שמעו שמוע ואל־תבינו וראו ראו ואל־תדעו
	LXX	ἀκοῇ ἀκούσετε καὶ οὐ μὴ συνῆτε καὶ **βλέποντες βλέψετε** καὶ οὐ μὴ ἴδητε.
Mt. 13.14		ἀκοῇ ἀκούσετε καὶ οὐ μὴ συνῆτε, καὶ **βλέποντες βλέψετε** καὶ οὐ μὴ ἴδητε.
Mk 4.12		ἵνα **βλέποντες βλέπωσιν** καὶ μὴ ἴδωσιν, καὶ **ἀκούοντες ἀκούωσιν** καὶ μὴ συνιῶσιν.
Acts 28.26		ἀκοῇ ἀκούσετε καὶ οὐ μὴ συνῆτε καὶ **βλέποντες βλέψετε** καὶ οὐ μὴ ἴδητε.

Mt. 13.13, Jn 9.39, and Lk. 8.10 also contain versions of Isa. 6.9, but do not contain the Greek verb + cognate participle construction.[2]

When these texts are compared, the following points are observed.

1. The LXX has translated the Hebrew verb + cognate infinitive absolute in the first clause by means of the finite verb + cognate dative noun. The Hebrew verb + cognate infinitive absolute in the second clause is rendered by the Greek verb + cognate participle. Both of these constructions are intensive, although the second one must be

1. Method for sorting through the 154 possibilities was admittedly somewhat subjective, but two main criteria were employed:

a. Instances were not considered where the participle has a clearly separate function in the sentence. For example, participles performing a substantive function were eliminated.

b. To be considered, the cognate participle had to have an obvious adverbial function, especially if it seemed to intensify the main verb.

2. All of these have a finite verb with a cognate participle, but either the participle or the verb is negated, that is, Matthew and Luke have something like 'while seeing, they do not see' (Matthew has present indicative, Luke has present subjunctive), John has 'that the ones not seeing might see', a negated substantival use of the participle. Cf. the examples from Aeschylus and Euripides above.

understood in light of the Hebrew construction to make sense. This does offer a good illustration of the freedom the LXX translators used in interpreting the Hebrew verb + cognate infinitive absolute.

2. The quotations in Matthew and Acts are verbatim from the LXX, whereas Mark differs considerably. The fidelity of Matthew as opposed to the Markan variation is noteworthy, because Matthew is known for his significant departure from the LXX in many places.[1] Here, Matthew's adherence even extends to the retention of the LXX's future indicative in contrast to the imperative of the Hebrew text.[2]

3. Mark has altered the LXX text considerably in the following ways:

    a.   Reversing the two clauses;

    b.   Giving the Greek verb + cognate participle construction for both clauses;

    c.   Changing the person from second to third;

    d.   Giving subjunctive verbs in the Greek verb + cognate participle construction rather than future indicative;

    e.   Using the second finite verb of each clause in third person rather than second person, with the οὐ being dropped, thus changing it from an emphatic negation to a simple negation of future possibility.

Beyond such differences, the major question for the student of New Testament Greek is this: how should this construction be grammatically understood? Further, how should it be translated into English? If the LXX and thus the Hebrew background of the Greek verb + cognate participle are taken into account, any interpretation must see this

---

1. See H.B. Swete, *An Introduction to the Old Testament in Greek* (rev. R.R. Ottley; Cambridge: Cambridge University Press, 1902; repr. New York: Ktav, 1968), p. 394. Swete notes that of Matthew's 16 Old Testament quotations not found in the other Synoptic Gospels, 4 are from the LXX, 4 are based on the LXX with significant variants, and '7 bear little or no resemblance' to the LXX. (Why this does not add up to 16 is not explained.) In comparison, 'Neither Mc. nor Lc. has any series of independent quotations'.

2. One author claims that this is in line with Matthew's 'purpose to emphasize human responsibility rather than divine intent' (R.H. Gundry, *Matthew: A Commentary on his Theological Art* [Grand Rapids: Eerdmans, 1982], p. 257). Additionally, Gundry sees Matthew's insertion of γάρ into the quotation in v. 15 as in keeping with this same purpose.

construction as intensive; any translation must attempt to bring this out.

A survey of the English translations of Mk 4.12 will be illustrative at this point. Unfortunately, the AV translators apparently did not understand the idiom and rendered the text very literally: 'seeing they may see and not perceive; and hearing they may hear and not understand'.

Subsequent translations have followed suit:

> NASB: 'while seeing they may see and not perceive; and while hear-
> ing, they may hear and not understand' (similarly ASV, NKJV).

Others have attempted to do something beyond such a literal translation:

> JB: 'they may see and see again, but not perceive; may hear and
> hear again but not understand';
> NEB: 'they may look and look, but see nothing, they may hear and
> hear and understand nothing'.

A few have apparently understood the intensive nature of this construction and tried to bring this out in translation:

> NIV: 'they may be ever seeing but never perceiving, and ever
> hearing but never understanding';
> NAB: 'they will look intently and not see, listen carefully and not
> understand';
> NRSV: 'they may indeed look, but not perceive, and may indeed listen,
> but not understand' (similarly RSV).

The translator should recognize the intensity of this construction and render it appropriately. The English method for intensifying a verb is frequently to use an adverb. The choice of adverb should be guided by the recognition that the Hebrew verb + cognate infinitive absolute construction seeks to intensify the verb's assertion, not its root meaning. Words like 'surely', 'certainly' (or, 'most certainly') and 'intently' are appropriate. A possible translation of Mk 4.12 might be:

> They are sure to look and not really see,
> They are sure to listen and not really understand.

A possible translation of Mt. 13.14 might be:

> You will surely listen but certainly not understand,
> You will surely look but certainly not see.

Such translations are merely illustrative, but do attempt to bring out the intensive sense of the construction.

Quotation of Exodus 3.7

As Swete says, the 'quotations from the Old Testament in the Acts are taken from the LXX exclusively'.[1] It is not surprising, then, to find Stephen's quotation of Exod. 3.7 at Acts 7.34 reproducing the LXX's Greek verb + cognate participle verbatim:

Acts 7.34   ἰδὼν εἶδον τὴν κάκωσιν τοῦ λαοῦ μου τοῦ ἐν Αἰγυπτῳ
Exod. 3.7   ראה ראיתי את־עני עמי אשר במצרים
LXX   ἰδὼν εἶδον τὴν κάκωσιν τοῦ λαοῦ μου τοῦ ἐν Αἰγυπτῳ

Luke records Stephen's fidelity to the LXX, down to such details as the New Testament *hapax legomenon* κάκωσις and the LXX's rendering of the אשר clause by means of an attributive articular construction with relative force.

Translation of the Greek verb + cognate participle should recognize the intensive force of the underlying Hebrew construction.[2] The emphasis is not upon the Lord's perceptive powers, but upon the certainty of his seeing. The AV translators misunderstood this completely.[3] Many of the more modern translations have understood the intensive nature of the Greek verb + cognate participle, and rendered it appropriately.[4] A possible translation might be:

> You may be sure that I have seen the misery of my people who are in Egypt...

---

1. Swete, *Introduction*, p. 398.
2. See F.F. Bruce, *The Acts of the Apostles: The Greek Text with Introduction and Commentary* (Grand Rapids: Eerdmans, 2nd edn, 1990), p. 200. This is one of the few commentaries which deals directly with this construction. Bruce calls this a 'Semitism' and sees it as a reflection of the Hebrew verb + cognate infinitive absolute. He also mentions Acts 4.17 and 5.28 as examples of the Hebrew verb + cognate infinitive absolute rendered with the Greek verb + cognate dative noun, possibly reflecting an underlying Semitic source at those points.
3. 'I have seen, I have seen the affliction of my people which is in Egypt...'
4. E.g., NRSV: 'I have surely seen the mistreatment of my people who are in Egypt...'

Quotation of Genesis 22.17

The author of Hebrews also shows general fidelity to the LXX in his
Old Testament quotations.[1] Considering the number and extent of the
quotations in Hebrews, it is not surprising to find one with the Greek
verb + cognate participle construction:

Heb. 6.14   εἰ μὴν **εὐλογῶν εὐλογήσω** σε
καὶ **πληθύνων πληθυνῶ** σε
Gen. 22.17   כי־ברך אברכך
והרבה ארבה את־זרעך כככובי השמים
LXX   ἦ μὴν **εὐλογῶν εὐλογήσω** σε
καὶ **πληθύνων πληθυνῶ** τὸ σπέρμα σου ὡς τοὺς
ἀστέρας τοῦ οὐρανοῦ

This quotation offers minor variations from the LXX (the truncated
object in the second clause, εἰ μήν rather than ἦ μήν),[2] but the Greek
verb + cognate participle constructions are reproduced exactly as in
the LXX.

As before, the intensive force of the underlying Hebrew verb +
cognate infinitive absolute should be brought out in translation. The
AV is at least consistent here in its failing to understand the intensive
nature of the Greek verb + cognate participle: 'Surely blessing I will
bless thee, and multiplying I will multiply thee'.[3] Most modern translations have attempted to render the Greek verb + cognate participle
as emphatic, avoiding a literal translation of the participle which
would be redundant in English.[4] A possible translation would be:

Certainly[5] I shall bless you tremendously,
And I shall multiply you prolifically.

1. Swete (*Introduction*, p. 402) describes Hebrews as 'in great part a catena of
quotations from the LXX'.
2. But this reading is textually uncertain, with ἦ being the reading in Ψ and in
the ˜ text.
3. The emphatic 'surely' is presumably the AV's way of expressing the ἦ μήν in
the text they were using, not a translation based on the Greek verb + cognate
participle.
4. NRSV is typical here: 'I will surely bless you and multiply you'. This,
however, loses the impact of the second Greek verb + cognate participle.
5. The 'certainly' reflects the εἰ μήν construction, commonly used with oaths in
classical Greek. See BAGD, s.v. εἰ μήν.

This type of translation uses the English adverb of corresponding meaning to convey the intensive sense of the Greek verb + cognate participle construction.

Possible Occurrences which are not LXX Quotations
In analyzing the GRAMCORD data, two other instances of Greek verb + cognate participle construction which seemed[1] out of the ordinary also emerged.

Heb. 6.10   διακονήσαντες τοῖς ἁγίοις καὶ διακονοῦντες.

This verse is in the context of the author's assurance that God does not overlook sincere works of love. The construction departs from the usual pattern being discussed, because it has two participles and no finite verb. However, it was shown above that the Hebrew verb + cognate infinitive absolute construction may occur with the Hebrew participle.

While the second participle does contain both an intensive and an adverbial sense, it need not be understood as reflecting the Hebrew verb + cognate infinitive absolute construction. The aorist participle emphasizes the total ministry to the saints; the present participle makes it clear that this ministry is still ongoing. A possible translation would be:

> your[2] ministry for the saints which is ongoing.

This should not be considered an example of the Greek verb + cognate participle construction as reflective of the Hebrew verb + cognate infinitive absolute.

Rev. 6.2   ἐξῆλθεν νικῶν καὶ ἵνα νικήσῃ.

This construction is generally overlooked in the commentaries.[3] The translation of the AV, 'he went forth conquering and to conquer', has basically been retained down to the most recent English translations,[4]

---

1. The subjective element is acknowledged here, but the basic criteria mentioned above apply.
2. Second person plural is the implied antecedent of the plural participles from the main verb of the clause, ἐνεδείξασθε.
3. The commentaries are much more concerned in this verse with unravelling the identity of the white horse and its rider.
4. E.g., NRSV: 'he came out conquering and to conquer'.

although some have attempted to nominalize the participle.[1]

Steven Thompson has recently proposed that this construction is among three 'true examples' of the use of the Hebrew verb + cognate infinitive absolute in Revelation.[2] Thompson claims that the text as it stands 'is neither Hebrew nor Greek', and suggests the following emendation:

$$\text{ἐξῆλθεν ἵνα νικῶν καὶ νικήσῃ.}^{3}$$

This alteration would bring the text more in line with a usual LXX method of interpreting the Hebrew verb + cognate infinitive absolute, that is, Greek verb + cognate participle. Thompson therefore suggests the following translation: 'he departed in order that he might thoroughly conquer'.[4]

One should always be suspicious of textual emendations without manuscript support, but even with the change Thompson fails to account for a pesky καί[5] in the middle of the construction. This could hardly be reflective of the Hebrew וֹ, for its presence would destroy the intensive cognate continuity of the double verb.

Thompson's argument aside, however, the construction is still not easily explained. Does the author mean something like 'he went out in order that while conquering he also might conquer'? This is an awkward use of καί, and seems too tautologous to be satisfactory. A little light might be shed by noting that the participle, νικῶν, is

---

1. E.g., NIV: 'he rode out as a conqueror bent on conquest'.
2. S. Thompson, *The Apocalypse and Semitic Syntax* (Cambridge: Cambridge University Press, 1985), pp. 80-81. The other two examples listed by Thompson, Rev. 3.17 and 18.16, are both verb + cognate adjective, and will not be considered here.
3. Thompson, *Apocalypse*, p. 80.
4. Thompson, *Apocalypse*, pp. 80-81. Thompson sees this and his examples at 3.17 and 18.6 as constructions 'owing their existence to Biblical Hebrew', thus buttressing the thesis of his entire book. This thesis (that the Greek of Revelation is heavily dependent upon a Semitic background, and that the particular Semitic background is not first-century Aramaic, but biblical Hebrew) has been heavily criticized recently. For general criticisms of Thompson's method, see Porter, *Verbal Aspect*, pp. 117, 119 and 138, and Porter's article, 'The Language of the Apocalypse in Recent Discussion', *NTS* 35 (1989), pp. 582-603.
5. The καί is omitted in some manuscripts and versions, but the principle of *lectio difficilior* combined with the superior manuscript attestation prevents us from disregarding it.

nominative, and should probably be tied to the subject of the verb. The ἵνα introduces a final purpose clause (simply νικήσῃ). The καί has an 'ascensive' function, leading to a heightened assertion.[1] A possible translation is

the conquering one left to conquer even more.

This is not a very satisfactory result, as the meaning remains somewhat esoteric, but may be what is intended. The successive use of a vigorous verb like νικάω is bound to be emphatic, but it is extremely doubtful that the author is intending a Greek parallel to the Hebrew verb + cognate infinitive absolute construction.

Eph. 5.5   τοῦτο γὰρ ἴστε γινώσκοντες

Finally, a construction will be considered that, while not a true Greek verb + cognate participle (because the verbs are not true cognates), is often mentioned in grammatical discussions as an example of an underlying Hebrew verb + cognate infinitive absolute.[2]

Commentators are divided at this point. T.K. Abbott insists that ἴστε γινώσκοντες cannot be seen as a reflection of the Hebrew verb + cognate infinitive absolute simply because the verbs are different. He translates it 'ye know full well of your own knowledge'.[3] Others disagree. J. Armitage Robinson takes this as a 'Hebraism' for 'ye know of a surety'. Robinson points out that the Hebrew verb + cognate infinitive absolute ידע ידוע appears 14 times in the Hebrew Bible. The usual LXX translation is with a Greek verb + cognate participle using forms of γινώσκω, but 1 Kgdms 20.3 has γινώσκοντες οἶδεν, and some manuscripts have ἴστε γινώσκοντες at Jer. 49.22.[4] Similarly, Markus Barth sees this as a clear Hebraism, because the two verbs are synonyms. He suggests the translation 'You had better keep this in mind'.[5]

1. See BAGD, s.v. καί, under definition II.2.
2. For example, see Turner, *Syntax*, p. 157; along with J.H. Moulton and W.F. Howard, *A Grammar of New Testament Greek*. II. *Accidence and Word Formation* (Edinburgh: T. & T. Clark, 1929), p. 444.
3. T.K. Abbott, *A Critical and Exegetical Commentary on the Epistles to the Ephesians and to the Colossians* (ICC; Edinburgh: T. & T. Clark, 1897), p. 150.
4. J.A. Robinson, *St Paul's Epistle to the Ephesians* (London: Macmillan, 2nd edn, 1904), p. 199.
5. M. Barth, *Ephesians: Translation and Commentary on Chapters 4–6* (AB; Garden City, NY: Doubleday, 1974), p. 563.

That ἴστε γινώσκοντες is a Semitism that can only be understood by resorting to the Hebrew verb + cognate infinitive absolute is certainly within the realm of possibility, but there may be another explanation. ἴστε can be understood as either a second person indicative *or* imperative. The antecedent of the τοῦτο should be understood as the preceding exhortation (that things like fornication and vulgarity are wholly out of place in the Christian community). The object of γινώσκοντες is the ὅτι clause (that certain types of persons have no inheritance in the Kingdom). A possible translation is

> You must understand these things (because) you know (that certain types have no inheritance).

This interpretation may be faulty, however it does show that the ἴστε γινώσκοντες does not necessarily have to be understood by retreating to an underlying Hebrew verb + cognate infinitive absolute understanding.[1]

Conclusions

First, while the Greek verb + cognate participle does occur in non-biblical Greek, it is very doubtful that it is used regularly (ever?) to express an intensive sense of a single verbal idea. The example from *1 Clement* may do this, but is not without problems. Many more unambiguous examples must be produced to warrant seeing this as any sort of regular Greek method for intensifying a verb.

Secondly, the construction Greek verb + cognate participle does occur in the New Testament with the sense of a single intensive verbal idea, but only in LXX quotations. The seven pure examples are found in Mt. 13.14, Mk 4.12 (2×), Acts 7.34, Acts 28.26 and Heb. 6.14 (2×). The three other suggested examples (Eph. 5.5; Heb. 6.10; Rev. 6.2) are dubious, and may be explained in other ways.

Thirdly, where the Greek verb + cognate participle appears in the New Testament, it should be understood as a translation of the Hebrew verb + cognate infinitive absolute, and the English translator should render it with intensive force. This does show the importance of

---

1. For a fuller discussion which sees ἴστε γινώσκοντες not as a single intensive construction, but as the pivot point of a chiastic structure embracing Eph. 5.3-5, see S.E. Porter, 'ἴστε γινώσκοντες in Ephesians 5.5: Does Chiasm Solve a Problem?', *ZNW* 81 (1990), pp. 271-76. Porter's analysis concludes that ἴστε and γινώσκοντες function as separate verbal ideas.

Hebrew Bible and LXX studies for the student of New Testament Greek.

Fourthly, this study does not overturn Porter's conclusion (that there is no instance of Semitic intervention for the verb of the Greek New Testament), for these examples are the result of the New Testament authors following the LXX, not a product of their usual grammatical patterns. Even so, the New Testament authors apparently felt that this construction could sometimes be presented without modification (as in *1 Clement*) and correctly understood by their audience. The small group of New Testament examples may be classed as examples of quotations of Semitically influenced translation, illustrating the LXX tradition which is often assumed by New Testament authors and apparently not beyond the ken of their readers.

Fifthly, grammars of New Testament Greek should include an understanding of the Greek verb + cognate participle as a reflection of the Hebrew verb + cognate infinitive absolute in LXX quotations. Otherwise, students of the Greek of the New Testament will not understand this phenomenon and will resort to inadequate translations such as are found in some earlier English Bibles.[1]

---

1.   While this may seem to be an obvious plea, note that two excellent recent surveys in *ANRW* II. 25.5 by J.W. Voelz ('The Language of the New Testament', pp. 893-977) and M. Wilcox ('Semitisms in the New Testament', pp. 978-1029) both omit discussion of the Greek verb + cognate participle. These treatments are not alone in such gaps.

INDEXES

INDEX OF REFERENCES

OLD TESTAMENT

Genesis			*1 Samuel*			*Amos*	
4	196		2.30	190		5.5	192
18.10	190, 192		20.3	192			
19.17	193					*Zechariah*	
22.17	201		*Job*			11.17	192
			13.17	190, 192			
Exodus						*Sirach*	
3.7	200		*Psalms*			28.1	191
11.9	193		118.18				
15.1	191		(LXX			LXX	
			117.18)	196		*1 Kingdoms*	
Leviticus						1.5	193
10.16	192		*Proverbs*			20.3	204
14.48	193		24.22	193			
						2 Kingdoms	
Numbers			*Isaiah*			17.11	193
5.6	193		6.9	197			
22.17	191		22.17	190		*3 Kingdoms*	
						11.34	193
Joshua			*Jeremiah*			22.6	193
2.9	195		1–28	191			
17.13	191		3.1	193			
			12.11	193			
Judges			22.24	193			
11.25	192		41.2	193			
20.39	190		49.22	204			

NEW TESTAMENT

Matthew			7.24	138, 145,		10.14	138, 144
2.9	138, 142			146		10.27	138, 145
6.7	148		7.26	138, 145		11.2	129, 138
6.32	147		9.4	148		11.4	138, 144
7.11	150		9.6	147		12.19	138, 144

12.25	148	1.43	148	*Luke*		
12.42	139, 144	2.10	147	1.2	163	
13.13	197	2.13	66	1.41	139, 144	
13.14	197, 199,	3.22	72	2.20	133, 139,	
	205	4.1	66		144	
13.15	198	4.12	197, 199,	2.25	173	
13.17	139, 144		205	2.46	139, 142	
13.18	139, 144	4.13	148	2.47	139, 142	
13.19	139, 144	4.16	139, 145	2.49	112, 147	
13.20	139, 145	4.18	139, 144	3.6	172	
13.22	139, 144	4.20	139, 145	3.11	72	
13.23	139, 145	4.24	139, 144	4.23	139, 144	
14.1	129, 138	4.27	149	4.28	139, 145	
15.12	139, 145,	4.39	72	4.34	149	
	147	5.1-20	66	5.1	139, 144	
17.5	138, 142	5.22-24	71	5.13	176	
18.15	138, 142	5.33	148	5.24	147	
19.22	139, 145	5.35	72	6.8	148	
20.22	149	6.8	72	6.18	131, 139,	
20.25	147	6.11	139, 142		142	
21.25	151	6.12	73	6.27	149	
21.27	150, 151	6.20	139, 142,	6.42	181	
21.33	139, 144		148	6.45	172	
21.45	139, 145	7.14	139, 142	6.47	132, 139,	
22.16	147	9.6	149		143, 146	
22.29	148	9.7	139, 142	7.9	139, 145	
24.6	129, 138	10.19	148	7.22	139, 144	
24.42	149	10.33	31	7.32	182	
24.43	149	10.38	149	7.42	173	
25.9	80	10.42	147	7.43	173, 174	
25.12	148	11.17	148	8.10	197	
25.13	148	11.27	70	8.15	139, 145	
25.26	147	11.30	151	8.16	172	
26.2	147	11.33	150, 151	8.21	139, 145	
26.45	31	12.4	147	8.42	51	
26.65-66	146	12.15	148	8.51	184	
26.65	139, 145	12.24	148	8.53	147	
26.70	149	12.28	139, 142	9.7	129, 138	
26.72	148	12.37	139, 142	9.9	139, 145	
26.74	148	13.7	129, 138	9.33	148	
27.18	147	13.33	149	9.35	139, 142	
27.65	149-51	13.35	149	9.39	182	
27.65b	151	14.40	149	10.11	181	
28.5	147	14.58	139, 142	10.16	139, 142	
		14.63-64	146	10.24	139, 144	
Mark		14.64	132, 139,	10.35	181	
1.24	149		143	10.39	139, 144	
1.32-33	67	14.71	148	10.42	181	

11.1	182	1.31	148	9.24	147
11.13	150	1.33	148	9.25	147, 149, 150
11.28	139, 145	1.37	139, 142	9.29	147
11.31	139, 144	2.9	149	9.30	149
11.33	172	3.2	147	9.31	140, 142, 147
11.44	150, 151	3.7	113		
11.44a	151	3.8	131, 139, 145, 149	9.39	197
12.12	113, 172			9.40	140, 146
12.30	147	3.11	148	10.3-4	132
12.39	149	3.27	189	10.3	130, 131, 140, 143
12.56	150	3.29	139, 142		
13.16	187	3.32	139, 145	10.4	143, 148
13.18	178	4.10	148	10.5	148
13.25	149	4.22	148	10.6	130
13.27	149	4.32	148	10.8	140, 142
13.31	172	4.42	147	10.16	132, 140, 143
14.15	139, 145	5.13	149		
15.1	139, 142	5.24	140, 146	10.20	130, 142
15.25-26	132	5.25	130-32, 140, 143	10.27	132, 140, 144
15.25	139, 143				
15.26	143	5.28-29	132	11.22	147
15.27	181	5.28	130, 140, 143	11.24	147
15.31	176			11.41	140, 142
15.32	51	5.29	143	11.42	140, 142, 147
16.6	174, 175	5.37	131, 140, 145		
16.14	139, 145			11.49	148
16.29	139, 142	6.6	149	12.34	113
16.31	139, 142	6.42	148	12.35	149
18.20	148	6.60	132, 140, 143	12.47	131, 132, 135, 140, 144
18.23	139, 145				
18.36	139, 142	6.61	147	12.50	147
19.11	139, 144	7.15	148, 149	13.1	147
19.22	147	7.27	149	13.3	147
19.48	139, 142	7.28	148, 149	13.7	148
20.7	149	7.29	148	13.11	148
20.9	180, 181	7.32	140, 142	13.17	148
20.21	147	7.40	131, 132, 140, 143	13.18	149
20.24	183			13.31	31
21.9	129, 138	8.14	149	14.4	148, 149
21.38	139, 142	8.19	148	14.5	149
22.15	191	8.37	147	14.24	14, 145
22.34	148	8.43	140, 145	15.5	149
22.57	148	8.47	135, 140, 145	15.21	148
22.60	148			16.18	149
23.34	149	8.55	148	16.30	147, 148
		9.10	147	18.2	148
John		9.12	149		
1.26	148	9.21	149		

18.4	148
18.21	148
18.37-38	132
18.38	144
19.8	140, 146
19.10	147
19.13	132, 140, 144
19.28	147
19.35	147
20.9	113, 148
20.24	147
21.4	147
21.12	147
21.15	147
21.16	147
21.17	148
21.24	147

Acts

1.5	173
2.6	140, 142
2.11	140, 142
2.22	140, 145, 150, 151
2.22a	151
2.30	147
3.16	148
3.17	147
3.22	140, 143
3.23	140, 143
4.4	140, 146
4.17	200
4.19	140, 143
5.5	51, 140, 146
5.7	148
5.11	129, 138
5.21	182
5.24	140, 146
5.28	200
5.29	113
5.39	51
6.11	140, 143
6.14	140, 143
7.17	148
7.26	51
7.34	132, 140, 144, 200, 205
7.40	149
7.54	140, 146
8.1	171
8.30	140, 143
9.4	131, 140, 146
9.7	131, 132, 134, 135, 140, 144
9.16	113
10.33	140, 145
10.37	148
10.44	140, 145
10.46	140, 142
11.7	131, 132, 140, 144, 146
12.9	147
12.11	147
13.7	140, 145
13.44	140, 145
14.9	140, 143
15.7	140, 146
15.12	140, 143
15.13	140, 143
15.37	181
16.3	147, 150
17.8	140, 146
17.10	176
17.21	140, 145
17.32	129, 138, 140, 143
18.26	140, 143
19.10	140, 145
19.32	149
20.22	148
20.25	147
20.29	147
21.12	140, 146
22.1-2	132
22.1	140, 144
22.2	144
22.7	131, 132, 140, 144, 146
22.8	1133
22.9	131, 134, 135, 140, 145
22.14	140, 146
22.22	140, 143
23.5	147
23.11	113
23.16	129, 130, 138
24.4	140, 143
24.22	148
24.24	141, 143
25.22	141, 143
26.3	141, 145
26.4	148
26.14	131, 140, 146
26.27	147
26.29	141, 143
27.21	113
28.15	129, 138
28.26	197, 205

Romans

1–8	41
1.1	115
1.13	110
1.9-10	176
2.2	147
2.12	41, 42
3.19	147
3.21-26	154
3.23	41, 42
5.3	147
5.12	41, 42
6.9	147
6.16	147
7.7	148
7.9	51
7.14	147
7.18	147
8.22	147
8.26	149
8.27	149
8.28	147
10.14	141, 143
11.2	149
11.25	110

12.3	113
13.11	148
14.14	147, 148
15.29	147
16	79
16.20	98, 99

1 Corinthians

1.1	115
1.16	149
2.2	148
2.9	141, 145
2.11	148
2.12	148
3.16	147
4.19	114
5.6	147
6.2	147
6.3	147
6.9	147
6.15	147
6.16	147
7.16	149
8.1	113, 147
8.4	147
9.13	147
9.24	147
10.1	110
11.3	110, 147
11.23	182
11.28	55
12.1	110
12.2	147
13.2	148
14.11	148
14.16	149
15.1-11	94
15.58	147, 176
16.13-14	55
16.15	150
16.23	98

2 Corinthians

1.1	115
1.7	147
1.8	110
1.12	110
3.13	182

4.14	147
5.1	147
5.2ff.	154
5.6	147
5.11	148
5.16	148
9.2	148
11.31	147
12.2	148-51
12.2a	151
12.3	148-51
12.3a	151
12.4	141, 145
12.14	114
12.20-21	114
13.13	98

Galatians

1.1	115
1.11	110
1.13	129, 138
2.9	114
2.16	147
4.8	148
4.13	147
4.20	114
4.21	141, 145
6.1	55
6.18	98

Ephesians

1.13	141, 146
1.15	129, 138
1.18	149
2.3	110
3.2	129, 138
4–6	204
4.21	129, 138
5.3-5	205
5.5	148, 197, 204, 205
6.8	147
6.9	147
6.20	113
6.21	148
6.24	98

Philippians

1.12	110
1.16	147
1.19	147
1.25	147
1.27	129, 138
2.24	114
4.9	141, 146
4.12	150
4.15	147
4.23	98, 99

Colossians

1.4	129, 138
1.23	132, 133, 141, 145
2.1	149
3.24	147
4.1	147
4.4	113
4.6	149
4.18	98, 99

1 Thessalonians

1.4	148
1.5	148
2.1	110, 148
2.2	151
2.2a	151
2.5	151
2.5a	151
3.3	148
3.4	151
3.4a	151
3.11	114
4.1	113
4.2	149
4.4	148, 150
4.13	110
5.2	147
5.12	148
5.28	98, 99

2 Thessalonians

1.8	148
2.6	148
3.7	113, 149
3.9	113
3.11	129, 138

3.18   98, 99

1 Timothy
1.1-2   97
1.1   97, 102, 105, 106, 115
1.1a   105
1.1b   105
1.2   97, 102, 105, 106
1.3ff.   109
1.3   104, 107, 108
1.4   106, 108
1.5   104, 107
1.6   106, 108
1.7   106
1.8   104, 105
1.9   104, 150
1.10-11   103
1.10   104, 108
1.11   104
1.12-17   103
1.12   104
1.13   104
1.14   97, 104-106
1.15   104
1.16   102, 104
1.18-19   102
1.18   104, 105, 107, 108, 147
1.19   97, 102, 106
1.20   104, 106-108
2-3   108
2.1-3.13   108
2   90
2.1   104, 107
2.2   103-106
2.4   104
2.7   97, 101, 104, 107
2.8   104, 107
2.10   104

2.11   104
2.12   104, 107
2.13   104
2.14   104
2.15   104, 106
3   90
3.1-13   108
3.1   102, 104
3.2   104
3.5   104, 113, 150
3.6   102, 104
3.7   103, 104, 110
3.8   102
3.10   106
3.11   102
3.12   106
3.13   106
3.14-16   109
3.14-15   86, 94, 108, 110, 114, 115, 117
3.14   104, 107
3.15   103, 104, 112-15, 149
3.16   102, 104
4-6   104
4.1   102, 104, 106, 107
4.3   104
4.5   104
4.6   100, 102, 104, 108, 112
4.7   104, 116
4.8   104
4.10   102-105
4.11   104, 107, 108, 112
4.12   104, 113
4.13   102, 104, 107
4.14   104
4.15   104
4.16   104, 107, 108, 141, 143

5   96
5.1   102, 104
5.2   102, 103
5.3-16   103
5.4   103, 104
5.5   104, 105
5.6   104
5.7   104, 107, 108, 112
5.8   97, 104, 106
5.9   104
5.10   104
5.11   103, 104, 106
5.12   106, 108
5.13   106, 108
5.14   104, 107
5.15   106, 108
5.16   104
5.17   103, 106
5.18   104
5.19   104
5.20   104, 106, 107
5.21   104, 107
5.22   104
5.23   104
5.24   106
5.25   106
6.1   103, 104, 106
6.2   103, 104, 106, 107
6.3   103, 104, 108
6.4   104
6.6   104
6.7-8   105, 106
6.9   103, 106
6.10   106
6.11   97, 104
6.12   104, 105
6.13   104, 107
6.14   105-107
6.15   104

6.16	104
6.17	104-107
6.19	106
6.20	99, 104, 107, 108
6.21	86, 98-100, 106, 108
6.21b	99

2 Timothy

1.13-14	132
1.13	132, 141, 144
1.41	132
1.15	150
1.16	113
2.6	110
2.23	147
2.24	110
3.14	149
3.15	148
4.19-21	98
4.22	98

Titus

1.11	110
1.16	148
3.11	147
3.15	98

Philemon

3	100
5	129
21-22	114
21	147
22	100
25	98-100

Hebrews

1.1-4	94
3.7-8	132
3.7	141, 144
3.8	144
3.15	132, 141, 144
4.7	132, 141, 144

4.14-16	94
6.10	202, 205
6.14	201,205
8.11	148
10.30	148
12.12	147
12.19	132, 141, 144
13.18	110

James

1.11	31
1.18	151
1.19	151
3.1	147
4.4	147
4.17	150
5.11	129, 138

1 Peter

1.3-13	94
1.18	147
1.24	131
5.9	150

2 Peter

1.12	151
1.12a	151
1.14	147
1.18	141, 145
2.9	150
3.9	116
3.10	116
3.11	110

1 John

1.1	141, 145
1.3	141, 146
1.5	141, 146
2.7	141, 145
2.11	150
2.19	137
2.19b	151
2.20	87, 119, 136, 137, 151
2.21	148
2.24	141, 145

2.29	147
3.2	147
3.5	147
3.11	141, 145
3.14	147
3.15	147
4.5	141, 143
4.6	141, 143
5.13	147
5.14	141, 143
5.15	141, 143, 147
5.18	147
5.19	147
5.20	147

3 John

4	129, 138
12	147

Jude

5	148
10	148
14	31

Revelation

1.3	141, 146
1.4	168
1.10	141, 146
2.2	148
2.9	148
2.13	150
2.17	148
2.19	148
3.1	148
3.8	148
3.12	114
3.15	148
3.17	203
3.20	132, 141, 144
4.1	141, 146
5.11	141, 145
5.13	130, 141, 143
6.1	141, 143
6.2	202, 205
6.3	141, 143

6.5	141, 143	11.12	131, 132,	18.16	203
6.6	141, 145		141, 144	19.1	131, 142,
6.7	141, 146	12.10	142, 144		145
7.4	141, 145	12.35	150	19.6	142, 145
7.13b	151	14.2	142, 145	19.12	148
7.14	151	14.13	132, 141,	20.2	150
8.3	141, 143		144, 146	20.13	150
9.13	142, 145	16.1	131, 133,	21.3	132, 142,
9.16	142, 145		141, 144		144, 146
10.4	142, 146	16.2	133	22.8	142, 146
10.8	142, 146	16.5	142, 143	22.18	142, 145
10.11	113	16.7	142, 143	22.20	80
11.5	113	18.4	142, 145		

PAPYRI

BGU
III, 846   97

P.Abinn.
19.30   116

P.Amh.
37   99
144   99

P.Berl. Leihg.
II, 46.9   116

P.Cairo Zen.
V, 59816   109

P.Fay.
117   99

P.Hamb.
5   96

P.Mich.
VIII, 464   109
VIII, 506.8   116

P.Oxy.
I, 118.37   116
II, 300   100
IX, 1188   96
XIX, 2228.
1.20   116

P.Ryl.
166   96
167   96
171   96
II, 231   97

P.Tebt.
55   99
58   99
421.12   195

Sel.Pap.
I, 104   97
I, 121   109

OTHER ANCIENT REFERENCES

Aeschylus
Prometheus Bound
477   195

1 Clement
4   196
12   195, 196
12.1   196
12.5   195, 196

16.11   196
32.1   196
56.3   196

Euripides
The Bacchanals
1050   195

Julius Victor
Ars Rhetorica
25 (*De Epistolis*)   96

Xenophon
Cyropaedia
8.4.9   195

INDEX OF AUTHORS

Abbott, T.K. 204
Aland, K. 136
Allerton, D.J. 127
Arndt, W.F. 201, 204

Bach, E. 120
Bache, C. 20, 30, 48, 50-52, 54, 59, 64, 70
Bahr, G.J. 95
Bakker, W.F. 19, 20
Barr, J. 154
Barrett, C.K. 91, 98, 116
Barth, M. 204
Bauckham, R. 96
Bauer, W. 201, 204
Beaugrande, R. de 92, 93
Bernard, J.H. 108, 111
Black, D.A. 29, 94, 154, 187
Black, M. 136
Blass, F. 18, 19, 39, 42, 55, 112, 114, 129, 130, 135, 172, 191, 194
Bloomfield, L. 167
Botha, R.P. 153, 164
Bresnan, J. 156
Brinton, L.J. 65, 66, 71
Brooks, J.A. 177
Brown, G. 92, 93
Brox, N. 91, 98, 111
Bruce, F.F. 200
Brugmann, K. 18, 37, 40, 41
Burton, E.D.W. 37
Bush, P. 92
Bybee, J. 50

Callow, K. 101
Carson, D.A. 29, 41, 60

Chatterjee, R. 78
Chomsky, N. 167
Comrie, B. 20, 23, 29-31, 50, 59, 61, 63, 64, 70, 77
Conybeare, F.C. 194
Conzelmann, H. 90, 91, 98, 99, 109, 111, 116-18
Cook, D. 91
Cotterell, P. 29, 92, 94, 154
Coulthard, M. 93
Cowley, A.E. 190
Cronje, J.v.W. 94
Crystal, D. 70, 158
Curtius, G. 36

Dahl, Ö. 20, 30, 62
Dana, H.E. 39
Danker, F.W. 201, 204
Danove, P. 87, 88
Davis, W.H. 188
Debrunner, A. 18, 19, 39, 42, 55, 112, 114, 129, 130, 135, 172, 191, 194
Denio, F.B. 42
Dibelius, M. 90, 91, 98, 99, 109, 111, 116-18
Dijk, T.A. van 94
Donelson, L.R. 91, 92, 111
Donovan, J. 19, 20
Doty, W.G. 95, 96
Dowty, D. 61
Dressler, W. 92
Dunn, J.D.G. 41-43, 90

Easton, B.S. 111
Eckman, F.R. 164, 165
Einstein, A. 163, 165

Ellicott, C.J. 109, 111
Erdman, C.R. 100

Fanning, B.M. 21-25, 30-46, 52, 53,
    55-57, 60, 61, 63-82, 154
Fee, G.D. 101, 109, 111, 114
Fillmore, C.J. 87, 119, 120-25, 127
Fiore, B. 91, 92, 109
Firth, J.R. 23, 69, 77
Forsyth, J. 30
Friedrich, P. 50
Fromkin, V.A. 165, 168
Funk, R.W. 19, 39, 42, 55, 112, 114,
    129, 130, 135, 154, 172, 191, 194

Gazdar, G. 156
Gesenius, W. 189, 190
Gingrich, F.W. 201, 204
Givón, T. 93
Goetchius, E.V.N. 152, 154
Grimes, J.E. 93, 101, 113
Gundry, R.H. 198
Guthrie, D. 91, 99, 109, 111, 114

Halliday, M.A.K. 23, 24, 69, 70, 107
Hammershamb, E. 189, 190
Hankamer, J. 127
Hanson, A.T. 91, 98, 111
Harris, Z. 167
Hasan, R. 107
Hermann, E. 36, 48, 59
Holt, J. 20
Holtz, G. 99, 111
Houlden, J.L. 91, 113, 116
Howard, W.F. 204
Hudson, R. 27

Jacobsohn, H. 36
Jelf, W.E. 41, 194
Johns, A.F. 188
Jones, H.S. 195

Kaplan, R. 156
Karleen, P.S. 189
Karris, R.J. 92, 118
Kautzsch, E. 190
Kay, P. 120, 121

Kelly, J.N.D. 98, 101, 105, 109, 111,
    114
Kenny, A. 23, 25, 53, 61, 65
Klein, E. 156
Koskenniemi, H. 115
Krause, M.S. 88, 89
Kuhn, T. 26, 43, 153
Kümmel, W.G. 90, 91

Lambdin, T.O. 189
Larson, D.N. 154
Levinson, S.C. 40, 101, 104
Liddell, H.G. 195
Lightfoot, D.W. 157-60, 163
Lips, H. von 112
Lloyd, A.L. 50
Lock, W. 99, 108-11, 114, 117
Longacre, R.E. 93
Louw, J.P. 19, 20, 28, 29, 30, 32, 38,
    66, 72, 94, 116, 154, 169
Lyons, J. 44, 61, 63, 64, 106

Mandilaras, B.G. 20
Mantey, J.R. 39
Martini, C.M. 136
Mateos, J. 20, 53, 61
Matthews, P. 127
McKay, K.L. 20, 21, 28, 30, 37, 44
Metzger, B.M. 136
Miller, P.A. 162
Mittwoch, A. 127
Moule, C.F.D. 90, 177, 188
Moulton, J.H. 18, 41, 99, 100, 204
Mueller, T.H. 131, 154
Mullins, T.Y. 110

Naylor, H.D. 19, 20
Nida, E.A. 29, 66, 72, 94, 116, 154,
    155, 169

O'Connor, M.C. 120, 121, 189, 190
Osgood, C.E. 155

Packard, D.W. 160
Palmer, M.W. 88, 156, 157, 159, 160,
    163, 166, 169, 171, 178-80
Pike, E. 156, 167
Pike, K.L. 156, 167

Porter, S.E. 21-25, 27-32, 34, 35, 38, 40-42, 45, 46, 49, 50, 52, 53, 55, 57-63, 69-82, 94, 116, 153, 154, 187-89, 194, 203, 205, 206
Porzig, W. 48, 59
Poutsma, A. 19, 20
Poythress, V. 26
Prior, M. 91, 111
Pullum, G. 156

Quinn, J.D. 99

Radford, A. 156, 167
Reed, J.T. 28, 35, 86, 87, 94
Rehkopf, F. 19
Ringen, J.D. 165
Robertson, A.T. 18, 37, 79, 177, 178, 188, 189
Robinson, J.A. 204
Roetzel, C.J. 90
Rojo, G. 78
Ruipérez, M.S. 61
Rydbeck, L. 27, 34

Sag, I. 127, 156
Saussure, F. de 158
Schenk, W. 94
Schmidt, D.D. 25, 28, 66, 67, 73, 154, 156
Scott, R. 195
Seow, C.L. 189
Silva, M. 25, 28, 29, 35, 41, 74, 82, 154
Simpson, E.K. 98, 111, 114
Smith, C.R. 29, 60
Smith, C.S. 48, 52, 59
Smyth, H.W. 129, 135
Snyman, A.H. 94
Spicq, C. 91, 108, 109, 112
Stagg, F. 29, 42

Stahl, J.M. 36
Stock, StG. 194
Stork, P. 55
Suci, G.J. 155
Swete, H.B. 198, 200, 201

Tannenbaum, P.H. 155
Thackeray, H.StJ. 191-94
Thiselton, A.C. 29
Thompson, S. 203
Thorley, J. 29
Toit, A.B. du 94
Towner, P.H. 111
Trummer, P. 115, 116
Turner, M. 29, 92, 94, 154
Turner, N. 19, 20, 99, 110, 129-31, 134, 135, 190, 195, 204

Vendler, Z. 23, 25, 53, 61, 65
Verkuyl, H.J. 62
Verner, D.C. 92, 109, 111
Voelz, J.W. 206

Wackernagel, J. 36
Waltke, B. 189, 190
Wells, R. 167
Wendland, E. 155
Werner, J.R. 94
White, J.L. 95, 96, 109, 110, 115
Wikgren, A. 136
Wilcox, M. 206
Winbery, C.L. 177
Winer, G.B. 18, 41, 174, 177
Wonneberger, R. 154

Yule, G. 93

Zerwick, M. 129-31, 134, 135

JOURNAL FOR THE STUDY OF THE NEW TESTAMENT

Supplement Series

1   THE BARREN TEMPLE AND THE WITHERED TREE
    William R. Telford
2   STUDIA BIBLICA 1978
    II. PAPERS ON THE GOSPELS
    Edited by E.A. Livingstone
3   STUDIA BIBLICA 1978
    III. PAPERS ON PAUL AND OTHER NEW TESTAMENT AUTHORS
    Edited by E.A. Livingstone
4   FOLLOWING JESUS:
    DISCIPLESHIP IN THE GOSPEL OF MARK
    Ernest Best
5   THE PEOPLE OF GOD
    Markus Barth
6   PERSECUTION AND MARTYRDOM IN THE THEOLOGY OF PAUL
    John S. Pobee
7   SYNOPTIC STUDIES:
    THE AMPLEFORTH CONFERENCES OF
    1982 AND 1983
    Edited by C.M. Tuckett
8   JESUS ON THE MOUNTAIN:
    A STUDY IN MATTHEAN THEOLOGY
    Terence L. Donaldson
9   THE HYMNS OF LUKE'S INFANCY NARRATIVES:
    THEIR ORIGIN, MEANING AND SIGNIFICANCE
    Stephen Farris
10 CHRIST THE END OF THE LAW:
    ROMANS 10.4 IN PAULINE PERSPECTIVE
    Robert Badenas
11 THE LETTERS TO THE SEVEN CHURCHES OF ASIA IN THEIR LOCAL
    SETTING
    Colin J. Hemer
12 PROCLAMATION FROM PROPHECY AND PATTERN:
    LUCAN OLD TESTAMENT CHRISTOLOGY
    Darrell L. Bock
13 JESUS AND THE LAWS OF PURITY:
    TRADITION HISTORY AND LEGAL HISTORY IN MARK 7
    Roger P. Booth
14 THE PASSION ACCORDING TO LUKE:
    THE SPECIAL MATERIAL OF LUKE 22
    Marion L. Soards

15 HOSTILITY TO WEALTH IN THE SYNOPTIC GOSPELS
    Thomas E. Schmidt
16 MATTHEW'S COMMUNITY:
    THE EVIDENCE OF HIS SPECIAL SAYINGS MATERIAL
    Stephenson H. Brooks
17 THE PARADOX OF THE CROSS IN THE THOUGHT OF ST PAUL
    Anthony Tyrrell Hanson
18 HIDDEN WISDOM AND THE EASY YOKE:
    WISDOM, TORAH AND DISCIPLESHIP IN MATTHEW 11.25-30
    Celia Deutsch
19 JESUS AND GOD IN PAUL'S ESCHATOLOGY
    L. Joseph Kreitzer
20 LUKE
    A NEW PARADIGM (2 Volumes)
    Michael D. Goulder
21 THE DEPARTURE OF JESUS IN LUKE–ACTS:
    THE ASCENSION NARRATIVES IN CONTEXT
    Mikeal C. Parsons
22 THE DEFEAT OF DEATH:
    APOCALYPTIC ESCHATOLOGY IN 1 CORINTHIANS 15 AND ROMANS 5
    Martinus C. de Boer
23 PAUL THE LETTER-WRITER
    AND THE SECOND LETTER TO TIMOTHY
    Michael Prior
24 APOCALYPTIC AND THE NEW TESTAMENT:
    ESSAYS IN HONOR OF J. LOUIS MARTYN
    Edited by Joel Marcus & Marion L. Soards
25 THE UNDERSTANDING SCRIBE:
    MATTHEW AND THE APOCALYPTIC IDEAL
    David E. Orton
26 WATCHWORDS:
    MARK 13 IN MARKAN ESCHATOLOGY
    Timothy J. Geddert
27 THE DISCIPLES ACCORDING TO MARK:
    MARKAN REDACTION IN CURRENT DEBATE
    C. Clifton Black
28 THE NOBLE DEATH:
    GRAECO-ROMAN MARTYROLOGY
    AND PAUL'S CONCEPT OF SALVATION
    David Seeley
29 ABRAHAM IN GALATIANS:
    EPISTOLARY AND RHETORICAL CONTEXTS
    G. Walter Hansen
30 EARLY CHRISTIAN RHETORIC AND 2 THESSALONIANS
    Frank Witt Hughes

31 THE STRUCTURE OF MATTHEW'S GOSPEL:
A STUDY IN LITERARY DESIGN
David R. Bauer

32 PETER AND THE BELOVED DISCIPLE:
FIGURES FOR A COMMUNITY IN CRISIS
Kevin Quast

33 MARK'S AUDIENCE:
THE LITERARY AND SOCIAL SETTING OF MARK 4.11-12
Mary Ann Beavis

34 THE GOAL OF OUR INSTRUCTION:
THE STRUCTURE OF THEOLOGY AND ETHICS
IN THE PASTORAL EPISTLES
Philip H. Towner

35 THE PROVERBS OF JESUS:
ISSUES OF HISTORY AND RHETORIC
Alan P. Winton

36 THE STORY OF CHRIST IN THE ETHICS OF PAUL:
AN ANALYSIS OF THE FUNCTION OF THE HYMNIC MATERIAL
IN THE PAULINE CORPUS
Stephen E. Fowl

37 PAUL AND JESUS:
COLLECTED ESSAYS
Edited by A.J.M. Wedderburn

38 MATTHEW'S MISSIONARY DISCOURSE:
A LITERARY CRITICAL ANALYSIS
Dorothy Jean Weaver

39 FAITH AND OBEDIENCE IN ROMANS:
A STUDY IN ROMANS 1–4
Glenn N. Davies

40 IDENTIFYING PAUL'S OPPONENTS:
THE QUESTION OF METHOD IN 2 CORINTHIANS
Jerry L. Sumney

41 HUMAN AGENTS OF COSMIC POWER:
IN HELLENISTIC JUDAISM AND THE SYNOPTIC TRADITION
Mary E. Mills

42 MATTHEW'S INCLUSIVE STORY:
A STUDY IN THE NARRATIVE RHETORIC OF THE FIRST GOSPEL
David B. Howell

43 JESUS, PAUL AND TORAH:
COLLECTED ESSAYS
Heikki Räisänen

44 THE NEW COVENANT IN HEBREWS
Susanne Lehne

45   THE RHETORIC OF ROMANS:
ARGUMENTATIVE CONSTRAINT AND STRATEGY AND PAUL'S
DIALOGUE WITH JUDAISM
Neil Elliott

46   THE LAST SHALL BE FIRST:
THE RHETORIC OF REVERSAL IN LUKE
John O. York

47   JAMES AND THE Q SAYINGS OF JESUS
Patrick J. Hartin

48   TEMPLUM AMICITIAE:
ESSAYS ON THE SECOND TEMPLE PRESENTED TO ERNST BAMMEL
Edited by William Horbury

49   PROLEPTIC PRIESTS
PRIESTHOOD IN THE EPISTLE TO THE HEBREWS
John M. Scholer

50   PERSUASIVE ARTISTRY:
STUDIES IN NEW TESTAMENT RHETORIC
IN HONOR OF GEORGE A. KENNEDY
Edited by Duane F. Watson

51   THE AGENCY OF THE APOSTLE:
A DRAMATISTIC ANALYSIS OF PAUL'S RESPONSES
TO CONFLICT IN 2 CORINTHIANS
Jeffrey A. Crafton

52   REFLECTIONS OF GLORY:
PAUL'S POLEMICAL USE OF THE MOSES–DOXA TRADITION IN
2 CORINTHIANS 3.12-18
Linda L. Belleville

53   REVELATION AND REDEMPTION AT COLOSSAE
Thomas J. Sappington

54   THE DEVELOPMENT OF EARLY CHRISTIAN PNEUMATOLOGY
WITH SPECIAL REFERENCE TO LUKE–ACTS
Robert P. Menzies

55   THE PURPOSE OF ROMANS:
A COMPARATIVE LETTER STRUCTURE INVESTIGATION
L. Ann Jervis

56   THE SON OF THE MAN IN THE GOSPEL OF JOHN
Delbert Burkett

57   ESCHATOLOGY AND THE COVENANT:
A COMPARISON OF 4 EZRA AND ROMANS 1–11
Bruce W. Longenecker

58   NONE BUT THE SINNERS:
RELIGIOUS CATEGORIES IN THE GOSPEL OF LUKE
David A. Neale

59 CLOTHED WITH CHRIST:
THE EXAMPLE AND TEACHING OF JESUS IN ROMANS 12.1–15.13
Michael Thompson

60 THE LANGUAGE OF THE NEW TESTAMENT:
CLASSIC ESSAYS
Edited by Stanley E. Porter

61 FOOTWASHING IN JOHN 13 AND THE JOHANNINE COMMUNITY
John Christopher Thomas

62 JOHN THE BAPTIZER AND PROPHET:
A SOCIO-HISTORICAL STUDY
Robert L. Webb

63 POWER AND POLITICS IN PALESTINE:
THE JEWS AND THE GOVERNING OF THEIR LAND 100 BC–AD 70
James S. McLaren

64 JESUS AND THE ORAL GOSPEL TRADITION
Edited by Henry Wansbrough

65 THE RHETORIC OF RIGHTEOUSNESS IN ROMANS 3.21-26
Douglas A. Campbell

66 PAUL, ANTIOCH AND JERUSALEM:
A STUDY IN RELATIONSHIPS AND AUTHORITY IN EARLIEST CHRISTIANITY
Nicholas Taylor

67 THE PORTRAIT OF PHILIP IN ACTS:
A STUDY OF ROLES AND RELATIONS
F. Scott Spencer

68 JEREMIAH IN MATTHEW'S GOSPEL:
THE REJECTED PROPHET MOTIF IN MATTHAEAN REDACTION
Michael P. Knowles

69 RHETORIC AND REFERENCE IN THE FOURTH GOSPEL
Margaret Davies

70 AFTER THE THOUSAND YEARS:
RESURRECTION AND JUDGMENT IN REVELATION 20
J. Webb Mealy

71 SOPHIA AND THE JOHANNINE JESUS
Martin Scott

72 NARRATIVE ASIDES IN LUKE–ACTS
Steven M. Sheeley

73 SACRED SPACE
AN APPROACH TO THE THEOLOGY OF THE EPISTLE TO THE HEBREWS
Marie E. Isaacs

74 TEACHING WITH AUTHORITY:
MIRACLES AND CHRISTOLOGY IN THE GOSPEL OF MARK
Edwin K. Broadhead

75 PATRONAGE AND POWER:
STUDIES ON SOCIAL NETWORKS IN CORINTH
John Kin-Man Chow

76   THE NEW TESTAMENT AS CANON:
A READER IN CANONICAL CRITICISM
Robert Wall and Eugene Lemcio

77   REDEMPTIVE ALMSGIVING IN EARLY CHRISTIANITY
Roman Garrison

78   THE FUNCTION OF SUFFERING IN PHILIPPIANS
L. Gregory Bloomquist

79   THE THEME OF RECOMPENSE IN MATTHEW'S GOSPEL
Blaine Charette

80   BIBLICAL GREEK LANGUAGE AND LINGUISTICS:
OPEN QUESTIONS IN CURRENT RESEARCH
Edited by Stanley E. Porter and D.A. Carson